THE TRANSFORMATION
OF AMERICAN SOCIETY,
1870-1890

THE

TRANSFORMATION

OF AMERICAN

SOCIETY, 1870-1890

Edited by
John A. Garraty

University of South Carolina Press
Columbia, S.C.

THE TRANSFORMATION OF AMERICAN SOCIETY,
1870-1890

First edition: HARPER TORCHBOOKS, 1968, Harper & Row,
Publishers, Incorporated, 49 East 33rd Street, New York,
N.Y. 10016.

This edition published by the University of South Carolina
Press, Columbia, S.C., 1969, by arrangement with Harper
Torchbooks, from whom a paperback edition is available
(TB/1395) .

Standard Book Number: 87249-124-2

Library of Congress Catalog Card Number: 68–65043.

Contents

Introduction

Few periods in the history of any nation saw such rapid and startling changes as those which occurred in the United States in the decades of the 1870's and 1880's. During those years, what we think of as modern American civilization was born. Industrialization was pushing society in new directions. The economy was revolutionized: manufacturing expanded at a fantastic rate and took on many fundamentally new characteristics, but agriculture changed almost as radically. And economic change was accompanied by drastic adjustments in how men lived and how they conceptualized their relationships to one another. Even the American political system, which seemed to contemporaries corrupt and so archaically inefficient as to be incapable of dealing effectively with current needs, was undergoing important alterations, the effects of which would only be clear in the next century.

Many Americans of that time were more impressed by the confusion and waste resulting from the speed and pervasiveness of the changes that were taking place than by the constructive achievements of the era, and many later historians have adopted this point of view. To such persons this was a Gilded Age, ruthlessly materialistic, selfishly individualistic, fraudulent, hypocritical, coarse. This view of the era is myopic more than false. In proper focus the constructive aspects of the period appear far more significant. It was not a Golden Age, for men, being human, do not create perfect civilizations. But neither was it a base age, veneered with a thin, flawed layer of gilt or tinsel.

Essentially, what was happening was that industrialization was making life more complicated. First of all, the way things were made was becoming more intricate and specialized. The artisan with his simple hand tools was being replaced by the factory hand who tended an expensive machine. This new worker was more productive, in the sense that each hour of his labor yielded a larger volume of goods, but he was also much less independent. His ability to produce was closely related to what many other per-

sons were doing—his fellow workers, the inventors and techni-
cians who designed the machines, the capitalists who paid for
their construction, and the managers who organized and directed
the manufacturing process. Farmers were only slightly less
restricted by this new trend than industrial workers; if the typical
farmer still ran an individual enterprise, he was nevertheless more
dependent on others—bankers who lent him money to buy the
machines that were now necessary if he was to operate efficiently,
government experts who supplied him with information about
crop and market conditions, and new plant varieties, railroad men
who transported his harvest to distant markets, and the host of
middlemen who graded, stored, and traded farm products.

Everyone engaged in producing goods found his activities
closely affected by the actions of many other persons, for the
entire economy was becoming more integrated. For this the railroad was chiefly responsible. On the eve of the Civil War the
United States already had the largest railroad system in the world,
some 30,000 miles of track. But by 1890 this figure had soared to
over 166,000 miles and, even more significant, the system had
been welded into a unified network, thus vastly speeding the
movement of goods and sharply reducing transportation costs.
The nation had developed a truly national economy. Men could
produce goods in one section and dispose of them in markets
thousands of miles away. This expanded their opportunities but
limited their independence. Competition became more intense
and also more widespread. Manufacturers could no longer muddle
along with out-of-date techniques, secure in their own localities
because they were protected against the competition of more
efficient producers in distant regions by high transportation costs.
Workers in areas where labor was scarce saw themselves losing this
"natural" advantage in the same way, and so did farmers in the
older sections, who had to sell their crops in competition with
those in the West. In general, everyone had to meet a higher
standard in order to succeed. Success offered more glittering
rewards, thus stimulating men to work hard, but it became more
difficult to achieve, with the result that many failed and others
were tempted to engage in shady practices to avoid failure. The
cutthroat competition of the age rose not so much from greed as
from fear.

Expansion of the arena and of the number of gladiators

engaged in the competition do not alone explain the particular character of the era. New techniques were altering the rules of the contest in countless ways, but always with the effect of increasing both the stakes and the odds against winning them. The invention of new machines and processes was the most obvious of the many forms that technological innovation took in these years. In steel making, in petroleum refining, in railroading, and in dozens of other fields, techniques were being transformed at a rapid rate. The smallest improvements in efficiency might have enormous effects upon the fortunes of those who made them. A change in the placement of a few machines might yield dramatic reductions in labor costs, a new advance in chemical knowledge might make possible the use of cheaper raw materials. In nearly every case, the men who were astute enough to take advantage of the new machines and methods and lucky enough to choose the right ones from among dozens available were those who emerged as leaders in their industries. In the new electrical industry, for example, the arc light and the incandescent lamp provided alternative means of lighting city streets, but which one would in the long run be adopted was not immediately apparent. Edison lost much of the advantage gained by his pioneering in the development of the dynamo and the distribution of electric power by failing to grasp at once the superiority of alternating current over direct current in the transmission of electricity.

New methods of business organization played a perhaps equally important role in determining success, for as businesses became larger and more complex, keeping track of what was actually being done and providing intelligent direction to the enterprise became ever more essential. Rockefeller's Standard Oil trust was far more than a device for swallowing up competitors, circumventing state laws, and preventing the public from realizing how large a share of the oil business Rockefeller controlled. It was also the nerve center of a huge industrial complex encompassing refineries, pipe lines, laboratories, clerical staffs, and sales organizations in more than a dozen states. New methods of advertising, of distributing goods, even of keeping records were vital not only to the making of profits but also to mere survival under the new order. And again, these changes required the subordination of the individual to the group. In this sense the most domineering of the industrialists, for all their wealth and self-confidence, do not really fit the "robber baron" stereotype. Although some of them were as rapacious and unprincipled as any medieval tyrant, they lacked arbitrary authority. Their baronies were too large, too complicated to be run by any individual. Rockefeller was plainly the head of a committee. Carnegie personally owned the lion's share of his great iron-and-steel empire, but he was perfectly aware of his dependence on what he called his "clever partners," whose special skills and talents made the functioning of that empire possible.

Industrial growth went hand in hand with the growth of cities, and in the cities the complexities of life were especially noticeable and vexing. No other American environment presented so many paradoxes. Wealth and poverty, beauty and ugliness, culture and ignorance, charity and crime—each of these contradictions could be found in abundance in the metropolises of the 1880's. Graceful new skyscrapers and majestic bridges, marvels of art and engineering, towered beside crumbling slum tenements. New museums and libraries displayed priceless, timeless treasures next door to whorehouses and gambling dens. Sordid politicians traded cheap favors to the poor for their votes in the same wards where idealistic young college graduates were founding settlement houses and trying to teach the poor the true meaning of democracy and community service.

Whether sordid or enlightened, ignoble or inspired, urban life put a premium on corporate existence. The cities offered unparalleled opportunities for every kind of talent, attracted the most ambitious, intelligent, and imaginative persons the nation produced. Yet the most unique of these individualists could no more escape the interdependence imposed by the city on its denizens than the dullest clod or the most downtrodden slavy.

Political institutions were also being affected by the pressures of the new complexities. Superficially politics seemed divorced from contemporary realities. It was not an age of great statesmen. Politicos postured and vaporized, refought the Civil War on the stump, belabored dead issues, and tried to ignore the live problems that industrialization had produced in such abundance. Yet inexorably the system was adjusting itself to meet the demands of the times. One by one the federal government took on new functions—the collection of statistics, scientific research, the regulation of the railroads, the restriction of monopolistic corporations. The federal bureaucracy expanded steadily—from 53,000 employees immediately after the Civil War to 166,000 in the early 1890's. State and city governments experienced a similar proliferation in size and function. And as the political system grew, it also changed its character. The old patronage system began to give way, the tenured professional bureaucrat replacing the unspecialized, ephemeral political appointee. Congress streamlined its procedures; the parties tightened their organizations and found new sources of revenue; the Presidents moved fumblingly toward more aggressive and imaginative types of leadership.

All these trends, and many others, inevitably affected men's ideas as well as their behavior. As society became more complex, it became necessary to think about social questions in a more systematic and specialized way if the new order was to be understood, the questions answered. Political economy, originally a branch of philosophy, now divided itself into political science and economics, and new disciplines like sociology, anthropology, and psychology began rapidly to evolve. And nearly all of these social sciences broke sharply with individualistic explanations of human behavior. Laissez faire, once an American axiom, came under attack from every quarter. In the universities, in the churches, everywhere that men were studying the structure of society and the meaning of life, the most creative and intelligent minds were reaching the conclusion that communal problems had to be solved by the community, that for all its admitted virtues, individualism was, if not undesirable, at least inadequate both as a philosophy and as a tactic in modern social relations.

* * *

To describe adequately the character of the transformation that American civilization underwent in the 1870's and 1880's within the pages of a single volume of contemporary sources is an impossible task. Complexity, after all, defies brief summary; it can be illustrated but not perfectly defined. What follows is only a selection (it is not even a sample in the scientific sense) from the immense mass of documentation left by that generation for historians to ponder over. The broad views of the period here presented as Part I, Mark Twain's dating from the early 1870's, the other, Andrew Carnegie's, from the middle of the 1880's, are personal impressions, important chiefly because of the historical significance of the authors and the contemporary popularity of the works themselves. They provide the reader with a flavor of the times rather than brilliant insights or profound analyses.

The selections dealing with agriculture illustrate first of all the diversity of what was still the largest sector of the American economy. The testimony of John C. Calhoun, II (Document 3) throws light both on southern farming after the Civil War and on the relations between black worker and white landowner and merchant. Major Powell's essay on western land policy (Document 4), on the other hand, illustrates how the dynamic expansion of the period produced new problems—in this case the need for revising long-established thinking about how the federal government should dispose of public lands. Everyone realized that conditions in the West were radically different from those in the older settled regions, and as Powell showed, it was possible to devise intelligent and practical policies to cope with these differences. Putting new policies into effect, however, was another matter. William Godwin Moody's description of "bonanza" wheat farming on the plains (Document 5) supplies an example of the new importance of machinery in agriculture, while Rodney Welch's article on "The Farmer's Changed Condition" (Document 6) deals broadly with the impact of commercial agriculture on rural values and practices.

The task of describing the transformation of industry is especially difficult in the limited space available. A selection from David A. Wells's *Recent Economic Changes* (Document 7) is almost mandatory; few Americans understood the significance of industrialization so well as he, and still fewer possessed his talent for generalization and for exemplification by means of vivid detail. The particular section from Wells's great book included here has the added advantage of showing how even this gifted expert was baffled by the multitudinous and varied phenomena he was attempting to comprehend.

Of the many industrial developments that merit coverage, the growth of the railroad network is surely outstanding, and Charles Francis Adams, Jr.'s *Railroads: Their Origin and Problems* is an easy choice among the contemporary discussions of this subject (Document 8). Adams was a scholarly authority on the history and technology of railroads in the United States, and as the former chairman of the Massachusetts Railroad Commission he was thoroughly familiar with the practical side of railroading; his book summarizes his experience during a crucial decade of railroad development. The first report of the Interstate Commerce Commission, excerpts from which make up the next document (9), is a logical supplement to Adam's observations about railroad regulation and offers an exceptionally good illustration of the generalization that the economic changes of the era were producing problems of enormous complexity.

The choice of Samuel C. T. Dodd's essay on trusts to represent the vast literature on corporate concentration was made more because of Dodd's position as the drafter of the famous Standard Oil trust agreement than because of the particular line of argument in defense of combinations that he developed. "Trusts" (Document 10) is a typical rather than an outstanding example of this position, but it does present the case clearly and in brief compass.

All the passages dealing with industrial workers and the conditions under which they labored are drawn from the reports of state bureaus of labor statistics. These bureaus, which illustrate the point made above—that government was taking on new functions in response to industrialization—collected masses of statistical information that is of great value to historians; but they also conducted many investigations of particular problems related to labor and industry which are not only historically important but also fascinating to read. The 1878 study of the Massachusetts bureau was a landmark of sorts—certainly one of the earliest American examples of the use of questionnaires to collect social data. The actual statements of ordinary workingmen recorded here (Document 11) tell us a great deal about how these workers felt about their jobs and about the society in which they lived. The report could not pretend to provide a balanced picture because the men whose opinions were collected did not represent a cross-section even of Massachusetts workers, but it nevertheless supplies a remarkable impressionistic survey of what *some* workers felt, and evidence of this kind for the period is rare indeed. The excerpts from the Massachusetts investigation of conditions in three textile towns present similar material, although in this case we must rely on the reports of field workers rather than the actual words of the mill hands. This is true also of the Illinois study of workingmen's income, expenditures, and living conditions (Document 12).

However, this magnificent Illinois report, based on a large and well-chosen sample of laboring men throughout the state, enables us to generalize about rather than merely to guess what it was like to be a wage earner in the 1880's. The Ohio report on the use of company scrip in the payment of wages (Document 13) lacks the objectivity and scope of the pioneering Illinois study, but it discusses an important problem faced by many workingmen and by implication reveals a great deal about the attitudes of many employers toward the labor force. Out of all these reports comes further evidence of the complexity of life; the variations of both income and attitude of workers in the same or similar trades, for example, points up the inadequacy of all glib generalizations on the subject.

Labor unions receive less space in this volume than workingmen in general, not because of any scarcity of material but because only a tiny fraction of the labor force belonged to unions in the 1870's and 1880's.[1] Nevertheless, the union movement was important; the growth of large corporations and the expansion of industrial activity were producing new conditions out of which the modern labor movement was to evolve. The two major points of view presented here, those of Terrence V. Powderly of the Knights of Labor and Adolph Strasser, a founder of the American Federation of Labor, define the limits within which the ideological battles of those years were fought by labor leaders. The brief selection (16) which concludes the section on unions explain how the trade unionists finally confronted the Knights and established their national organization.

Americans were of course well aware that the nation was becoming inceasingly urbanized and that the growth of cities was anything but an unmixed blessing. This is demonstrated by the selection from Samuel Lane Loomis's volume, *Modern Cities and Their Religious Problems*. (Document 17). Loomis also understood the many paradoxical aspects of urban life and had a sound grasp of the causes of most of the cities' problems. Being a minister, he saw these problems in moral terms, but he avoided the error of blaming them on the depravity of the city dwellers. He called upon the churches to take the lead in improving condi-

---

[1] The subject of labor unions will be treated in depth in the forthcoming two-volume *Documentary History of Labor,* edited by Herbert G. Gutman.

tions, but recognized that improvement could not be achieved merely by exhortation or prayer. The two contemporary descriptions of the model town of Pullman, Illinois, included here (Document 18) are important not because Pullman was either a typical city or a harbinger of the future. They tell us a good deal about the advantages of urban planning, but they also highlight through their contrasting points of view the conflict between individualism and social control that was beginning to be fought out in these years. George Pullman saw clearly—too clearly—the advantages of a rigidly regulated, tightly organized social system, but he failed to see that too much control was antithetical to democracy and human liberty. Like most contemporary observers, the labor commissioners, despite their sympathies for workingmen, were overly impressed by the beauty and efficiency of the town of Pullman. Richard T. Ely, however, was one of the first to warn of the dangers lurking behind Pullman's benevolent paternalism.

One of the most striking characteristics of the American response to new urban problems was the enthusiasm of the many persons working to improve the lot of the poor forced to live in squalor in the city slums. The selections by Robert Treat Paine, Jr., Jane Addams, and Alfred T. White (Documents 19, 20, and 21) describe some of the many ways in which well-to-do and middle-class citizens sought to accomplish this worthy task. How little was achieved, however, is graphically illustrated in the excerpt included here from Jacob Riis's famous description of New York City's slums, *How the Other Half Lives,* published in 1890 (Document 22).

Although the partisan political battles of these years do not seem particularly relevant to the underlying problems of the era, the contemporary writing about the political system was of extraordinarily high quality. Perhaps because of the inability of the politicians to confront the major issues of the day, the political analysts were challenged to dig deeply into the character of the system that appeared to frustrate them. James Bryce's *American Commonwealth* is so full of insights that almost any section of it merits inclusion, but his chapters on the presidency are particularly important. The passages chosen (Document 23) tell us much about the inherent character of the office and also a great deal about its particular state in the 1880's—why it is a great office

and why, at that time, it seemed such a feeble one in some respects; why, as Bryce said, great men are not often presidential candidates and why, nevertheless, men sometimes achieve greatness
by becoming President. Woodrow Wilson's comments on the
House of Representatives, drawn from his book *Congressional
Government* (Document 24), help explain why both contemporaries and many later critics believed that American politics had
become stalled at dead center. Indeed, Wilson's devastating criticisms of the committee system probably influenced the drive to
strengthen party leadership in the House, a drive which culmi-
nated in Speaker Thomas B. Reed's famous coup of 1890 and the
formulation of the "Reed Rules," which made the Speaker almost
a dictator in the regulation of House business.

When Wilson pointed out that the federal government was not
adjusting to the needs of the times, he was merely adding his
weight to a heavy barrage of criticism. Much of this criticism was
aimed at the spoils system, the practice of handing out jobs in the
federal bureaucracy to party workers in return for their services in
winning elections. President Hayes's executive order forbidding
the levying of assessments on officeholders, a common practice
which represented a sort of spoils system in reverse, marked an
early stage in the fight for civil service reform (Document 25).
The bitterness of the old-fashioned politicians, who, aside from
the benefits they received from their control of patronage gen-
uinely believed that the party system could not exist without
patronage, is reflected in Senator Roscoe Conkling's diatribe
against George W. Curtis, one of the most vociferous of the
reformers (Document 26).

Actually, the arguments employed by both sides in the battle
for civil-service reform were more often than not directed at relatively unimportant aspects of the question, such as corruption and
unfair influence, which were not likely to be eliminated merely by
making government workers pass tests, or by giving them tenure.
Reform came, in the Pendleton Act of 1883, in part because of the
assassination of President Garfield by a demented spoilsman, but
it would have had to come soon in any case. (Document 27). The
growth of the bureaucracy and its increasing need for professional
skills as the government took on highly specialized new functions
were making the old system completely unworkable. George W.
Curtis's analysis of the work of the reformers does not give this

aspect of the subject enough attention, but it provides a good summary both of what was accomplished and of the ideas and attitudes of the reformers.

In a sense, the rich literature analyzing the American political system was part of a far broader body of writing on the general subject "What is wrong with American society and what can be done about it?" Nothing so thoroughly explodes the hypothesis that the people of that generation were coarse, anti-social individualists as the persistent, imaginative, and forceful arguments for reform devised by large numbers of thinkers, and the great interest which their writings aroused among the public at large. Henry George's *Progress and Poverty* (Document 29) is probably the most famous of the attacks on existing conditions. The fact that so many readers found his drastic plan for expropriating all unearned increment in the form of rent worth serious consideration is evidence that the people of the country were deeply concerned about the growing disparity between the rich and the poor, and uneasy about the enormous changes that were taking place in the social and economic structure of the United States. George, however, was really arguing for a retreat from contemporary realities to a simpler world. Laurence Gronlund, on the other hand, sought in his book *The Cooperative Commonwealth* to domesticate the ideas of Karl Marx, that is, to prove that Marxian socialism was not antithetical to the American faith in individualism and democracy (Document 30). Despite his playing down of class conflict, however, Gronlund accepted wholeheartedly the idea that the economy should be closely controlled by the state and that the public interest must take precedence over that of any individual or group.

That the emerging social sciences also adopted the point of view that laissez faire must give way to social control is shown in the concluding selections. Lester Frank Ward, the sociologist, presents a powerful argument for social planning (Document 31), based on his application of Darwin's theory of evolution to the development of social institutions. The thinking of the younger generation of economists is revealed in the selection from the discussions that led to the formation of the American Economic Association (Document 32), and in the excerpt from Henry Carter Adams's monograph, "Relation of the State to Industrial Action" (Document 33), which applies the general ideas of these "new" economists to the specific question of state regulation of the economy. Finally, Woodrow Wilson's discussion of the proper role of government, drawn from his book *The State*, places the new philosophy in the broad framework of political science (Document 34). Wilson was not concerned with particular measures. He was not even temperamentally a reformer. Unlike Henry George, he offered no panacea; unlike Gronlund he eschewed denunciation of what already existed. But he argued that government should be free to take all necessary steps to deal with contemporary problems. His dispassionate insistence that the nation must confront the complexities of the modern world makes a fitting conclusion to this volume.

Part I

Mark Twain and Andrew Carnegie— Gilt or Pure Gold?

1. Mark Twain—*The Gilded Age* (1873)

What was the general spirit and character of the 1870's and 1880's? There is probably no satisfactory answer to this superficially simple question; the country was too large and diverse to submit to any single categorization. Contemporaries who tried to generalize about the age inevitably presented only part of the picture. Documents 1 and 2 present extreme views, but ones that were widely held, as the popularity of the books from which they are taken testifies. *The Gilded Age* (1873), written by Mark Twain with the aid of Charles Dudley Warner, was first of all a novel, and far from the best of Twain's work. It was written hurriedly, more or less on a dare, and did not pretend to be a serious analysis of the American character. Yet it caught several facets of the era perfectly—its coarse materialism, bombastic boosterism, speculative fever, and corruption. Its title has become a cliché, a universal symbol of the age, and has been used by many scholarly historians to epitomize several decades of American history.

Toward evening, the stage-coach came thundering into Hawkeye with a perfectly triumphant ostentation—which was natural and proper, for Hawkeye was a pretty large town for interior Missouri. Washington, very stiff and tired and hungry, climbed out, and wondered how he was to proceed now. But his difficulty was quickly solved. Col. Sellers came down the street on a run and arrived panting for breath. He said:

"Lord bless you—I'm glad to see you, Washington—perfectly delighted to see you, my boy! I got your message. Been on the look-out for you. Heard the stage horn, but had a party I couldn't

SOURCE: Mark Twain and C. D. Warner, *The Gilded Age: A Tale of To-day* (Hartford, Conn., 1874), pp. 76-90.

shake off—man that's got an enormous thing on hand—wants me to put some capital into it—and I tell you, my boy, I could do worse, I could do a deal worse. No, now, let that luggage alone; I'll fix that. Here, Jerry, got anything to do? All right—shoulder this plunder and follow me. Come along, Washington. Lord, I'm glad to see you! Wife and the children are just perishing to look at you. Bless you, they won't know you, you've grown so. Folks all well, I suppose? That's good—glad to hear that. We're always going to run down and see them, but I'm into so many operations, and they're not things a man feels like trusting to other people, and so somehow we keep putting it off. Fortunes in them! Good gracious, it's the country to pile up wealth in! Here we are— here's where the Sellers dynasty hangs out. Dump it on the door-step, Jerry—the blackest niggro in the State, Washington, but got a good heart—mighty likely boy, is Jerry. And now I suppose you've got to have ten cents, Jerry. That's all right—when a man works for me—when a man—in the other pocket, I reckon—when a man—why, where the mischief *is* that portmonnaie!—when a—well now that's odd—Oh, now I remember, must have left it at the bank; and b'George I've left my check-book, too—Polly says I ought to have a nurse—well, no matter. Let me have a dime, Washington, if you've got—ah, thanks. Now clear out, Jerry, your complexion has brought on the twilight half an hour ahead of time. Pretty fair joke—pretty fair. Here he is, Polly! Washington's come, children!—come now, don't eat him up—finish him in the house. Welcome, my boy, to a mansion that is proud to shelter the son of the best man that walks on the ground. Si Hawkins has been a good friend to me, and I believe I can say that whenever I've had a chance to put him into a good thing I've done it, and done it pretty cheerfully, too. I put him into that sugar specula-tion—what a grand thing that was, if we hadn't held on too long!"

Washington was greatly pleased with the Sellers mansion. It was a two-story-and-a-half brick, and much more stylish than any of its neighbors. He was borne to the family sitting room in triumph by the swarm of little Sellerses, the parents following with their arms about each other's waists.

The whole family were poorly and cheaply dressed; and the clothing, although neat and clean, showed many evidences of having seen long service. The Colonel's "stovepipe" hat was nap-less and shiny with much polishing, but nevertheless it had an almost convincing expression about it of having been just purchased new. The rest of his clothing was napless and shiny, too, but it had the air of being entirely satisfied with itself and blandly sorry for other people's clothes. . . .

A dreary old hair-cloth sofa against the wall; a few damaged chairs; the small table the lamp stood on; the crippled stove— these things constituted the furniture of the room. There was no carpet on the floor; on the wall were occasional square-shaped interruptions of the general tint of the plaster which betrayed that there used to be pictures in the house—but there were none now. There were no mantel ornaments, unless one might bring himself to regard as an ornament a clock which never came within fifteen strokes of striking the right time, and whose hands always hitched together at twenty-two minutes past anything and traveled in company the rest of the way home.

"Remarkable clock!" said Sellers, and got up and wound it. "I've been offered—well, I wouldn't expect you to believe what I've been offered for that clock. Old Gov. Hager never sees me but he says, 'Come now, Colonel, name your price—I *must* have that clock!' But my goodness I'd as soon think of selling my wife." . . .

He began to tell about an enormous speculation he was thinking of embarking some capital in—a speculation which some London bankers had been over to consult with him about—and soon he was building glittering pyramids of coin, and Washington was presently growing opulent under the magic of his eloquence. But at the same time Washington was not able to ignore the cold entirely. He was nearly as close to the stove as he could get, and yet he could not persuade himself that he felt the slightest heat, notwithstanding the isinglass door was still gently and serenely glowing. He tried to get a trifle closer to the stove, and the consequence was, he tripped the supporting poker and the stove-door tumbled to the floor. And then there was a revelation—there was nothing in the stove but a lighted tallow-candle!

The poor youth blushed and felt as if he must die with shame. But the Colonel was only disconcerted for a moment—he straightway found his voice again:

"A little idea of my own, Washington—one of the greatest things in the world! You must write and tell your father about it—don't forget that, now. I have been reading up some European Scientific reports—friend of mine, Count Fugier, sent them to me—sends me all sorts of things from Paris—he thinks the world of me, Fugier does. Well, I saw that the Academy of France had been testing the properties of heat, and they came to the conclusion that it was a nonconductor or something like that, and of course its influence must necessarily be deadly in nervous organizations with excitable temperaments, especially where there is any tendency toward rheumatic affections. Bless you, I saw in a moment what was the matter with us, and says I, out goes your fires!—no more slow torture and certain death for me, sir. What you want is the *appearance* of heat, not the heat itself—that's the idea. Well how to do it was the next thing. I just put my head to work, pegged away a couple of days, and here you are! Rheumatism? Why a man can't any more start a case of rheumatism in his house than he can shake an opinion out of a mummy! Stove with a candle in it and a transparent door—that's it—it has been the salvation of this family. Don't you fail to write your father about it, Washington. And tell him the idea is mine—I'm no more conceited than most people, I reckon, but you know it is human nature for a man to want credit for a thing like that." . . .

"I intend to look out for you, Washington, my boy. I hunted up a place for you yesterday, but I am not referring to that, now— that is a mere livelihood—mere bread and butter; but when I say I mean to look out for you I mean something very different. I mean to put things in your way that will make a mere livelihood a trifling thing. I'll put you in a way to make more money than you'll ever know what to do with. You'll be right here where I can put my hand on you when anything turns up. I've got some prodigious operations on foot; but I'm keeping quiet; mum's the word; your old hand don't go around pow-wowing and letting everybody see his k'yards and find out his little game. But all in good time, Washington, all in good time. You'll see. Now there's an operation in corn that looks well. Some New York men are trying to get me to go into it—buy up all the growing crops and just boss the market when they mature—ah, I tell you it's a great thing. And it only costs a trifle; two millions or two and a half will do it. I haven't exactly promised yet—there's no hurry—the more indifferent I seem, you know, the more anxious those fellows will get. And then there is the hog speculation—that's bigger still. We've got quiet men at work," [he was very impressive here] "mousing around, to get propositions out of all the farmers in the whole west and northwest for the hog crop, and other agents quietly getting propositions and terms out of all the manufacto-ries—and don't you see, if we can get all the hogs and all the slaughter houses into our hands on the dead quiet—whew! it would take three ships to carry the money.—I've looked into the thing—calculated all the chances for and all the chances against, and though I shake my head and hesitate and keep on thinking, apparently, I've got my mind made up that if the thing can be done on a capital of six millions, that's the horse to put up money on! Why Washington—but what's the use of talking about it—any man can see that there's whole Atlantic oceans of cash in it, gulfs and bays thrown in. But there's a bigger thing than that, yet—a bigger————"

"Why Colonel, you can't want anything bigger!" said Washing-ton, his eyes blazing. "Oh, I wish I could go into either of those speculations—I only wish I had money—I wish I wasn't cramped and kept down and fettered with poverty, and such prodigious chances lying right here in sight! Oh, it is a fearful thing to be poor. But don't throw away those things—they are so splendid and I can see how sure they are. Don't throw them away for something still better and maybe fail in it! I wouldn't, Colonel. I would stick to these. I wish father were here and were his old self again—Oh, he never in his life had such chances as these are. Colonel, you *can't* improve on these—no man can improve on them!"

A sweet, compassionate smile played about the Colonel's fea-tures, and he leaned over the table with the air of a man who is "going to show you" and do it without the least trouble:

"Why Washington, my boy, these things are nothing. They *look* large—of course they look large to a novice, but to a man who has been all his life accustomed to large operations—shaw! They're well enough to while away an idle hour with, or furnish a bit of employment that will give a trifle of idle capital a chance to earn its bread while it is waiting for something to *do*, but—now just listen a moment—just let me give you an idea of what we old veterans of commerce call 'business.' Here's the Rothschilds' prop-osition—this is between you and me, you understand————"

Washington nodded three or four times impatiently, and his glowing eyes said, "Yes, yes—hurry—I understand————"

————"for I wouldn't have it get out for a fortune. They want me to go in with them on the sly—agent was here two weeks ago about it—go in on the sly" [voice down to an impressive whisper, now] "and buy up a hundred and thirteen wildcat banks in Ohio, Indiana, Kentucky, Illinois and Missouri—notes of these banks are at all sorts of discount now—average discount of the hundred and thirteen is forty-four per cent—buy them all up, you see, and then all of a sudden let the cat out of the bag! Whiz! the stock of every one of those wildcats would spin up to a tremendous premium before you could turn a handspring—profit on the speculation not a dollar less than forty millions!" [An eloquent pause, while the marvelous vision settled into W.'s focus.] "Where's your hogs now! Why my dear innocent boy, we would just sit down on the front door-steps and peddle banks like lucifer matches!"

Washington finally got his breath and said:

"Oh, it is perfectly wonderful! Why couldn't these things have happened in father's day? And I—it's of no use—they simply lie before my face and mock me. There is nothing for me but to stand helpless and see other people reap the astonishing harvest."

"Never mind, Washington, don't you worry. I'll fix you. There's plenty of chances. How much money have you got?"

In the presence of so many millions, Washington could not keep from blushing when he had to confess that he had but eighteen dollars in the world.

"Well, all right—don't despair. Other people have been obliged to begin with less. I have a small idea that may develop into something for us both, all in good time. Keep your money close and add to it. I'll make it breed. I've been experimenting (to pass away the time,) on a little preparation for curing sore eyes—a kind of decoction nine-tenths water and the other tenth drugs that don't cost more than a dollar a barrel; I'm still experimenting; there's one ingredient wanted yet to perfect the thing, and somehow I can't just manage to hit upon the thing that's necessary, and I don't dare talk with a chemist, of course. But I'm progressing, and before many weeks I wager the country will ring with the fame of Beriah Sellers' Infallible Imperial Oriental Optic Liniment and Salvation for Sore Eyes—the Medical Wonder of the Age! Small bottles fifty cents, large ones a dollar. Average cost, five and seven cents for the two sizes. The first year sell, say, ten thousand bottles in Missouri, seven thousand in Iowa, three thousand in Arkansas, four thousand in Kentucky, six thousand in Illinois, and say twenty-five thousand in the rest of the country. Total, fifty-five thousand bottles; profit clear of all expenses, twenty thousand dollars at the very lowest calculation. All the capital needed is to manufacture the first two thousand bottles—say a hundred and fifty dollars—then the money would begin to flow in. The second year, sales would reach 200,000 bottles—clear profit, say, $75,000—and in the meantime the great factory would be building in St. Louis, to cost, say, $100,000. The third year we could easily sell 1,000,000 bottles in the United States and———"

"Oh, splendid!" said Washington. "Let's commence right away—let's———"

"———1,000,000 bottles in the United States—profit at least $350,000—and then it would begin to be time to turn our attention toward the real idea of the business."

"The real idea of it! Ain't $350,000 a year a pretty real———"

"Stuff! Why what an infant you are, Washington—what a guileless, short-sighted, easily-contented innocent you are, my poor little country-bred know-nothing! Would I go to all that trouble and bother for the poor crumbs a body might pick up in this country? Now do I look like a man who—does my history suggest that I am a man who deals in trifles, contents himself with the narrow horizon that hems in the common herd, sees no further than the end of his nose? Now you know that that is not me—couldn't be me. You ought to know that if I throw my time and abilities into a patent medicine, it's a patent medicine whose field of operations is the solid earth! its clients the swarming nations that inhabit it! Why, what is the republic of America for an eye-water country? Lord bless you, it is nothing but a barren highway that you've got to cross to get to the true eye-water market! Why, Washington, in the Oriental countries people swarm like the sands of the desert; every square mile of ground upholds its thousands upon thousands of struggling human creatures—and every separate and individual devil of them's got the ophthalmia! It's as natural to them as noses are—and sin. It's born with them, it stays with them, it's all that some of them have left when they die. Three years of introductory trade in the Orient and what will be the result? Why, our headquarters would be in Constantinople and our hindquarters in Further India! Factories and warehouses in Cairo, Ispahan, Bagdad, Damascus, Jerusalem, Yedo, Peking, Bangkok, Delhi, Bombay and Calcutta! Annual income—well, God only knows how many millions and millions apiece!"

Washington was so dazed, so bewildered—his heart and his eyes had wandered so far away among the strange lands beyond the seas, and such avalanches of coin and currency had fluttered and jingled confusedly down before him, that he was now as one who has been whirling round and round for a time, and, stopping all at once, finds his surroundings still whirling and all objects a dancing chaos. However, little by little the Sellers family cooled down and crystalized into shape, and the poor room lost its glitter and resumed its poverty. Then the youth found his voice and begged Sellers to drop everything and hurry up the eye-water; and he got his eighteen dollars and tried to force it upon the Colonel—pleaded with him to take it—implored him to do it. But the Colonel would not; said he would not need the capital (in his native magnificent way he called that eighteen dollars Capital) till the eye-water was an accomplished fact. He made Washington easy in his mind, though, by promising that he would call for it just as soon as the invention was finished, and he added the glad tidings that nobody but just they two should be admitted to a share in the speculation. . . .

2. Andrew Carnegie— *Triumphant Democracy* (1886)

On the other hand, Andrew Carnegie's *Triumphant Democracy* (1886) also reflected a point of view common in the United States, and not merely one held by men of wealth like the great iron master. Carnegie marvelled at the energy and creativity of his generation. He celebrated the enormous material achievements of Americans, but also their accomplishments in cultural and intellectual areas. As the following selection shows, he saw the United States as a kind of Utopia, its citizens marching (one might say galloping) into a Golden, rather than a Gilded Age. The truth, of course, lies somewhere between his view and Twain's, but no one has yet located its exact resting place.

The American at home, spinning along with his country, can obtain little idea of the amazing rate at which she is moving in

SOURCE: Andrew Carnegie, *Triumphant Democracy: Sixty Years' March of the Republic* (New York, 1886), pp. 494-7, 500, 503-9.

comparison with other parts of the world. It is only when he sits
down and studies statistics that he becomes almost dizzy at discovering the velocity with which she is rushing on. The prayer
cannot be repressed, that as this unparalleled material development proceeds there may come with it a like growth in the arts,
in knowledge, in education, in national virtue, and in all the
refinements of life. Happily, evidences abound on every hand that
such is the case. . . .

. . . It is only a few years since a clergyman wrote a book in
which he announced seven perils impending over the Republic.
One of these was Mormonism, which has thus so suddenly van-
ished into air. Another of the seven perils was intemperance,
which is also passing away. One may travel for months and never
see a man under the influence of liquor, and if he sees one it is a
poor foreigner. The native American is a sober man.

The third peril which was so terrible for the Republic, according to the reverend alarmist, was immigration; yet but fourteen
per cent of the present population, a proportion which must rapidly decline, is of foreign birth, and these have, almost without
exception, readily adapted themselves to republican conditions
and become good citizens. The growth of the Catholic Church was
another of the perils of the Republic, and of course the direst of
all; but it does not increase relatively to the population, and even
if it did, no peril to the Republic would ensue. So fade away these
imaginary perils of this overexcited preacher, and thus the
Republic ever confounds her prophets of evil. Anxious as this
writer no doubt was to obtain the publication of his pessimistic
alarm, which figures readily accessible would have entirely dis-
proved, one wonders how much more anxious he must now be to
recall it.

In theology, as noted in the chapter on religion, there have
been during the decade most encouraging signs of the coming of
the day when brethren will dwell together in unity. The bonds of
sectarianism are relaxing, and less attention is being paid to what
a man believes and more to what he does. . . .

The sums, amounting to many millions, bequeathed by individuals for educational and philanthropic ends; and what is much
more encouraging, the great sums given by an unusual number of
men during life for these and kindred objects, have been notable
in the decade just past. Millionnaires are beginning to realize more

and more the force of Seneca's words, "However owned, all is but a trust"—a trust to be administered during life for the good of the public from whom it came.

The change and advance made in education, in deference to modern ideas, has almost transformed our universities. These now give degrees for scientific instruction upon the same footing as for classics. In several universities the scientific has already become the most important course. No university or college could stand to-day which had not changed its methods and realized at last that its duty was to make our young men fit to be American citizens and not to waste their time trying to make poor imitations of Greeks and Romans. The study of English literature is now given proper precedence in the curriculums of several colleges, and Williams college has just discarded the knowledge of Latin and Greek as a test of admission. The widening of instruction in the public schools is also notable. Several States have embraced manual training, sewing, cookery, etc., and the schools of the city of New York are about to experiment with the kindergarten. The instruction given in the free public schools, formerly limited to the three R's, has been steadily extended to embrace other branches. . . .

In the field of invention we have to chronicle many achievements. The telephone has come into general use, and electricity, not only for light but as a motor, is now one of our most useful agents. Five thousand miles of cable and electric railway have been built. The phonograph and graphophone are coming into use. The kodak has made photography universal. Through several important inventions the new metal, aluminum, has conquered many fields and promises great results. We can claim for the decade that this article, which formerly cost ninety dollars per pound, is now sold for sixty cents. We may some day "buy gold cheap" through this sorceress, Science.

In material prosperity no previous decade has approached that under review. It has been almost incredible. Population has increased twelve and a half millions; all the rest of the English-speaking race increased only four and a quarter millions. Wealth has risen from $43,642,000,000 in 1880 to $65,000,000,000 in 1890. The wealth per habitant has increased from $366 in 1850 and $870 in 1880, to over $1,000 in 1890, an increase of nearly two hundred percent in forty years. . . .

Touching the material condition of the great mass of the people between 1889 and 1890, we may safely say that no nation ever enjoyed such universal prosperity. The producers, in agriculture and manufactures, have not made exceptional gains. Indeed, these have not been as prosperous as usual, owing to the great fall in the prices of products. But the masses of the people have never received compensation so high or purchased commodities so cheaply. Never in any country's history has so great a proportion of the products of labor and capital gone to labor and so little to capital. And this furnishes the best proof of a most satisfactory condition of affairs. It is probable that in many future decades the citizen is to look back upon this as the golden age of the Republic and long for a return of its conditions.

A general increase of wages marks the decade, these having risen in almost every branch of industry, while the cost of the necessaries of life has fallen below any recorded. In agriculture good crops have been the moving cause of the low prices of cereals, and in the manufacturing field improved methods have increased the product and thus increased the earnings of the worker. . . .

This is also the greatest decade ever known for railway building, there having been built between 1880 and 1890 almost as many miles as during the entire period from 1830 to 1880. Here are the figures: Total mileage in 1890, 163,562; miles built during the decade, 75,838. No clearer idea of the size and progress of the Republic can be obtained than by remembering that it continues to build every year about as many miles of railway as all the rest of the world. It has in completed railway lines to-day within twenty thousand miles as much as the rest of the world. . . .

The reduction of rates of postage to two cents, and for double the weight, is a notable event, and the credit of this belongs to the decade. We also have to credit the introduction of special-delivery stamps, by which, for the payment of ten cents, a letter is delivered at once by special messenger. . . .

The introduction of steam-pipes through cities for supplying steam, both for mechanical power and heating purposes, is another of the improvements for which we have to thank the period under review.

Reference has been made to the bad cookery formerly prevalent. A decided improvement is to be noted in this important matter. Schools have been created for the teaching of cooking, and students from the East have established themselves in the Western cities throughout the country, and a great improvement is now manifest as a result of their teaching.

We must not fail to note the triumphs of American surgery, and the great advance made in preventive medicine. In many branches the American surgeons have been the first, until now we are not surprised that in reviewing a recent text-book of American surgery the leading medical publication of Great Britain, *The Lancet,* ends with these significant words:

> If this text-book is a fair reflex of the present position of American surgery, we must admit it is of a very high order of merit, and that English surgeons will have to look very carefully to their laurels if they are to preserve a position in the van of surgical practice.

In no country was the importance of trained nurses so instantly recognized as in the United States, during the past decade. It is doubtful if there has been a more important step in advance in all the province of medicine than in properly educating suitable men and women for the office of nurse. The success of the movement throughout the United States has been phenomenal. In every city the patient has now at his call an agency for his cure only less potent than the physician. The character and attainments of the young women who have been drawn to this most useful vocation cause us to read without surprise of the marriage of several to remarkable men who have had an opportunity to become acquainted with them. . . .

No record of the decade would be complete without noting the triumphs of America in the region of astronomy. Professors Barnard, Burnham, Sedgwick, Rowland, Brashear, and others have rendered the decade illustrious, and placed the Republic in the front rank.

Our country has won many other notable triumphs. The Cuvier medal of the French Academy was presented to the Geological Survey of the United States in token of its invaluable work.

The Lalande medal for astronomical discoveries was presented to Professor Barnard, of the Lick Observatory.

Mr. Richard M. Hunt, of New York, has received the Royal gold medal for architecture, a gift of the Queen, awarded by the Royal Institute of British Architects.

Professor Rowland, of John Hopkins University, has recently been honored by the French Academy of Sciences, which has elected him a corresponding member.

The Bessemer gold medal has been presented to Hon. Abram S. Hewitt; and as I write, the cable informs us that it has this year also fallen to America, having been awarded to John Fritz, the mechanical Nestor of the iron and steel industry.

At the annual meeting of the Royal Geographical Society this year the gold medal was given to the United States chargé d'affaires, for presentation to an American citizen, W. Woodville Rockhill, "in recognition of the services rendered by him to geography by his travels and explorations in Western China, Koko Nor, Tsaidam, and Thibet, and his observations on the ethnology and languages of countries visited by him, and published in his book, 'The Land of the Lamas;' for the enterprise and intrepidity shown by him, and for his years of study of the native languages to prepare him for those travels."

All these are cheering evidences that the Republic is no longer compelled to rest its claims for recognition upon its vast material resources. It now challenges the older nations in the higher domain of intellectual, scientific, and artistic development. . . .

Part II

Agriculture

3. John C. Calhoun, II—Life and Labor in the New South (1883)

In 1883 the Senate Committe on Education and Labor conducted an investigation of the relations between labor and capital. Hearings were held in New York, New England, and in the South. Dozens of witnesses came forward to testify: great industrialists and ordinary workingmen, union leaders, social scientists, reformers, politicians, and fanatics. The bulk of the testimony collected concerned problems related to industrialization, but some witnesses spoke about the condition of agricultural workers too. The most interesting of these was John Caldwell Calhoun, grandson of the great South Carolina senator. This Calhoun had settled after the Civil War in Arkansas and become a cotton planter. His testimony offers an excellent picture of the labor system of the South and of the condition of the southern Negro in the 1870's and 1880's as seen by a conservative but well-intentioned white farmer. He is questioned here by the chairman of the committee, Republican Senator Henry W. Blair of New Hampshire.

SEN. BLAIR: Not having had a personal acquaintance with Mr. Calhoun, and learning of his rare opportunities to give valuable information to the committee, and of his presence in the city, I addressed him a letter, calling attention to the subject-matter upon which we should like information, and which I had reason to think he could give us better than almost any one else, indicating certain questions which I would like to have him prepared to answer, and receiving a courteous reply, expressing a willingness to oblige the committee, I have called him before the committee. . . .

SOURCE: U.S. Senate Committee on Education and Labor, *Report on the Relations Between Labor and Capital* (Washington; D.C., 1885), II, 157-61, 163-4, 169, 172-3, 186-7.

Q. What is the condition of the laborers in your section?—A. The laborers in the Mississippi Valley are agricultural. But few whites are employed; they soon become land-owners or tenants. Your question, therefore, reduces itself to, What is the condition of the negroes? I should say good, as compared with a few years ago, and improving. You must recollect that it has only been 18 years since the negroes emerged from slavery without a dollar and with no education, and that for generations they had been taught to rely entirely upon others for guidance and support. They became, therefore, at once the easy prey of unscrupulous men, who used them for their personal aggrandizement, were subjected to every evil influence, and did not discover for years the impositions practiced upon them. They were indolent and extravagant, and eager to buy on a credit everything the planter or merchant would sell them. The planter had nothing except the land, which, with the crop to be grown, was mortgaged generally for advances. If he refused to indulge his laborers in extravagant habits during the year, by crediting them for articles not absolutely necessary, his action was regarded as good grounds for them to quit work, and there were those present who were always ready to use this as an argument to array the negroes against the proprietors. This, of course, demoralized the country to a very great extent, and it has only been in the past few years the negro laborers have realized their true condition and gone to work with a view of making a support for themselves and families. There is yet much room for improvement, but they will improve just as they gain experience and become self-reliant.

Considering their condition after emancipation and the evil influences to which they have been subjected, even the small advancement they have made seems surprising.

Q. Under what systems are the laborers in your section employed?—A. There are three methods: we hire for wages for a part of the crop, or we rent. . . .

Q. What division is made between labor and capital of their joint production when you work on shares?—A. I doubt if there is greater liberality shown to laborers in any portion of the world than is done under this system. The proprietor furnishes the land and houses, including dwelling, stables, and out-houses, pays the taxes, makes all necessary improvements, keeps up repairs and insurance, gives free of cost a garden spot, fuel, pasturage for the stock owned by the laborers, and allows the use of his teams for hauling fuel and family supplies, provides mules or horses, wagons, gears, implements, feed for teams, the necessary machinery for ginning, or, in short, every expense of making the crop and preparing it for market, and then divides equally the whole gross proceeds with the laborers. In addition to all this, the proprietor frequently mortgages his real estate to obtain means to advance to the laborers supplies on their portion of the crop yet to be grown, thus mortgaging what he actually possesses, and taking a security not yet in existence, and which depends not only upon the vicissitudes of the seasons, but the faithfulness of the laborers themselves. Under this system thrifty, industrious laborers ought soon to become land-owners. But, owing to indolence, the negroes, except where they are very judiciously managed and encouraged, fail to take advantage of the opportunities offered them to raise the necessaries of life. They idle away all the time not actually necessary to make and gather their corn and cotton, and improvidently spend what balance may remain after paying for the advances made to them.

Q. When you rent, what division is made?—A. Where the laborer owns his own teams, gears, and implements necessary for making a crop, he gets two-thirds or three-fourths of the crop, according to the quality and location of the land.

Under the rental system proper, where a laborer is responsible and owns his team, &c., first-class land is rented to him for $8 or $10 per acre. With the land go certain privileges, such as those heretofore enumerated.

Q. How many hours do the laborers work?—A. This is an extremely difficult question to answer. Under the wages system, from sunrise to sunset, with a rest for dinner of from one and one-half to three hours, according to the season of the year.

Under the share or rental system there is much time lost; for instance, they seldom work on Saturday at all, and as the land is fertile, and a living can be made on a much smaller acreage than a hand can cultivate, they generally choose one-third less than they should, and it is safe to say that one-third of the time which could and would be utilized by an industrious laborer is wasted in fishing, hunting and idleness.

Q. Under what system do you work?—A. We are forced to adopt all of the systems heretofore stated. We prefer, however, the tenant system. We wish to make small farmers of our laborers, and bring them up as nearly as possible to the standard of the small white farmers. But this can only be done gradually, because the larger portion of the negroes are without any personal property. We could not afford to sell mules, implements, &c., where a laborer has nothing. Therefore the first year we contract to work with him on the half-share system, and require him to plant a portion of the land he cultivates in corn, hay, potatoes, &c. For this portion we charge him a reasonable rent, to be paid out of his part of the cotton raised on the remainder. In this way all of the supplies raised belong to him, and at the end of the first year he will, if industrious, find himself possessed of enough supplies to support and feed a mule. We then sell him a mule and implements, preserving, of course, liens until paid. At the end of the second year, if he should be unfortunate, and not quite pay out, we carry the balance over to the next year, and in this way we gradually make a tenant of him. We encourage him in every way in our power to be economical, industrious, and prudent, to surround his home with comforts, to plant an orchard and garden, and to raise his own meat, and to keep his own cows, for which he has free pasturage. Our object is to attach him as much as possible to his home. Under whatever system we work, we require the laborer to plant a part of his land in food crops and the balance in cotton with which to pay his rent and give him ready money. We consider this system as best calculated to advance him. Recognizing him as a citizen, we think we should do all in our power to fit him for the duties of citizenship. We think there is no better method of doing this than by interesting him in the production of the soil, surrounding him with home comforts, and imposing upon him the responsibilities of his business. Who will make the best citizen or laborer, he who goes to a home with a week's rations, wages spent, wife and children hired out, or he who returns to a home surrounded with the ordinary comforts, and wife and children helping him to enjoy the products of their joint labor? We recognize that no country can be prosperous unless the farmers are prosperous. Under our system, we seek to have our property cultivated by a reliable set of tenants, who will be able to always pay their rent and have a surplus left.

Again, a large portion of the cotton crop of the country is made by small white farmers. These to a great extent are raising their own supplies, and making cotton a surplus crop. The number who do this will increase year by year. It must be apparent that the large planters cannot afford to hire labor and compete with those whose cotton costs nothing except the expenditure of their own muscle and energy. The natural consequence resulting from this condition of things is that the negro, if he is to prosper, must gradually become a small farmer, either as a tenant or the owner of the soil, and look himself upon cotton as a surplus crop.

Q. What is the relation existing between the planters and their employés?—A. Friendly and harmonious. The planter feels an interest in the welfare of his laborers, and the latter in turn look to him for advice and assistance.

Q. What danger is there of strikes?—A. Very little. As a rule the laborers are interested in the production of the soil, and a strike would be as disastrous to them as it would be to the proprietors. There is really very little conflict between labor and capital. The conflict in my section, if any should come in the future, will not assume the form of labor against capital, but of race against race.

Q. How can the interest of the laborers of your section be best subserved?—A. By the establishment by the States of industrial schools, by the total elimination from Federal politics of the so-called negro question, and by leaving its solution to time, and a reduction of taxation, both indirect and incidental. It is a noteworthy fact that the improvement of my section has kept pace, *pari passu*, with the cessation of the agitation of race issues. The laborers share equally with the land owners the advantages of the improvement, and there is every reason to expect increasing and permanent prosperity if all questions between the land-owners and their laborers in our section are left to the natural adjustment of the demand for labor. For many years the negroes regarded themselves as the wards of the Federal Government, and it were well for them to understand that they have nothing more to expect from the Federal Government than the white man, and that, like him, their future depends upon their own energy, industry, and economy. This can work no hardship. The constant demand for their labor affords them the amplest protection. Nothing, probably, would contribute so immediately to their prosperity as the reduction of the tariff. They are the producers of no protected articles. The onerous burdens of the tariff naturally fall heaviest upon those who are large consumers of protected articles and produce only the great staples, grain and cotton, which form the basis of our export trade, and which can, from their very nature in this country, receive no protection from a tariff. . . .

Q. About the store system; how extensive is it, and how great an evil does it constitute?—A. It constitutes a very considerable evil, but you cannot blame the storekeeper for it, for this reason, or he can only be blamed partially: Capital in that country is very limited, and capital in New Orleans is very limited. When you consider the fact that New Orleans, which handles the cotton crop of that country, has a smaller banking capital than any one of your little towns in Massachusetts or New Hampshire, it shows at once that there is not enough capital to be advanced to the country people at reasonable enough rates of interest for those people to conduct a strictly legitimate business. I have known capital to cost in New Orleans, counting the commissions, 15 or 20 per cent, for money loaned. The storekeeper who borrows that money to conduct his business with has to buy his goods from some merchant at some point who must make his profit. He cannot go directly to the producer, because he has got to have somebody to help him out if his capital falls short. Therefore, before the goods get down to him, they have cost him perhaps 30, 40, or 50 per cent more than the first price. Therefore he has to tack on an enormous profit to bring himself out whole and pay his expenses in order to meet his obligations with the factor in New Orleans. There is, however, among a certain class, as there would be in all sections of the country, as exists right here in New York, or anywhere else, a set of people who will always prey upon ignorance. The best protection that can be afforded to the laborer of that country is education; fit him for his condition of life, that he may protect himself.

Q. Do you anticipate in the near or remote future any further difficulty from the race question?—A. Not at all, and if we are left to ourselves things will very soon equalize themselves.

Q. You are left to yourselves now, are you not?—A. We are now.

Q. All you ask is to continue to be let alone?—A. Just to be let alone. The South, with her natural resources and advantages of climate and soil, feels that she is perfectly able to take care of herself and her affairs, and all she wants is that the legislation of the country, both Federal and State, should be that which will mete out justice to all her citizens, colored as well as white. . . .

Q. You were speaking of the necessity of the education of the labor of the South, the negro especially. Will you not describe to us the actual condition of the masses of the colored people in the matter of education, to what extent it has progressed, and what facilities and opportunities exist, and what additional are required?—A. It varies in different sections. For instance, Georgia and Tennessee are probably ahead of any of the Southern States in point of educating the colored people; they have more facilities; they have negro primary schools and colleges where a man is educated. The education that I was speaking of, more particularly for the negro, is a plain English education, sufficient to enable him to read and write.

Q. What we call up North a common-school education?—A. A common-school education. I will illustrate that. Suppose a negro comes to me to make a contract that I have written for him, and he cannot read or write. I offer that contract to him, and I read it to him. He touches a pen and signs his mark to it; there is no obligation attached at all. He says at once, "That man is an educated man; he has the advantage of me; he shows me that contract. I do not know what is in it; I cannot even read it." Therefore a contract made with a negro in that way is almost a nullity; but if he could read that contract himself and sign his own name to it, it would be a very different thing. I never allow a negro to sign a written contract with me before he has taken it home with him and had some friend to read it over and consult with him about it, because I want some obligation attached to my contracts. . . .

Q. What do you think of his intellectual and moral qualities and his capacities for development?—A. There are individual instances I know of where negroes have received and taken a good education. As a class, it would probably be several generations, at any rate, before they would be able to compete with the Caucasian. I believe that the negro is capable of receiving an ordinary English education, and there are instances where they enter professions and become good lawyers. For instance, I know in the town of Greenville, Miss., right across the river from me, a negro attorney, who is a very intelligent man, and I heard one of the leading attorneys in Greenville say he would almost have anybody on the opposite side of a case rather than he would that negro. The sheriff of my county is from Ohio, and a negro, and he is a man whom we all support in his office, because he is capable of administering his office. We are anxious that the negroes should have a fair representation. For instance, you ask for the feeling existing between the proprietor and the negroes. The probate judge of my county is a negro and one of my tenants, and I am here now in New York attending to important business for my county as an appointee of that man. He has upon him the responsibilities of all estates in the county; he is probate judge.

Q. Do you think the feelings between the planter and the colored laborer, as a rule, are more amicable and friendly than on the part of the small white farmers toward the negro population; how is it in that regard?—A. I think that the white farmer is not so dependent upon the negroes as the large planter is for his labor, and he is not brought so much in contact with the negro laborer as the large proprietor. Probably he has not the same experience with him; but if a small white farmer became a planter and would have to employ laborers I do not know that there would be any difference in his treatment from that of an ordinary planter. . . .

4. John Wesley Powell—A New Policy for the Arid Lands of the West (1890)

Major John Wesley Powell, called by the historian William H. Goetzmann "the greatest explorer-hero since the days of Fremont," was a largely self-taught naturalist, a man of enormous curiosity and energy. Few Americans of any age equaled him in dedication both to the pursuit of scientific knowledge and to serving the public interest. Although he had lost an arm in the battle of Shiloh, he became after the war an active explorer and mapper of the Rocky Mountain region, his most famous achievement being his descent of the Colorado River through the gorges of the Grand Canyon.

Powell was in addition, however, an original thinker of the first order; he saw the West not only as a challenge to the geologist and geographer, but also as the seat of a new civilization with its own particular character. His interest, in other words, was social as well as scientific. His remarkable *Report on the Lands of the Arid Regions of the West* (1878) outlined a comprehensive plan of development based on the cooperative use of limited supplies of water and the employ-

SOURCE: J. W. Powell, "Institutions for the Arid Lands," *The Century Magazine*, XVIII (1890), 111-15.

ment of areas unfit for farming as grazing land. His proposals seemed too revolutionary for the Congress of that day, although from the perspective of the present they appear eminently reasonable. The following article, written in 1890 when Powell was director of the United States Geological Survey, was an attempt to marshal public support for his scheme.

In the East the log cabin was the beginning of civilization; in the West, the miner's camp. In the East agriculture began with the settler's clearing; in the West, with the exploitation of wealthy men. In the log cabin years a poor man in Ohio might clear an acre at a time and extend his potato-patch, his cornfield, and his meadow from year to year, and do all with his own hands and energy, and thus hew his way from poverty to plenty. At the same time his wife could plant hollyhocks, sweet-williams, marigolds, and roses in boxed beds of earth around the cabin door. So field and garden were all within the compass of a poor man's means, his own love of industry, and his wife's love of beauty. . . .

The farming of the arid region cannot be carried on in this manner. Individual farmers with small holdings cannot sustain themselves as individual men; for the little farm is, perchance, dependent upon the waters of some great river that can be turned out and controlled from year to year only by the combined labor of many men. And in modern times great machinery is used, and dams, reservoirs, canals, and many minor hydraulic appliances are necessary. These cost large sums of money, and in their construction and maintenance many men are employed. In the practice of agriculture by irrigation in high antiquity, men were organized as communal bodies or as slaves to carry on such operations by united labor. Thus the means of obtaining subsistence were of such a character as to give excuse and cogent argument for the establishment of despotism. The soil could be cultivated, great nations could be sustained, only by the organization of large bodies of men working together on the great enterprises of irrigation under despotic rulers. But such a system cannot obtain in the United States, where the love of liberty is universal.

What, then, shall be the organization of this new industry of agriculture by irrigation? Shall the farmers labor for themselves and own the agricultural properties severally? or shall the farmers be a few capitalists, employing labor on a large scale, as is done in the great mines and manufactories of the United States? The history of two decades of this industry exhibits this fact: that in part the irrigated lands are owned and cultivated by men having small holdings, but in larger part they are held in great tracts by capitalists, and the tendency to this is on the increase. When the springs and creeks are utilized small holdings are developed, but when the rivers are taken out upon the lands great holdings are acquired; and thus the farming industries of the West are falling into the hands of a wealthy few.

Various conditions have led to this. In some portions of the arid region, especially in California, the Spanish land grants were utilized for the purpose of aggregating large tracts for wholesale farming. Sometimes the lands granted to railroads were utilized for the same purpose. Then, to promote the irrigation of this desert land, an act was passed by Congress giving a section of land for a small price to any man who would irrigate it. Still other lands were acquired under the Homestead Act, the Preemption Act, and the Timber-Culture Act. Through these privileges title could be secured to two square miles of land by one individual. Companies wishing to engage in irrigation followed, in the main, one of two plans: they either bought the lands and irrigated their own tracts, or they constructed irrigating works and supplied water to the farmers. Through the one system land monopoly is developed; through the other, water monopoly. . . .

Where agriculture is dependent upon an artificial supply of water, and where there is more land than can be served by the water, values inhere in water, not in land; the land without the water is without value. A stream may be competent to irrigate 100,000 acres of land, and there may be 500,000 acres of land to which it is possible to carry the water. If one man holds that water he practically owns that land; whatever value is given to any portion of it is derived from the water owned by the one person. In the far West a man may turn a spring or a brook upon a little valley stretch and make him a home with his own resources, or a few neighbors may unite to turn a small creek from its natural channel and gradually make a cluster of farms. This has been done, and the available springs and brooks are almost exhausted. But the chief resource of irrigation is from the use of the rivers and from the storage of waters which run to waste during a greater part of the year; for the season of irrigation is short, and during most of the months the waters are lost unless held in reservoirs. In the development of these water companies there has been much conflict. In the main improvident franchises have been granted, and when found onerous the people have impaired or more or less destroyed them by unfriendly legislation and administration. The whole subject, however, is in its infancy, and the laws of the Western territory are inadequate to give security to capital invested in irrigating works on the one hand and protection to the farmer from extortion on the other. For this reason the tendency is to organize land companies. At present there is a large class of promoters who obtain options on lands and make contracts to supply water, and then enlist capital in the East and in Europe and organize and control construction companies, which, sometimes at least, make large profits. There seems to be little difficulty in interesting capitalists in these enterprises. The great increase in value given to land through its redemption by irrigation makes such investments exceedingly attractive. But at present investors and farmers are alike badly protected, and the lands and waters are falling into the hands of "middlemen." If the last few years' experience throws any light upon the future the people of the West are entering upon an era of unparalleled speculation, which will result in the aggregation of the lands and waters in the hands of a comparatively few persons. Let us hope that there is wisdom enough in the statesmen of America to avert the impending evil.

Whence, then, shall the capital come? and how shall the labor be organized by which these 100,000,000 acres of land are to be redeemed? This is the problem that to-day confronts our statesmen and financiers. Capital must come, for the work is demanded and will pay. Let us look at the statistics of this subject in round numbers, and always quite within probable limits. Let us speak of 100,000,000 acres of land to be redeemed by the use of rivers and reservoirs. This will cost about ten dollars per acre, or $1,000,-000,000. In the near future a demand for this amount will be made, and it will be forthcoming beyond a peradventure. The experience obtained by the redemption of 6,000,000 acres of land, already under cultivation, abundantly warrants the statement that an average of fifty dollars per acre is a small estimate to be placed upon the value of the lands yet to be redeemed as they come to be used. Thus there is a prize to be secured of $5,000,-000,000 by the investment of $1,000,000,000. Such vast undertakings will not be overlooked by the enterprising men of America. . . .

. . . The waters of to-day have values and must be divided; the waters of the morrow have values, and the waters of all coming time, and these values must be distributed among the people. How shall it be done?

It is proposed to present a plan for the solution of these problems, and others connected therewith, in an outline of institutions necessary for the arid lands. Some of these problems have been discussed in former articles, and it may be well to summarize them all once more, as follows:

First. The capital to redeem by irrigation 100,000,000 acres of land is to be obtained, and $1,000,000,000 is necessary.

Second. The lands are to be distributed to the people, and as yet we have no proper system of land laws by which it can be done.

Third. The waters must be divided among the States, and as yet there is no law for it, and the States are now in conflict.

Fourth. The waters are to be divided among the people, so that each man may have the amount necessary to fertilize his farm, each hamlet, town, and city the amount necessary for domestic purposes, and that every thirsty garden may quaff from the crystal waters that come from the mountains.

Fifth. The great forests that clothe the hills, plateaus, and mountains with verdure must be saved from devastation by fire and preserved for the use of man, that the sources of water may be protected, that farms may be fenced and homes built, and that all this wealth of forest may be distributed among the people.

Sixth. The grasses that are to feed the flocks and herds must be protected and utilized.

Seventh. The great mineral deposits—the fuel of the future, the iron for the railroads, and the gold and silver for our money— must be kept ready to the hand of industry and the brain of enterprise.

Eighth. The powers of the factories of that great land are to be created and utilized, that the hum of busy machinery may echo among the mountains—the symphonic music of industry.

A thousand millions of money must be used; who shall furnish it? Great and many industries are to be established; who shall control them? Millions of men are to labor; who shall employ them? This is a great nation, the Government is powerful; shall it engage in this work? So dreamers may dream, and so ambition may dictate, but in the name of the men who labor I demand that the laborers shall employ themselves; that the enterprise shall be controlled by the men who have the genius to organize and whose homes are in the lands developed, and that the money shall be furnished by the people; and I say to the Government: Hands off! Furnish the people with institutions of justice, and let them do the work for themselves. The solution to be propounded, then, is one of institutions to be organized for the establishment of justice, not of appropriations to be made and offices created by the Government.

In a group of mountains a small river has its source. A dozen or a score of creeks unite to form the trunk. The creeks higher up divide into brooks. All these streams combined form the drainage system of a hydrographic basin, a unit of country well defined in nature, for it is bounded above and on each side by heights of land that rise as crests to part the waters. Thus hydraulic basin is segregated from hydraulic basin by nature herself, and the landmarks are practically perpetual. In such a basin of the arid region the irrigable lands lie below; not chiefly by the river's side, but on the mesas and low plains that stretch back on each side. Above these lands the pasturage hills and mountains stand, and there the forests and sources of water supply are found. Such a district of country is a commonwealth by itself. The people who live therein are interdependent in all their industries. Every man is interested in the conservation and management of the water supply, for all the waters are needed within the district. The men who control the farming below must also control the upper regions where the waters are gathered from the heavens and stored in the reservoirs. Every farm and garden in the valley below is dependent upon each fountain above.

All of the lands that lie within the basin above the farming districts are the catchment areas for all the waters poured upon the fields below. The waters that control these works all constitute one system, are dependent one upon another, and are independent of all other systems. Not a spring or a creek can be touched without affecting the interests of every man who cultivates the soil in the region. All the waters are common property until they reach the main canal, where they are to be distributed among the people. How these waters are to be caught and the common source of wealth utilized by the individual settlers interested therein is a problem for the men of the district to solve, and for them alone.

But these same people are interested in the forests that crown the heights of the hydrographic basin. If they permit the forests to be destroyed, the source of their water supply is injured and the timber values are wiped out. If the forests are to be guarded, the people directly interested should perform the task. An army of aliens set to watch the forests would need another army of aliens to watch them, and a forestry organization under the hands of the General Government would become a hotbed of corruption; for it would be impossible to fix responsibility and difficult to secure integrity of administration, because ill-defined values in great quantities are involved.

Then the pasturage is to be protected. The men who protect these lands for the water they supply to agriculture can best protect the grasses for the summer pasturage of the cattle and horses and sheep that are to be fed on their farms during the months of winter. Again, the men who create water powers by constructing dams and digging canals should be permitted to utilize these powers for themselves, or to use the income from these powers which they themselves create, for the purpose of constructing and maintaining the works necessary to their agriculture.

Thus it is that there is a body of interdependent and unified interests and values, all collected in one hydrographic basin, and all segregated by well-defined boundary lines from the rest of the world. The people in such a district have common interests, common rights, and common duties, and must necessarily work together for common purposes. Let such a people organize, under national and State laws, a great irrigation district, including an entire hydrographic basin, and let them make their own laws for the division of the waters, for the protection and use of the forests, for the protection of the pasturage on the hills, and for the use of the powers. This, then, is the proposition I make: that the entire arid region be organized into natural hydrographic districts, each one to be a commonwealth within itself for the purpose of controlling and using the great values which have been pointed out. There are some great rivers where the larger trunks would have to be divided into two or more districts, but the majority would be of the character described. Each such community should possess its own irrigation works; it would have to erect diverting dams, dig canals, and construct reservoirs; and such works would have to be maintained from year to year. The plan is to establish local self-government by hydrographic basins. . . .

But the General Government must bear its part in the establishment of the institutions for the arid region. It is now the owner of most of the lands, and it must provide for the distribution of these lands to the people in part, and in part it must retain possession of them and hold them in trust for the districts. It must also divide the waters of the great rivers among the States. All this can be accomplished in the following manner. Let the General Government make a survey of the lands, segregating and designating the irrigable lands, the timber lands, the pasturage lands, and the mining lands; let the General Government retain possession of all except the irrigable lands, but give these to the people in severalty as homesteads. Then let the General Government declare and provide by statute that the people of each district may control and use the timber, the pasturage, and the water powers, under specific laws enacted by themselves and by the States to which they belong. Then let the General Government further declare and establish by statute how the waters are to be divided among the districts and used on the lands segregated as irrigable lands, and then provide that the waters of each district may be distributed among the people by the authorities of each district under State and national laws. By these means the water would be relegated to the several districts in proper manner, interstate problems would be solved, and the national courts could settle all interstate litigation.

But the mining industries of the country must be considered. Undeveloped mining lands should remain in the possession of the General Government, and titles thereto should pass to individuals, under provisions of statutes already existing, only where such lands are obtained by actual occupation and development and then in quantities sufficient for mining purposes only. Then mining regions must have mining towns. For these the townsite laws already enacted provide ample resource.

It is thus proposed to divide responsibility for these institutions between the General Government, the State governments, and the local governments. Having done this, it is proposed to allow the people to regulate their own affairs in their own way—borrow money, levy taxes, issue bonds, as they themselves shall determine; construct reservoirs, dig canals, when and how they please; make their own laws and choose their own officers; protect their own forests, utilize their own pasturage, and do as they please with their own powers; and to say to them that "with wisdom you may prosper, but with you must fail.". . .

5. William Godwin Moody— Bonanza Farming (1883)

The most spectacular agricultural development of the post-Reconstruction years occurred on the northern plains, where the vast, flat, treeless country was ideally suited to mechanized farming. Huge "bonanza" wheat farms, ranging in size from 3,000 to 100,000 acres, were put together by enterprising capitalists and run by professional agricultural managers. By the early 1880's there were about ninety of these giant farms in North Dakota alone; in good years some of them yielded harvests of several hundred thousand bushels of wheat. Bonanza operators used the latest machinery and employed small armies of migrant workers. Although this type of agriculture was never typical, even on the plains, the method alarmed many observers, for it seemed to presage the demise of the small independent farmer, so long considered the backbone of the nation.

William Godwin Moody was interested in bonanza farming primarily because of his concern for the workingman. The government had a duty, he insisted, to provide every man with an opportunity to work. Believing, like so many of his contemporaries, that "overproduction" was the chief symptom of the industrial malaise of the times, he advocated the 6-hour day as a means of spreading available jobs equitably and at the same time preventing the glutting of markets. The following account of bonanza farming, taken from Moody's book *Land and Labor in the United States* (1883), was based on a tour of the northern plains in 1879.

Within the past year or two a new development in agriculture, in the great Northwest, has forced itself upon the public attention, that would seem destined to exercise a most potent influence on the production of all food products, and work a revolution in the great economies of the farm. But not enough is known of this new development to enable one to form any just estimate of either its force or extent. For the purpose of obtaining the data necessary to assist to a more correct understanding of the opera-

SOURCE: W. G. Moody, *Land and Labor in the United States* (New York, 1883), pp. 31-2, 39-41, 43-8, 51-2, 55-9.

tions of what are known as the "Bonanza Farms," and their present and probable future effects, the writer went upon the ground
to make them a study.

On reaching St. Paul I visited the Land Office of the St.
Paul and Sioux City Railroad, to gather some facts in regard to
Southern Minnesota. The Land Commissioner, James H. Drake,
Esq., learning of the purpose of my tour in the Northwest,
expressed a strong desire that I should go over their road, visit
some of the great farms in its neighborhood, and see for myself. . .

. . . The farm of the Rock County Farming Company . . . contains 21,000 acres, of which 4,625 are now under cultivation, with
a large amount of land newly broken that will be seeded for next
year's crop. Of this amount 3,251 acres are in wheat; 312 acres in
flax; 550 acres in oats; 312 acres in barley; and 200 in corn. There
are 96 horses and mules, 26 harvesters, 3 straw burning steam
thrashers, and other farming implements to the total value of
$15,000. On the place are two stations, about two miles apart,
each having one house and two large barns, and other buildings
for the care of tools, stock, etc. The house at Station One is of
wood, two stories, double, painted white, and lathed and plas-
tered, containing the office of the superintendent and boarding
accommodation for a large number of men. At Station Two the
house is smaller, of one and a half stories, painted brown, without
lath or plaster, and fitted up specially as a boarding house for the
farm hands. The farm is immediately on the line of the railroad
and has two railroad stations.

The number of men employed is, for the month of March, 20;
April and May, 56; June to July 20th, 40; July 21st to August
20th, 115; August 21st to November 15th, 70; November 16th to
the end of February, 12. . . .

. . . In a number of places there were gangs of a dozen or more
plows engaged in breaking new ground for next year's crop. Each
plow was of the sulky pattern, with disc coulter, drawn by three
mules or horses, the driver occupying a seat between the wheels.
One of the plows was of a new pattern, being without a landslide,
and cutting a sixteen inch furrow four and a half inches deep,
which it cut and turned more beautifully than any I had before
seen.

On this farm, and at other points on this road, grasshoppers
were doing some damage. Earlier in the season the superintendent

had made a raid upon them, and showed me some heaps of a black mass, which he said were fifty-six bushels of that insect plague which he had caught in a tar machine, from the side of one quarter section.

Everywhere fruit growing appeared to be altogether neglected, and vegetable gardens and poultry were scarce.

I was informed that the large farmers on the road obtained special rates for their transportation, and that those rates were fifty per cent below the rates charged to the small farmers; and that their farming implements were obtained at thirty-three and one-third per cent discount from published prices, which the small farmers were compelled to pay.

The buildings of some of the small farmers who have been there located for some four or five years, or more, had a quite comfortable appearance; but the new settlers were generally without a sign of comfort. So far as I could learn, in conversation with them and upon inquiry, there was the same distress that I had found in Kansas and other places. . . .

Oliver Dalrymple, of St. Paul, the pioneer in the great farm development in this country in the Northwest, began his first operation seventeen years ago, in Minnesota, near St. Paul, where, for a number of years, he successfully cultivated a farm of 2,500 acres. At the time he commenced his work near St. Paul, in 1866, he paid $2.00 a bushel for his seed wheat, and sold his crop for $1.83; from his first crop paying for the whole investment and leaving a large surplus. After the Northern Pacific lands had passed into individual hands, as above referred to, Mr. Dalrymple entered into an arrangement with some of the holders, by which he was to undertake the management of their lands in the growing of wheat and other products. The proprietors of the lands to furnish land, stock, tools, and the capital required for seed, labor, and improvements, upon condition that when the products of the farms had paid all expenditures, with an agreed interest, he was to receive a clear title of one half .of each farm with its stock and improvements.

In the spring of 1876 he commenced his operations near Castleton, upon what are now known as the Cass farm, of 6,355 acres; and the Cheney farm, of 5,200 acres. The following year work was begun on what is known as the Grandin farm, at Grandin, of

40,000 acres. Subsequently Mr. Dalrymple obtained, in his own right, the Alton farm, of 4,000 acres, adjoining the Cass farm.

On arriving at Fargo, July 12th, I at once attempted to find Mr. Dalrymple at his office in that town, but did not succeed, he being at Castleton. Most fortunately I encountered Mr. J. L. Grandin, who at once cordially invited me to a seat in his carriage and a visit to his farm, at Grandin, thirty-six miles to the north of Fargo. . . .

J. L. Grandin is the principal owner of the 40,000 acre, or Grandin farm. At present there are on the place three stations, or points where are located the buildings necessary for the operations in their sections. Station One is located in the northeastern part of the farm, about 250 yards distant from the river. At this station are two dwellings, both of two stories and good size; one is painted white, being the residence of the farm superintendent and the foreman at that section; the other, painted brown, is fitted up specially as a boarding house for the hands. There are also two large barns, the general farm office, a large building for the storage and care of the tools, known as machinery hall, a steam feed mill, blacksmith shop, granary, vegetable storehouses, piggery, sheds, etc., in all thirteen good, substantial, well painted buildings, having the appearance, at a short distance, of a considerable village. At this station are two large wind mills, one near the superintendent's residence, the other on the bank of the river, about 300 yards distant, that forces water into a tank at the station. On the bank of the river is a storehouse for the shipment of grain, with two cars to run on a double wooden tramway, so arranged that the loaded car in descending to the boat will draw up the empty one.

Station Two is two and a half miles to the south of Station One, containing the dwelling of the foreman at that portion of the farm, and a boarding house, both smaller than at Station One; a machinery hall, a large barn, and a blacksmith shop, with other buildings, eight in all, substantial and well painted. At this station is a large water tank, filled by a wind mill on the bank of the river one half mile to the east. On the river bank, at that point, is another storehouse like that at Station One, and for the same purpose.

Station Three, one half mile south and one mile west of Station Two has one dwelling of one and a half stories for the foreman there located, and cooking arrangements for the men there employed, who find sleeping room in the loft over machinery hall; beside which there is a large barn and other small buildings. At this station there was being erected a granary of the capacity of 50,000 bushels. The buildings of this station are of the same substantial character as the others upon the farm. The three stations are connected by telegraph and telephone, and with the general office at Station One. . . .

There are 1,200 acres of new land now broken, to be seeded next year, in addition to the amount already under cultivation, giving 6,500 acres for the crop of 1880. It is the avowed intention to add to the amount under cultivation from year to year, and construct additional stations as required.

The men are called at four o'clock in the morning, breakfast, and get to work a little after five, and work till seven in the evening, with one hour at noon for dinner, making nearly thirteen hours of labor per day.

Going to the Grandin farm from the way of Fargo, one mile from the place, upon the left hand, a field of one mile square of wheat was seen, belonging to Dr. Garrett, of Philadelphia. Passing that field, with no visible division between, the wheat fields of the Grandin farm are reached, lying on both sides of the road for four continuous miles; that on the left hand being two miles wide and on the right about a half mile to the river. A row of young elms has been set out on both sides of the road for the full four miles, and, also, about the yard of the superintendent's dwelling, at Station One. But not a fruit tree or bush was to be seen. Mr. Grandin informed me it was the intention to divide the whole farm into section lots of 640 acres each, opening roads on the section lines and planting elms on all the roads.

Every facility was afforded for the fullest observation, and to give me all the information desired. It would be difficult to find a finer sight than was presented by those magnificent fields of grain, standing breast high, taking on the golden yellow that precedes the harvest, their heads, as far as the eye could reach, standing as level and smooth as the top of a great table; and when fanned by the wind moving in ripples and waves like the waters of a sea.

It was believed that the yield of wheat would be at least twenty bushels to the acre. Some portions, it was said, would give more than thirty bushels. It certainly was very fine. The grain grown upon the farm, and by others near the river, was shipped to Fargo by way of the Grandin line of steamers. . . .

Most persons in reading of fields described by hundreds and thousands of acres can form but little idea of their actual or comparative sizes. To assist to a better understanding of the sizes of these fields and farms I will state that Manhattan Island, the site of the City of New York, has an area of about twenty-two square miles, or 14,000 acres. The fields of grain of the three farms lying together contain an area of 10,477 acres, or about three fourths of the area of the City of New York. The Grandin farm of 40,000 acres has nearly space enough for three cities like New York; and the whole farm property of the Grandins would furnish sites for five such cities. Whatever else may be said of these operations, they certainly are not wanting in grandeur. . . .

To well weigh the economic effects of the developments here considered, it must be remembered that they are yet in their infancy—that they are mainly the growth of the last half of the past and the present decade—and must make some effort to estimate the probable future development of the same forces and effects under the present rate of acceleration. All parties engaged in these enterprises concurred in the statement that great numbers of capitalists who are already large holders of agricultural lands, as well as others who have not yet obtained any, are only waiting the results of the present harvest before they also enter into the business. The amounts of new land broken, in all directions, for future seeding, are very great.

The two great facts developed by these observations are, that those who have gone into wheat growing upon a large scale, making use of the most improved machinery and cheap labor, are making colossal fortunes at seventy cents per bushel for wheat, limited only by the number of acres cultivated and the skill with which the work is done; and that it may also be grown, at large profits, for less than twenty-five cents per bushel.

But that, on the other hand, the small farmers, depending mainly on their own labor, with limited capital and less machinery, are not making a comfortable subsistence, but are running behind hand and must go under; and that a further reduction in the market price for food products must hasten their end.

Before agricultural machinery had come into general use, and before the age of railroads, the farms of our fathers would average, in size, but little more than one hundred acres, with an amount of plowland equalling about fifty acres each. Very rarely did they exceed double that amount. On every such farm was there a family home, with all the ties, endearments, advantages, and improvements that the word "home" conveys to our minds. They furnished not alone homes, but employment, abundance, and comfort for a family of at least a dozen persons. Go through New England, New York, New Jersey, Pennsylvania, and Ohio, and see the great numbers of such places, all of them formerly family homesteads, lying within sight and hailing distance of each other. From a half dozen to an hundred may be seen from almost any elevated point.

Now mark the change that has already taken place and is fast obtaining in all our new and great agricultural regions. Under the power of machinery and capital the farms have grown from the size of 100 acres, as formerly, to 1,000 acres, to 10,000 acres, to 100,000 acres, even to 500,000 acres, or nearly 800 square miles, and more, with not one home upon their vast areas; with no one surrounding a family rooftree with all that made the old home a paradise. Yet these huge tracts are being developed, cultivated, and made to yield as was no farm in the days of our fathers. Now, machinery and a few score or a few hundred hirelings and animals, to run and attend the machines, do the work under the eye of overseers. The hirelings—the human animals—are worked for a few weeks or a few months in the year, paid barely enough to live upon for the time being, and then are turned out and driven from the place, to tramp or live as best they can, no matter what may be the want and misery of their lives, whilst the brute animals and machines are well housed and cared for. The owner of the farm has a property interest in the brute, but no interest whatever in the human animal other than that of getting the greatest possible amount of work for the least amount of compensation. The most valuable improvements are for the protection of the brutes and the machinery, whilst the human tillers of the soil have neither right nor interest in anything they see, or touch, or produce. In this way the finest sections of our country, in tracts running up to the size of eight hundred or more square miles— areas that would give fifty acres of plowland to more than a thousand families, and to our fathers would have furnished homes, ample employment, and comfort to more than ten thousand peo-

ple—are now without even one home, and furnish but transient
and uncertain employment to a few hundreds.

This state of things is made possible, and is obtaining, solely by
and under the power and use of machinery; first in the hands of
individual capitalists; then in the hands of companies; and, lastly,
by corporations.

The owners of these large tracts have bonanzas, yielding great
profits, not one dollar of which is expended in beautifying and
permanently improving their vast estates, beyond that necessary
for the care of the stock and tools, nor in sustaining a permanent
population. Their homes, their pleasures, their family ties, are not
upon their farms. Their wealth is flaunted in the gaieties and dis-
sipations, or expended in building and developing some distant
city or country. But the owner and cultivator of the small farm in
its neighborhood, upon which he has planted his rooftree, and
around which are gathered all his hopes and ambitions, finds it
impossible to pay his taxes, clothe and educate, or find any comfort for his wife and little ones. The case of the small farmer is
steadily going from bad to worse. The two can not exist together;
the small farmer can not successfully compete with his gigantic
neighbor under present conditions. He will inevitably be swal-
lowed up. It is at best but a question of time.

Thus are vast areas, in the very heart of our country, barred
and closed to the occupation and ownership of our people in
small tracts, and the making of homes for a strong and thrifty population, but are made centers of weakness that are sure, soon or
late, under present tendencies, to spread over the whole land. . . .

6. Rodney Welch—
The Changing World of the Farmer (1891)

More basic than the machine itself as a revolutionary force in agriculture was the increasing commercialization of farming. American farmers had always produced for the market; except in the most isolated
frontier districts, real self-sufficiency was a myth even in colonial times.
But nineteenth-century improvements in transportation, especially the

SOURCE: Rodney Welch, "The Farmer's Changed Condition," *The Forum*, X
(1891), 689-90, 692-5, 697-9.

spread of the railroad network, enabled farmers in every section to sell their produce in national and even in international markets and to obtain the manufactured goods they desired from equally distant sources. This "commercial revolution" wrought a fundamental change in the way of life of the agriculturalist. It provided him with creature comforts and opened up to him a host of intellectual and cultural opportunities, but it also made him more dependent upon outside influences for both his prosperity and his psychological wellbeing. It raised his hopes and expectations, but then caused him to be dissatisfied when his new ambitions were not entirely achieved. In the following essay a contemporary observer, Rodney Welch, describes the transformation that was sweeping over agriculture in the United States and comments upon some of its effects.

During my childhood, which was passed on a rocky hillside farm in New England, farmers constituted a class more nearly independent than any other in the community. They were engaged in domestic husbandry, which embraced the care of cultivated fields, pastures, gardens, orchards, and forests. They produced nearly all the food that was necessary for their families. The owner of a small farm not infrequently raised corn, wheat, rye, barley, and buckwheat, as well as potatoes and all kinds of garden vegetables. The sweets for the table were often limited to the sugar and molasses that he made from the sap on the maple, and to the honey collected by his bees. Small game was obtained from the forest, and trout were caught in the streams that flowed among the hills. The lake afforded larger fish, like perch and pickerel. Every farmer's intention was to raise each needful article of food that the climate and soil enabled him to produce. Even condiments, like pepper, caraway seed, sage, and other sweet herbs, were not below his attention. As a considerable portion of every farm was covered with forest trees of various kinds, the owner was at no expense for fuel or for materials to be used in making fences or in erecting ordinary buildings.

In those times most of the trade of farmers was carried on by barter. Eggs, butter, cheese, and smoked hams were taken by country store-keepers in exchange for groceries, dry goods, and notions. Nearly every farmer went to the seashore once a year, and exchanged apples, cider, potatoes, and garden vegetables for fish. The products of farm, garden, and orchard often paid the salary of the minister, the fees of the doctor, and the subscription price of the newspaper. A thrifty farmer generally managed to have the skins of the animals that he slaughtered at home tanned and dressed on shares, as by so doing he obtained leather for making shoes and boots for his family, without the payment of money. Shoe-makers then went from house to house, taking a kit of tools with them and often remaining for several days at a time. In many cases they made their shoe pegs from blocks of birch wood that the farmer had in readiness, used thread that the farmer's wife had spun from flax grown on the farm, and smoothed it with wax saved from the honey comb that had been taken from the bee hive. They were often paid for their services in cord wood, hay, grain, potatoes, butter, cheese, stocking yarn, or other articles that were useful in a family. Tailoresses also went from house to house and cut and made the garments worn by the men and boys. Wheelwrights held themselves in readiness to go to farmers' homes and make the running gear of the ox carts that were then generally employed to draw heavy articles on the farm and to haul them to market. Pump-makers, too, plied their art on farms at the call of the owners.

Every farm house was then a manufactory, not of one kind of goods, but of many. All day long in the chamber or attic the sound of the spinning wheel and loom could be heard. Carpets, shawls, bed spreads, table covers, towels, and cloth for garments were made from materials produced on the farm. Many of these kinds of cloth were marvels of beauty and utility. The kitchen of the house was a baker's shop, a confectioner's establishment, and a chemist's laboratory. Every kind of food for immediate use was prepared there daily; and on special occasions sausages, head cheese, pickles, apple butter, and preserves were made. It was also the place where soap, candles, and vinegar were manufactured. In one of the buildings attached to the house, or near it, the farmer had a workshop in which he made ox yokes, bows for fastening cattle to stanchions, milking stools, the handles for farming tools, and often the tools themselves. Agricultural implements were then few and simple, and farmers made as many of them as they could. . . .

There was little of what could be called commercial farming in the northern States at that time. Farmers who were located near the seacoast, or near a navigable river, could always dispose of their surplus products to good advantage and at fair prices. But such was not the case with farmers who lived a long distance from water communications. They could drive their cattle to market, but the price of their grain was consumed in hauling it a hundred miles, while their apples and potatoes would not be accepted as gifts. There was often great scarcity of some product of which there was an abundance in a locality two hundred miles away. Wool was almost the only article that could be transported a long distance without having its price absorbed in the cost of cartage. . . .

At present little remains to remind one of the condition of farmers during the time I have referred to. They now generally occupy the great prairies of the West instead of the hills and valleys of the eastern States. They are no longer engaged in domestic farming. Like manufacturers and the operators of mines, they are producing articles for supplying the market. They buy almost as many things as do persons who live in towns. They do not take their wheat and corn to a custom mill to be converted into flour and meal, but they sell their grain and buy the materials to make bread for their familes. They have given up raising small products for the supply of their tables, and as a consequence their grocery bills are large. As there are few trees in the prairie regions, and as the area occupied by forests in other parts of the country has been greatly reduced, farmers are compelled to purchase their fuel, which is generally bituminous coal, and to buy all the materials used in the construction of fences and buildings. The owners of many western farms are obliged to buy even pea sticks and bean poles.

The farmer of the present day has no necessity for bartering his products. He has no occasion to use eggs instead of coins when he is making small purchases. Everything he raises commands a price, though it may be small. In many of the western States—Illinois, for instance—nine tenths of the farm houses are within five miles of railway stations, and at most of these stations are grain elevators and yards for holding cattle and hogs till they can be loaded upon stock cars. There is no occasion for a farmer to go to a city market with his stock, grain, wool, or other products. He generally finds it to his advantage to consign them to some commission merchant, thus saving the cost of travel. . . .

The farm house is no longer a manufactory; the sound of the loom and the spinning wheel is never heard in it, and the socks and mittens used by members of the family are not knit at home. If many cows are kept on the place, their milk is generally sent to a creamery or to a cheese factory. The making of candles, soap, beer, and vinegar, the bleaching of cloth, straw hats, and bonnets, and the dyeing of garments, are numbered among the lost arts of the household. The introduction of machinery has revolutionized almost every branch of work on farms, and has greatly reduced the number of laborers required. In the great grain-producing sections of the country, farming has almost become a sedentary occupation. The soil is turned by a gang plow drawn by four horses, while the driver is mounted on a spring seat covered with a cushion. The sower no longer goes forth to scatter seed which he carries in a bag or basket; he rides on a grain drill and holds the reins that guide a pair of matched bay or chestnut horses, handsome enough to draw a duchess through the streets of London. At harvest time the owner of the wheat fields mounts another cushioned spring seat, shaded by a canopy, and again takes the reins; the self-binding harvester does the rest. Corn is planted, cultivated, husked, and shelled by machines. Haymaking, once the most laborious occupation on the farm, has been rendered the easiest by the introduction of machines that cut the grass, spread it over the surface of the ground, rake it together when it has become dry, raise it upon the wagon, and carry it to the hay loft or stack. The flail has been laid aside with the distaff, the hand loom, and the spinning wheel. The steam-propelled threshing machine surpasses any other labor-saving device ever invented. . . .

Still, with all these apparently beneficial changes, with machines to do nearly all the work, with money for their products instead of "store pay," with a market at the door, with more leisure and less drudgery, I doubt if farmers are any better contented with their lot, or if they obtain more enjoyment from life, than they did in old times. I also question if they are more prosperous. They are generally in a condition of unrest, if not of discontent. Their social condition has not improved, as has that of mechanics and traders. Most of them are anxious to leave the farm for the store, the shop, the mine, or the locomotive. . . .

The migration from country to town commenced in our northern States near the close of the civil war, and it has been steadily increasing till the present time. It has included the most desirable and the least desirable of the inhabitants of the rural districts. It may sound strange to eastern readers, but it is nevertheless true, that in the States of Illinois, Wisconsin, and Iowa more farms have been deserted by their owners than in New Hampshire, Vermont, and Massachusetts. In the New England States owners leave their farms because the labor spent in cultivating them is no longer remunerative, but such is not the case in the prairie regions of the West. There the owners of farms leave them for the reason that they can obtain sufficient rent from tenants to enable them to support their families in towns. . . .

Wealthy farmers move to town because they wish better social, educational, and religious advantages than are afforded in the country. The desire for amusements also exerts an influence. When one family of refinement and culture leaves a farming neighborhood, several are likely to follow its example, till finally the desire for agreeable companionship causes nearly every farmer of intelligence and refinement to leave the place which he had fitted up for a home. The result of this is the formation of a distinct peasant class, such as is found in Bavaria and Bohemia. In entire counties in Illinois and Wisconsin the English language is scarcely ever heard outside of the large towns. The church services are conducted in a foreign tongue, and instruction is given in it in the schools. The intellectual condition of the people who occupy farms there is not above that of the lowest class of laborers in our large cities. The townships they inhabit seem like detached portions of central Europe put down near the center of the new world. Nominally these men may be citizens, for town politicians have had them passed through the naturalization mill; but they know little and care less about the institutions of the country.

Farmers have long been losing their place and influence in the councils of the State and nation. Our later Congresses have not contained enough farmers from the northern States to constitute the committees on agriculture. Our national law-makers have known so little about what would promote the prosperity of farmers that they have favored measures that have greatly injured agriculture. They have insisted on developing the national domain in advance of a demand for any more land for cultivation, and they have purchased Indian reservations of great size and have disposed of the land at a price that has scarcely paid the cost of surveying and the expenses of the land offices. By these means they have encouraged tens of thousands of persons to engage in farming who would otherwise have remained in other pursuits. The offer of free land, or of land at a nominal price, has tempted many to leave shops, mines, and vessels, and to engage in agriculture. These have become the competitors of the producers in the old States who had spent much time and money in improving farms. They have overstocked the home and foreign markets with grain, meat, vegetables, fruits, dairy products, and honey, and as a consequence the price of nearly every farm product has declined, sometimes below the cost of the labor required to produce it. . . .

Part III

Industry

7. David Ames Wells—
The American Industrial Revolution (1889)

One of the most interesting books published in the United States during the 1880's was David A. Wells's *Recent Economic Changes.* Wells was an economist of the free-trade, hard-money school, basically conservative but wide-ranging in his interests. He was capable of grasping the significance of seemingly trivial changes and of seeing the relationship between apparently unrelated trends. He understood clearly that industrialization was transforming not only the economy but also the whole character of American life. In his book he discussed such matters as the increased incidence of heart trouble and divorce, along with more conventional subjects like trends in production and prices. In the following section he deals with the "problem" of over-production—its causes and consequences—and with other aspects of the "almost total revolution" that was convulsing the American economy.

The most popular alleged cause of recent economic disturbances . . . is *"over-production."* In a certain sense there can be no over-production of desirable products so long as human wants for such products remain unsatisfied. But it is in accordance with the most common of the world's experiences that there is at times and places a production of most useful and desirable things in excess of any demand at remunerative prices to the producer. This happens, in some instances, through lack of progress or enterprise, and in others through what may be termed an excess of progress or enterprise. An example of the first is to be found in the circum-

SOURCE: D. A. Wells, *Recent Economic Changes* (New York, 1889), pp. 70-5, 78-80, 91-4, 105-9, 111.

stance that in the days of Turgot, the French Minister of Finance under Louis XVI, there were at times in certain departments of France such abundant harvests that wheat was almost unmarketable, while in other and not far-distant sections of the country there was such a lack of food that the inhabitants perished of hunger; and yet, through the absence of facilities for transportation and communication of intelligence, the influence of bad laws, and the moral inertia of the people, there was no equalization of conditions.

An example of the second, intensified to a degree never before experienced, is to be found in the results of the improvements in production and distribution which have been made especially effective within the last quarter of a century. A given amount of labor, operating through machinery, produces or distributes at least a third more product on the average, in given time, than ever before. Note the natural tendency of human nature under the new conditions. The machinery which thus cheapens and increases product is, as a rule, most costly, and entails a like burden of interest, insurance, and care, whether it is at work or idle; and the possessor of it, recognizing this fact, naturally desires to convert outlay into income by utilizing it to the greatest extent possible. Again, a man who has learned by experience that he can dispose of a certain amount of product or service at a profit, naturally reasons that a larger amount will give him, if not a proportionally greater, at least a larger aggregate profit; and as the conditions determining demand are not only imperfectly known, but to a certain extent incapable of exact determination, he discards the idea of any risk, even if he for a moment entertains it, and pushes industrial effort to its maximum. And as this process is general, and, as a rule, involves a steady increase in the improved and constantly improving instrumentalities of production and distribution, the period at length arrives when the industrial and commercial world awakens to the fact that there is a product disproportionate to any current remunerative demand. Here, then, is one and probably the best explanation of the circumstance that the supply of very many of the great articles and instrumentalities of the world's use and commerce has increased, during the last ten or fifteen years, in a far greater ratio than the contemporaneous increase in the world's population, or of its immediate consuming capacity.

Another interesting feature of the situation . . . is, that "over-production" in recent years has resulted largely from the establishment of many new industrial enterprises whose capacity for production far exceeds any concurrent market demand; as is especially exemplified in the case of the manufacture of iron. . . . It was formerly a general assumption that, when price no longer equaled the cost of production and a fair profit on capital, production would be restricted or suspended; that the less favored producers would be crowded out, and by the relief thus afforded to the market normal prices would be again restored. But this doctrine is no longer applicable to the modern methods of production. Those engaged in great industrial enterprises, whether they form joint-stock companies or are simply wealthy individuals, are invested with such economic powers that none of them can be easily pushed to the wall, inasmuch as they can continue to work under conditions that would not permit a small producer to exist. Examples are familiar of joint-stock companies that have made no profit and paid no dividends for years, and yet continue active operations. The shareholders are content if the plant is kept up and the working capital preserved intact, and even when this is not done, they prefer to submit to assessments, or issue preference shares and take them up themselves rather than go into liquidation, with the chance of losing their whole capital. Another feature of such a condition of things is, that the war of competition in which such industrial enterprises are usually engaged is mainly carried on by a greater and greater extension of the market supply of their products. An illustration of this is afforded in the recent history of the production of copper. When in 1885 the United States produced and put on to the market seventy-four thousand tons, as against forty thousand tons in 1882, the world's prices of copper greatly declined. A large number of the smaller producers were compelled to suspend operations, or were entirely crushed; but the great Spanish and other important mines endeavored "to offset the diminution of profit on the unit of quantity" by increasing their production; and thus the price of copper continued to decline until it reached a lower figure than ever before known in history.

Under such circumstances *industrial over-production*—manifesting itself in excessive competition to effect sales, and a reduction of prices below the cost of production—may become

chronic; and there appears to be no other means of avoiding such results than that the great producers should come to
some understanding among themselves as to the prices they will
ask; which in turn naturally implies agreements as to the extent
to which they will produce. Up to this point of procedure no
exception on the part of society can well be taken. But such an
agreement, once perfected and carried out, admits of an almost
entire control of prices and the establishment of monopolies, in
the management of which the rights of the public may be wholly
ignored. Society has practically abandoned—and from the very
necessity of the case has got to abandon, unless it proposes to war
against progress and civilization—the prohibition of industrial
concentrations and combinations. The world demands abundance
of commodities, and demands them cheaply; and experience
shows that it can have them only by the employment of great capital upon the most extensive scale. The problem, therefore, which
society under this condition of affairs has presented to it for solution is a difficult one, and twofold in its nature. To the producer
the question of importance is, How can competition be restricted
to an extent sufficient to prevent its injurious excesses? To the
consumer, How can combination be restricted so as to secure its
advantages and at the same time curb its abuses? . . .

If production exceeds, by even a very small percentage, what is
required to meet every current demand for consumption, the
price which the surplus will command in the open market will
govern and control the price of the whole; and if it can not be
sold at all, or with difficulty, an intense competition on the part of
the owners of accumulated stocks to sell will be engendered, with
a great reduction or annihilation of all profit. . . .

. . . From 1881 to 1884 the American nail manufacture was
exceedingly profitable; and during those years, as a natural consequence, most of the existing mills increased their capacity, and
some more than doubled it. New mills also were built East and
West, until the nail-producing power of the country nearly doubled, while the consuming capacity increased only about twenty
per cent. The further result was that prices were forced down by
an overstocked market, until nails were sold at from ten to fifteen
per cent below cost, and in some instances mills that "could stand
alone" were accused of intentionally forcing down prices in order
to bankrupt weaker competitors. In the end prices were in a meas-

ure restored by a combination and agreement among manufacturers to restrict production.

Another illustration to the same effect is to be found in the present remarkable condition of the milling (flour) interest of the
United States, which was thus described in an address before the
"National Millers' Association" by its vice-president, at their
annual meeting at Buffalo, in June, 1888:

"A new common enemy," he said, "has sprung up, which threatens
our property with virtual confiscation. . . . Large output, quick sales,
keen competition, and small profits are characteristics of all modern
trade. We have the advantage in our business of always being in fashion; the world requires so much bread every day, a quantity which can
be ascertained with almost mathematical accuracy. . . . But our ambition has overreached our discretion and judgment. We have all parti-
cipated in the general steeple-chase for pre-eminence; the thousand-
barrel mill of our competitor had to be put in the shade by a two-
thousand-barrel mill of our town construction; the commercial triumph of former seasons had to be surpassed by still more dazzling
figures. As our glory increased our profits became smaller, until now
the question is not how to surpass the record, but how to maintain our
position and how to secure what we have in our possession. . . . In the
general scramble we have gradually lost sight of the inexorable laws of
supply and demand. We have been guilty of drifting away from sound
trade regulations until our business has not only ceased to be profitable but carries with it undue commercial hazard."

As prices fall and profits shrink, producers working on insufficient capital, or by imperfect methods, are soon obliged, in order
to meet impending obligations, to force sales through a further
reduction of prices; and then stronger competitors, in order to
retain their markets and customers, are compelled to follow their
example; and this in turn is followed by new concessions alter-
nately by both parties, until gradually the industrial system
becomes depressed and demoralized, and the weaker succumb
(fail), with a greater or less destruction of capital and waste of
product. Affairs now having reached their maximum of depres-
sion, recovery slowly commences. Consumption is never arrested,
even if production is, for the world must continue to consume in
order that life and civilization may exist. The continued increase
of population also increases the aggregate of consumption; and,
finally, the industrial and commercial world again suddenly real-
izes that the condition of affairs has been reversed, and that now

the supply has become unequal to the demand. Then such producers as have "stocks on hand," or the machinery of production ready for immediate and effective service, realize large profits; and the realization of this fact immediately tempts others to rush into production, in many cases with insufficient capital (raised often through stock companies), and without that practical knowledge of the detail of their undertaking which is necessary to insure success, and the old experience of inflation and reaction is again and again repeated.

Hence the explanation of the now much-talked-of "periods" or "cycles" of panic and speculation, of trade activity and stagnation. . . .

. . . Consider next how potent for economic disturbance have been the changes in recent years in the relations of labor and capital, and how clearly and unmistakably these changes are consequents or derivatives from a more potent and antecedent agency.

Machinery is now recognized as essential to cheap production. Nobody can produce effectively and economically without it, and what was formerly known as domestic manufacture is now almost obsolete. But machinery is one of the most expensive of all products, and its extensive purchase and use require an amount of capital far beyond the capacity of the ordinary individual to furnish. There are very few men in the world possessed of an amount of wealth sufficient to individually construct and own an extensive line of railway or telegraph, a first-class steamship, or a great factory. It is also to be remembered that for carrying on production by the most modern and effective methods large capital is needed, not only for machinery, but also for the purchasing and carrying of extensive stocks of crude material and finished products. . . .

. . . In the manufacture of jewelry by machinery, one boy can make up nine thousand sleeve-buttons per day; four girls also, working by modern methods, can put together in the same time eight thousand collar-buttons. But to run an establishment with such facilities the manufacturer must keep constantly in stock thirty thousand dollars' worth of cut ornamental stones, and a stock of cuff-buttons that represents nine thousand different designs and patterns. Hence from such conditions have grown up great corporations or stock companies, which are only forms of associated capital organized for effective use and protection. They are regarded to some extent as evils; but they are necessary, as there is apparently no other way in which the work of production and distribution, in accordance with the requirements of the age, can be prosecuted. The rapidity, however, with which such combinations of capital are organizing for the purpose of promoting industrial and commercial undertakings on a scale heretofore wholly unprecedented, and the tendency they have to crystallize into something far more complex than what has been familiar to the public as corporations, with the impressive names of syndicates, trusts, etc., also constitute one of the remarkable features of modern business methods. It must also be admitted that the whole tendency of recent economic development is in the direction of limiting the area within which the influence of competition is effective. . . .

. . . Coincident with and as a result of this change in the methods of production, the modern manufacturing system has been brought into a condition analogous to that of a military organization, in which the individual no longer works as independently as formerly, but as a private in the ranks, obeying orders, keeping step, as it were, to the tap of the drum, and having nothing to say as to the plan of his work, of its final completion, or of its ultimate use and distribution. In short, the people who work in the modern factory are, as a rule, taught to do one thing—to perform one and generally a simple operation; and when there is no more of that kind of work to do, they are in a measure helpless. The result has been that the individualism or independence of the producer in manufacturing has been in a great degree destroyed, and with it has also in a great degree been destroyed the pride which the workman formerly took in his work—that fertility of resource which formerly was a special characteristic of American workmen, and that element of skill that comes from long and varied practice and reflection and responsibility. Not many years ago every shoemaker was or could be his own employer. The boots and shoes passed directly from an individual producer to the consumer. Now this condition of things has passed away. Boots and shoes are made in large factories; and machinery has been so utilized, and the division of labor in connection with it has been carried to such an extent, that the process of making a shoe is said to be divided into sixty-four parts, or the shoemaker of to-day is only the sixty-fourth part of what a shoemaker once was. It is also asserted that "the constant employment at one sixty-fourth part of a shoe not only offers no encouragement to mental activity, but dulls by its monotony the brain of the employé to such an extent that the power to think and reason is almost lost." . . .

Attention is next asked to the economic—industrial, commercial, and financial—disturbances that have also resulted in recent years from changes, in the sense of improvements, in the details of the distribution of products; and as the best method of showing this, the recent course of trade in respect to the practical distribution and supply of one of the great articles of commerce, namely, tin-plate, is selected.

Before the days of the swift steamship and the telegraph, the business of distributing tin-plate for consumption in the United States was largely in the hands of one of the great mercantile firms of New York, who brought to it large enterprise and experience. At every place in the world where tin was produced and tin-plate manufactured they had their confidential correspondent or agent, and every foreign mail brought to them exclusive and prompt returns of the state of the market. Those who dealt with such a firm dealt with them under conditions which, while not discriminating unfavorably to any buyer, were certainly extraordinarily favorable to the seller, and great fortunes were amassed. But to-day how stands that business? There is no man, however obscure he may be, who wants to know any morning the state of the tin-plate market in any part of the world, but can find it in the mercantile journals. If he wants to know more in detail, he joins a little syndicate for news, and then he can be put in possession of every transaction of importance that took place the day previous in Cornwall, Liverpool, in the Strait of Sunda, in Australia, or South America. What has been the result? There are no longer great warehouses where tin in great quantities and of all sizes, waiting for customers, is stored. The business has passed into the hands of men who do not own or manage stores. They have simply desks in offices. They go round and find who is going to use tin in the next six months. They hear of a railroad-bridge which is to be constructed; of a certain number of cars which are to be covered; that the salmon-canneries on the Columbia River or Puget's Sound are likely to require seventy thousand boxes of tin to pack the catch of this year, as compared with a requirement of sixty thousand last year—a business, by the way, which a few years ago was not in existence—and they will go to the builders, contractors, or business-managers, and say to them: "You will want at such a time so much tin. I will buy it for you at the lowest market price, not of New York, but of the world, and I will put it in your possession, in any part of the continent, on a given day, and you shall cash the bill and pay me a percentage commission"—possibly a fraction of one per cent; thus bringing a former great and complicated business of importing, warehousing, selling at wholesale and retail, and employing many middle-men, clerks, book-keepers, and large capital, to a mere commission business, which dispenses to a great extent with the employment of intermediates, and does not necessarily require the possession or control of any capital.

Let us next go one step farther, and see what has happened at the same time to the man whose business it has been not to sell but to manufacture tin-plate into articles for domestic use, or for other consumption. Thirty or forty years ago the tinman, whose occupation was mainly one of handicraft, was recognized as one of the leading and most skillful mechanics in every village, town, and city. His occupation has, however, now well-nigh passed away. For example, a townsman and a farmer desires a supply of milk-cans. He never thinks of going to his corner tinman, because he knows that in New York and Chicago and Philadelphia, and other large towns and cities, there is a special establishment fitted up with special machinery, which will make his can better and fifty per cent cheaper than he can have it made by hand in his own town.

The same influences have also to a great degree revolutionized the nature of retail trade, which has been aptly described as, "until lately, the recourse of men whose character, skill, thrift, and ambition won credit, and enabled them to dispense with large capital." Experience has shown that, under a good organization of clerks, shopmen, porters, and distributors, it costs much less proportionally to sell a large amount of goods than a small amount, and that the buyer of large quantities can, without sacrifice of satisfactory profit, afford to offer to his retail customers such advantages in respect to prices and range of selection as almost to preclude competition on the part of dealers operating on a smaller scale, no matter how otherwise capable, honest, and diligent they may be. The various retail trades, in the cities and larger towns of all civilized countries, are accordingly being rapidly superseded by vast and skillfully organized establishments—and in Great Britain and Europe by co-operative associations—which can sell at little over wholesale prices a great variety of merchandise, dry-goods, manufacturers of leather, books, stationery, furs, ready-made clothing, hats and caps, and sometimes groceries and hardware, and at the same time give their customers far greater conveniences than can be offered by the ordinary shop-keeper or tradesman. . . .

From these specimen experiences it is clear that an almost total revolution has taken place, and is yet in progress, in every branch and in every relation of the world's industrial and commercial system. Some of these changes have been eminently destructive, and all of them have inevitably occasioned, and for a long time yet will continue to occasion, great disturbances in old methods, and entail losses of capital and changes of occupation on the part of individuals. And yet the world wonders, and commissions of great states inquire, without coming to definite conclusions, why trade and industry in recent years have been universally and abnormally disturbed and depressed. . . .

8. Charles Francis Adams, Jr.—
The Railroad Problem (1879)

Like his brother Henry, Charles Francis Adams, Jr., bore the burden of having to live up to the famous Adams name. Also like Henry, he was appalled by the coarse, materialistic aspects of contemporary American life that Mark Twain satirized in *The Gilded Age*. He was not, however, content to remain aloof from the hectic, competitive society of his generation, as Henry was. Instead, he set out to make a place (and a fortune) for himself in what he called "the most developing force and the largest field of the day," the railroad business. He studied this highly technical industry intensely, wrote a sensational exposé of the practices of the railroad tycoons Jay Gould and Cornelius Vanderbilt, called *A Chapter of Erie,* and in the same year, 1869, persuaded the Massachusetts legislature to create the first state railroad commission. As chairman of this body, Adams exerted a great influence on the whole history of railroad regulation. His experiences while holding this office, along with his general view of the railroad

SOURCE: C. F. Adams, Jr., *Railroads: Their Origin and Problems* (New York, 1887), pp. 80-1, 116-20, 126-8, 131-2, 134-40, 186-90.

problem, are summarized in *Railroads: Their Origin and Problems* (1879), from which the following selection is taken.

The Railroad Problem

During the last ten years there has been so much vague discussion of what is commonly known as the Railroad Problem, that many people, and those by no means the least sensible, have begun gravely to doubt whether after all it is not a mere cant phrase, and whether any such problem does indeed exist. . . . Under these circumstances, before beginning to discuss the Railroad Problem, it might seem proper to offer some definition of what that problem is. To do this concisely is very difficult. As an innovating force the railroad has made itself felt and produced its problems in every department of civilized life. So has the steam-engine; so has the newspaper; so has gunpowder. Unlike all these, however, the railroad has developed one distinctive problem, and a problem which actively presses for solution. It has done so for the reason that it has not only usurped, in modern communities, the more important functions of the highway, but those who own it have also undertaken to do the work which was formerly done on the highway. Moreover, as events have developed themselves, it has become apparent that the recognized laws of trade operate but imperfectly at best in regulating the use made of these modern thoroughfares by those who thus both own and monopolize them. Consequently the political governments of the various countries have been called upon in some way to make good through legislation the deficiencies thus revealed in the working of the natural laws. This is the Railroad Problem. Thus stated, it hardly needs to be said that the questions involved in its solution are of great magnitude and extreme delicacy. . . .

The railroad system of the United States, with all its excellences and all its defects, is thoroughly characteristic of the American people. It grew up untrammelled by any theory as to how it ought to grow; and developed with mushroom rapidity, without reference to government or political systems. In this country alone were the principles of free trade unreservedly and fearlessly applied to it. The result has certainly been wonderful, if not in all respects satisfactory. Why it has not been wholly satisfactory remains to be explained.

Looked upon as a whole, the American railroad system may now be said to have passed, wholly or in part, through three distinct phases of growth the limits of which are merged in each other, though their order of succession is sufficiently clear. First was the period of construction, beginning with the year 1830 and closing with the completion of the Pacific railroad in 1869;—merged with this period and following upon it, was that of active competition, which reached its fullest development in 1876;—this naturally was followed by the period of combination, which first assumed a large and definite shape in 1873, and has since that gradually but surely been working itself out into something both definite and practical. To one now looking back and reviewing the whole course of events, cause and effect become apparent. Things could not have taken any course other than that which they did take,—the logic has been inexorable. The whole theory under which the railroad system was left to develop itself was founded on a theoretical error; and it was none the less an error because, even if it had been recognized as such, it could not have been remedied. That error lay in the supposition, then universally accepted as an axiom, that in all matters of trade, competition, if allowed perfectly free play, could be relied upon to protect the community from abuses. The efficacy of railroad competition,—expressing itself in the form of general laws authorizing the freest possible railroad construction everywhere and by any one,—at an early day became almost a cardinal principle of American faith.

. . . If the people, and through the people the government, had faith in competition, the private individuals who constructed the railroads seemed to have no fear of it. They built roads everywhere, apparently in perfect confidence that the country would so develop as to support all the roads that could be built. Consequently railroads sprang up as if by magic, and after they were constructed, as it was impossible to remove them from places where they were not wanted to places where they were wanted, they lived upon the land where they could, and, when the business of the land would not support them, they fought and ruined each other.

The country was of immense extent, and its development under the stimulus of the new power was unprecedentedly rapid. At first, and during the lives of more than one generation, it really seemed as if the community had not relied upon this fundamental law of competition without cause. Nevertheless, there never was a time, since the first railroad was built, when he who sought to look for them could not find in almost any direction significant indications of the violation of a natural law. Local inequalities always existed, and the whole system was built up upon the principle of developing competing points at the expense of all others. There were certain localities in the country known as railroad centres; and these railroad centres were stimulated into an undue growth from the fact that competition was limited to them. The principles of free trade did not have full play; they were confined to favored localities. Hence resulted two things: in the first place the community suffered; then the railroads. Under the hard stress of local and through competition the most glaring inequalities were developed. The work of the railroad centres was done at a nominal profit, while the corporations recompensed themselves by extorting from other points where competition did not have to be met, the highest profit which business could be made to pay. It thus gradually became apparent, although men were very slow to take in the fact, that immense and invaluable as were the results in many respects secured through unlimited railroad competition, yet so far as the essential matter of securing to all reasonable and equal rates of payment for similar services performed was involved, it did not produce the effect confidently expected of it. On the contrary, it led directly to systematic discriminations and wild fluctuations, and the more active the competition was, the more oppressive the discriminations became and the less possible was it to estimate the fluctuations. In other words, while the result of other and ordinary competition was to reduce and equalize prices, that of railroad competition was to produce local inequalities and to arbitrate . . .

. . . The natural results followed. In 1870 a popular agitation broke out which for the time being threatened to sweep down not only all legal barriers but every consideration of self-interest. . . .

Of the Granger episode little now needs to be said. That it did not originate without cause has already been pointed out. It is quite safe to go further and to say that the movement was a necessary one, and through its results has made a solution of the railroad problem possible in this country. At the time that movement took shape the railroad corporations were in fact rapidly assuming a position which could not be tolerated. Corporations, owning and operating the highways of commerce, they claimed for themselves a species of immunity from the control of the law-making power. When laws were passed with a view to their regulation, they received them in a way which was at once arrogant and singularly injudicious. The officers entrusted with the execution of those laws they contemptuously ignored. Sheltering themselves behind the Dartmouth College decision, they practically undertook to set even public opinion at defiance. . . .

. . . In other words, they had thoroughly got it into their heads that they as common carriers were in no way bound to afford equal facilities to all, and, indeed, that it was in the last degree absurd and unreasonable to expect them to do so. The Granger method was probably as good a method of approaching men in this frame of mind as could have been devised. They were not open to reason, from the simple fact that their ideas of what in their position was right or wrong, reasonable or unreasonable, were wholly perverted. They were part of a system founded on error; and that error they had all their lives been accustomed to look upon as truth. The Granger violence was, therefore, needful to clear the ground. . . . The Granger legislation, crude as it was and utterly as it lacked insight, did produce results. That it did so was due wholly to the fact that the states which enacted the Granger laws went further, and incorporated into them a special executory force. . . . The ingenuity of lawyers, working on the intricacies of a most complicated system, has never failed to make a broad path through the meshes of merely declaratory statutes. The Granger legislatures, though with great reluctance, recognized this fact. Boards of commissioners were accordingly provided, and to them was entrusted a general supervision over the railroads and the duty of making the new legislation effective. The organization and experience of these commissions is, from the governmental point of view, the most important and instructive phase in the development of the railroad problem during the last few years. . . .

. . . They were not judicial tribunals. They ever reflected the angry complexion of the movement out of which they had originated. They were where they were, not to study a difficult problem and to guide their steps by the light of investigation. Nothing of this sort was, as a rule, expected of them. On the contrary they were there to prosecute. The test of their performance of duty was to be sought in the degree of hostility they manifested to the railroad corporations. In a word they represented force.

That under these circumstances they succeeded at all is the true cause of astonishment; not that they succeeded but partially. That they did succeed was due solely to the incorrigible folly and passionate love of fighting which seems inherent in the trained American railroad official. Placed as they were, entirely unfamiliar with the difficult questions they were compelled to confront, lacking confidence in themselves and very much afraid of their opponents, had those opponents seen fit to be even moderately civil and deferential to them, the position of the commissioners would have been rendered extremely difficult. Had the representatives of the railroad corporations, with their vast resources and intimate acquaintance with the subject, been wise enough to take the initiative and meet the commissioners half way, it would have been strange indeed if they had not succeeded in impressing upon them a sense of the difficulty of their task, and so materially affected their action. Instead of this they simply ignored them. . . . Naturally this impolitic course not only incensed the commissioners, but, what was of far more consequence, it strengthened their hands. The popular feeling, strong enough before, was intensified. The agitation was thus kept alive until the decision of the courts of last resort was obtained, which fortunately placed the railroads completely at the mercy of the legislatures. Nothing short of this would apparently have sufficed to force them out of their attitude of stupid, fighting defiance. This result, however, once arrived at, they immediately recovered their senses, and with them their strength. They became at once compliant and—formidable. . . . It was no longer claimed that railroads were mere private business enterprises, and the abuses incident to their competition among themselves were at least softened down by the absence of that old arbitrary spirit which had so aggravated hardships. The laws were sufficiently complied with to remove the more flagrant causes of complaint, and the practical results thus secured through the Granger agitation were far more considerable than has been generally supposed.

Fortunately, while in the more western states of the Union years were being wasted in a mere preliminary struggle, the question in another part of the country had from the beginning taken a different shape, and one far more promising of results. Owing to other conditions of railroad ownership and a more composed state of the public mind, the East afforded a better field for profitable discussion than the West. Various state railroad commissions already existed in that section, but in 1869 one was organized in Massachusetts on a somewhat novel principle, and a principle in curious contrast with that which has just been described as subsequently adopted in the West. In the West the fundamental idea behind every railroad act was force;—the commission represented the constable. In the Massachusetts act the fundamental idea was publicity. . . . The board of commissioners was set up as a sort of lens by means of which the otherwise scattered rays of public opinion could be concentrated to a focus and brought to bear upon a given point. The commissioners had to listen, and they might investigate and report;—they could do little more. Accordingly they were compelled to study their subject, and with each question which came before them they had to stand or fall on the reasons they presented for their conclusions. They could not take refuge in silence. Whenever they attempted to do so they speedily found themselves in trouble. They had, as each case came up, to argue the side of the corporations or of the public, as the case might be; but always to argue it openly, and in a way which showed that they understood the subject and were at least honest in their convictions. . . . The result was necessarily as different from that reached at the West, as were the conditions under which it was reached. The board, in the first place, became of necessity a judicial in place of a prosecuting tribunal. It naturally had often to render decisions upon matters of complaint which came under its cognizance in favor of the railroad corporations;—whether it decided in their favor or against them, however, its decisions carried no weight other than that derived from the reasons given for them. The commissioners were consequently under the necessity of cultivating friendly relations with the railroad officials, and had to inspire them, if they could, with a confidence in their knowledge and fairness. Without that they could not hope to sustain themselves. On the other hand, their failure was imminent unless they so bore themselves as to satisfy the public that they were absolutely independent of corporate influence, and could always be relied upon to fearlessly investigate and impartially decide.

Undesignedly the Massachusetts legislators had rested their law on the one great social feature which distinguishes modern civilization from any other of which we have a record,—the eventual supremacy of an enlightened public opinion. . . .

Contrary to the general and popular conviction, an increasing number of those who have given most thought to the subject, whether as railroad officers or simply from the general economical and political points of view, are disposed to conclude that, so far from being necessarily against public policy, a properly regulated combination of railroad companies, for the avowed purpose of controlling competition, might prove a most useful public agency. These persons contend that railroad competition, if it has not already done its work, will have done it at a time now by no means remote. An enormous developing force, during the period of construction, its importance will be much less in the later periods of more stable adjustment. Under these circumstances, and recognizing the fact that the period of organization is now succeeding that of construction, these persons are disposed to see in regulated combination the surest, if not, indeed, the only way of reaching a system in which the advantages of railroad competition may, so far as possible, be secured; and its abuses, such as waste, discrimination, instability, and bankruptcy, be greatly modified if not wholly gotten rid of. In conducting its traffic, they argue, each road or combination of roads is now a law unto itself. It may work in concert with other roads or combinations, or it may refuse to do so. It may make rates to one place, where it may think it for its interest that business should go, and may refuse to make them to another place where it is for its interest that business should not go. All this is essentially wrong. Yet the business community of America, from one end of the country to the other, has been from the beginning so thoroughly accustomed to the extreme instabilities of railroad competition, that it has wholly lost sight of what its own interest requires. What it needs is certainty,—a stable economy in transportation,—something that can be reckoned on in all business calculations,—a fixed quantity in the problem. This, of all results the most desirable, is now even looked upon with apprehension. There is an idea, the result of long habit, in the public mind, that, so far as transportation is concerned, prosperity is to be secured through a succession of temporary local advantages,—an unending cutting of rates. The idea of a great system of internal transportation at once reasonable, equitable, and certain,—permitting traffic to flow and interchanges to be made just how and where the interests of buyer and seller dictate,—never discriminating,—rarely, and then only slowly, fluctuating,—this is a conception very far removed from the reality, and it may well be doubted whether now it even commends itself when stated to the average man of business. He clings, on the contrary, to the burden of inequalities to which he is accustomed, and is inclined to doubt whether he could live without them. . . .

If, however, any approach is ever to be made towards that ideal state of affairs which has just been suggested, it can apparently be made only in one way. The abuses incident to unhealthy railroad competition must cease; and undoubtedly the first step towards getting rid of those abuses is to render the railroad system, throughout all its parts, amenable to some healthy control. The present competitive chaos must be reduced into something like obedience to law. Yet this apparently can only be effected when the system is changed into one orderly, confederated whole. To attempt to bring it about during an epoch of wars, and local pools, and conflicts for traffic, would be as futile as it would have been to enact a code of laws unsupported by force, for the government of the Scotch Highland clans in the sixteenth century, or a parcel of native African tribes now. A confederation, or even a general combination among all the railroad corporations having some degree of binding force, might, therefore, as has been suggested, not improbably prove the first step in the direction of a better and more stable order of things. But to lead to any results at once permanent and good this confederation must, in three respects, differ radically from everything of the same sort which has hitherto preceded it: it must be legal; it must be public; it must be responsible.

9. Interstate Commerce Commission—
First Annual Report (1887)

In February 1887, after long and often acrimonious debate, Congress passed a law with the simple title "An act to regulate commerce."

Although wordy (it fills more than eight closely printed pages in the statute book) the law was straightforward and forthright in form. Railroad charges must be "reasonable and just." The granting of any "special rate, rebate, drawback, or other device" was declared to be "unlawful." No road could "charge or receive any greater compensation . . . for a shorter than a longer distance over the same line" or "enter into any contract . . . with any other common carrier . . . for the pooling of freights." The act went on to create a five-man Interstate Commerce Commission to see that these regulations were obeyed.

The task, however, proved extremely difficult, for railroading was a highly technical and complex business. The act, despite its sweeping phraseology, was hard to apply to specific situations. The character of the problem and some of the earliest decisions of the commission are described in the following selection from its first annual report.

Another question presenting itself immediately on the organization of the Commission was that respecting the proper construction of the fourth section of the act. . . .

The provision against charging more for the shorter than for the longer haul under the like circumstances and conditions over the same line and in the same direction, the shorter being included within the longer distance, is one of obvious justice and propriety. Indeed, unless one is familiar with the conditions of railroad traffic in sections of the country where the enactment of this provision is found to have its principal importance, he might not readily understand how it could be claimed that circumstances and conditions could be such as to justify the making of any exceptions to the general rule. . . .

A study of the conditions under which railroad traffic in certain sections of the country has sprung up is necessary to an understanding of the difficulties which surround the subject. The territory bounded by the Ohio and the Potomac on the north and by the Mississippi on the west presented to the Commission an opportunity, and also an occasion, for such a study. The railroad business of that section has grown to be what it is in sharp competition with water carriers, who not only have had the ocean at their service, but by means of navigable streams were able to penetrate the interior in all directions. The carriers by water were first in the field, and were having a very thriving business while railroads were coming into existence; but when the roads were built the competition between them and the water-craft soon

SOURCE: Interstate Commerce Commission, *First Annual Report* (Washington, D.C., 1887), pp. 15-19, 36-7, 41-2.

became sharp and close, and at the chief competing points the question speedily came to be, not what the service in transportation was worth, or even what it would cost to the party performing it, but at what charge for its service the one carrier or the other might obtain the business. In this competition the boat owners had great advantages; the capital invested in their business was much smaller; they were not restricted closely to one line, but could change from one to another as the exigencies of business might require; the cost of operation was less. But the railroads had an advantage in greater speed, which at some times, and in respect to some freight, was controlling.

In this competition of boat and railroad the rates of transportation which were directly controlled by it soon reached a point to which the railroads could not possibly have reduced all their tariffs and still maintain a profitable existence. They did not attempt such a reduction, but on the contrary, while reducing their rates at the points of water competition to any figures that should be necessary to enable them to obtain the freights, they kept them up at all other points to such figures as they deemed the service to be worth, or as they could obtain. It often happened, therefore, that the rates for transporting property over the whole length of a road to a terminus on a water highway would not exceed those for the transportation for half the distance only, to a way station not similarly favored with competition. The seeming injustice was excused on the plea of necessity. The rates to the terminus, it was said, were fixed by the competition and could not be advanced without abandoning the business to the boats. . . .

But the lower rates on the longer hauls have not been due altogether to water competition; railroad competition has been allowed to have a similar effect in reducing them. . . .

. . . By some persons it was assumed that the Commission had by the act been given a general authority to suspend altogether the operation of the fourth section, and upon this utterly baseless and unreasonable assumption the Commission was plied with arguments in support of a general suspension. Other views went to the opposite extreme, and while holding that the general rule must be enforced in all cases until the Commission had sanctioned exceptions, would restrict the power to make exceptions to individual shipments made under circumstances and conditions which were special and peculiar. Such a restriction would obviously render the authority to make exceptions of no practical utility. . . .

By others the fact was emphasized that the charging or receiving "any greater compensation in the aggregate for the transportation of passengers or of the like kind of property" "for a shorter than for a longer distance over the same line in the same direction, the shorter being included in the longer distance," was only declared by the section to be unlawful when both were "under substantially similar circumstances and conditions"; and they confidently affirmed that the carrier could require no order of relief from the Commission when the circumstances and conditions were in fact dissimilar, since the greater charge was not then unlawful and not forbidden. This view would leave the carrier at liberty to act on its own judgment of the conditions and circumstances in any case, subject to responsibility to the law if the greater charge were made for the shorter transportation when the circumstances and conditions were not in fact dissimilar, unless authorized to make such greater charge by the relieving order of the Commission.

When the Commission was called upon in the performance of its duty to give an interpretation to this section it was found on comparison of views that the interpretation last above mentioned seemed to all its members to be the one best warranted by the phraseology of the statute. Moreover, when it was considered how vast was the railroad mileage of the country, how numerous were the cases in different sections in which, for divers reasons, the general rule prescribed by the fourth section was then departed from, this interpretation seemed the only one which, in administering the law, would be found practical or workable. . . .

The act to regulate commerce was not passed to injure any interests, but to conserve and protect. It had for its object to regulate a vast business according to the requirements of justice. Its intervention was supposed to be called for by the existence of numerous evils, and the Commission was created to aid in bringing about great and salutary measures of improvement. The business is one that concerns the citizen intimately in all the relations of life, and sudden changes in it, though in the direction of improvement, might in their immediate consequences be more harmful than beneficial. It was much more important to move safely and steadily in the direction of reform than to move hastily, regardless of consequences, and perhaps be compelled to retrace important steps after great and possibly irremediable mischief had been done. The act was not passed for a day or for a year; it had permanent benefits in view, and to accomplish these with the least possible disturbance to the immense interest involved seemed an obvious dictate of duty.

Acting upon these views, and in order to give opportunity for full discussion, the Commission, after having made sufficient investigation into the facts of each case to satisfy itself that a prima facie case for its intervention existed, made orders for relief under the fourth section, where such relief was believed to be most imperative. . . .

Of the duties devolved upon the Commission by the act to regulate commerce, none is more perplexing and difficult than that of passing upon complaints made of rates as being unreasonable. The question of the reasonableness of rate involves so many considerations and is affected by so many circumstances and conditions which may at first blush seem foreign, that it is quite impossible to deal with it on purely mathematical principles, or on any principles whatever, without a consciousness that no conclusion which may be reached can by demonstration be shown to be absolutely correct. . . .

The public interest is best served when the rates are so apportioned as to encourage the largest practicable exchange of products between different sections of our country and with foreign countries; and this can only be done by making value an important consideration, and by placing upon the higher classes of freight some share of the burden that on a relatively equal apportionment, if service alone were considered, would fall upon those of less value. . . .

It may be truly said, also, that while railroad competition is to be protected, wars in railroad rates unrestrained by competitive principles are disturbers in every direction; if the community reaps a temporary advantage, it is one whose benefits are unequally distributed, and these are likely to be more than counterbalanced by the incidental unsettling of prices and interference with safe business calculations. The public authorities at the same time find that the task of regulation has been made more troublesome and difficult through the effect of war rates upon the public mind. These are consequences which result so inevitably from this species of warfare, that it would naturally be expected they would be kept constantly in mind by railroad managers. It is inevitable that the probability that any prescribed rates will be accepted by the public as just shall to some extent be affected by the fact that at some previous time they have been lower; perhaps considerably lower. . . .

The act to regulate commerce has now been in operation nearly eight months. One immediate effect was to cause inconvenience in many quarters, and even yet the business of some parts of the country is not fully adjusted to it. Some carriers also are not as yet in their operations conforming in all respects to its spirit and purpose. Nevertheless the Commission feels justified in saying that the operation of the act has in general been beneficial. In some particulars, as we understand has also been the case with similar statutes in some of the States, it has operated directly to increase railroad earnings, especially in the cutting off of free passes on interstate passenger traffic, and in putting an end to rebates, drawbacks, and special rates upon freight business. The results of the law in these respects are also eminently satisfactory to the general public, certainly to all who had not been wont to profit by special or personal advantages. In connection with the abolition of the pass system, there has been some reduction in passenger fares, especially in the charge made for mileage tickets in the Northwest, the section of the country where they are perhaps most employed.

Freight traffic for the year has been exceptionally large in volume, and is believed to have been in no small degree stimulated by a growing confidence that the days of rebates and special rates were ended, and that open rates on an equal basis were now offered to all comers. The reflex action of this development of confidence among business men has been highly favorable to the roads.

In some localities the passage of the act was made the occasion on the part of dissatisfied and short-sighted railroad managers for new exactions, through a direct raising of rates, by change in classification and otherwise. The manifestation of the spirit which induced such action is now but seldom observed, and the wrongs resulting from it have in general been corrected. The effect of the operation of the fourth section has been specially described above, and the Commission repeats in this place its opinion that, however serious may have been the results in some cases, the general effect has been beneficial. The changes in classification made since the act took effect have been in the direction of greater uniformity, and have also in general, it is believed, been concessions to business interests.

The tendency of rates has been downward, and they have seldom been permanently advanced except when excessive competition had reduced them to points at which they could not well be maintained. No destructive rate wars have occurred, but increased stability in rates has tended in the direction of stability in general business. There is still, however, great mischief resulting from frequent changes in freight rates on the part of some companies; changes that in some cases it is difficult to suggest excuse for.

The general results of the law have been in important ways favorable to both the roads and the public; while the comparatively few complaints that have been heard of its results are either made with imperfect knowledge of the facts, or spring from the remembrance of practices which the law was deliberately framed to put an end to.

10. Samuel C. T. Dodd—*Trusts* (1890)

Samuel C. T. Dodd was a lawyer in the oil regions of western Pennsylvania. Experience with the results of cutthroat competition in the petroleum business made him a firm believer in the virtue of industrial combination as a device for orderly economic development. In 1881 he became chief counsel for John D. Rockefeller's Standard Oil Company. In that capacity he was responsible for the creation of the Standard Oil Trust, a legal device designed to get around state laws preventing corporations from owning businesses incorporated in other states. More important in Dodd's eyes than any particular form of organization, however, was his conviction that large-scale industrial combinations were both essential and in the public interest. He devoted much time and energy in the 1880's and 1890's to advocating this idea. The following essay, entitled "Trusts," appeared originally in the *New York Tribune* in 1890.

Business in this country is now carried on through combina-

SOURCE: S. C. T. Dodd, *Trusts* (n. p., 1900), pp. 108-10, 114-16.

tions, and cannot be carried on otherwise. Slowly but surely the law has recognized their necessity and utility. . . .

The last quarter of a century has been emphatically an era of combination in business. Has competition been destroyed? On the contrary, it was never so strong. Effort impels to effort—combination begets combination. New industries are built up—new markets are opened—new methods of manufacture invented. It is the law of life. By each striving to get ahead, all make better progress.

Have prices been increased? On the contrary, combination in business and low prices have ever gone hand in hand. Combination has never been so great as in the last fifteen years, and prices have never ruled so low. Much of this decrease may be attributed to improved methods of manufacture, new machinery and lower transportation. It is still true that aggregated capital was essential to the adoption of new machinery and improved methods of manufacture, and that lower transportation is the direct result of combination of railroads, which has taken place in defiance of public opinion.

Has the individual been crushed out? To some extent, undoubtedly, as a solitary individual. But he has found a larger sphere for his efforts through association with other individuals. No day has ever equalled to-day in the business opportunities offered intelligent and industrious men. Employes can, and many do, invest their savings in stocks of industrial corporations and associations, and thus share in the profits of the business. In this direction lies the ultimate solution of the problem of profit-sharing between employer and employe. Legislators can wisely turn their attention to such measures as shall tend to make such investments free from all risks except legitimate risks. Prevention of stock-watering, with its progeny of stock manipulation and corporation-wrecking, will encourage workmen to share the profits of business.

Has the wage earner suffered? On the contrary, new avenues of labor have been opened; the demand for labor, and particularly skilled labor, has increased, wages are higher, the cost of living is lower, and the condition of the laboring man never so good as to-day. If there are exceptions, they arise out of excessive competition in certain classes of the labor market, caused in this country by excessive immigration of unskilled laborers. . . .

With such a quarter-century of experience of the advantages of association in business behind us, the man who still fears the combination will destroy competition and produce high prices would have feared a conflagration during Noah's flood.

The question remains, should the right of association be limited? If so, where shall the line be drawn? When is an association dangerously large? . . .

The magnitude of business associations cannot be limited until the magnitude of the business is limited. As business increases and markets widen, greater combinations of capital will be required, and the magnitude of the business associations will increase. Any attempt to limit association will be as ineffectual as an attempt to limit the tides.

If combinations are formed, as no doubt they have been and will be, for evil purposes, or if evil effects are produced by association, the law must direct its attention to the remedy of the specific evils. It is vain to hope to eradicate them by destroying or limiting the right of association.

No association, call it trust or what you may, is defensible unless formed for legitimate business. Their legitimate purpose and effect is that of increasing production, opening wider markets and increasing consumption, lessening expenses of manufacture and sale, adopting the latest improvements and best methods of business, and thus giving to the public the best product at the smallest remunerative prices. This is the legitimate purpose of a trust, and every trust formed and operated upon any other idea is doomed to inevitable failure. . . .

The influence of trusts on business has not differed from that exercised by partnerships and corporations. Since the petroleum trust was formed, petroleum has decreased in price; the product is safer and better; the output has increased; exports have increased in spite of foreign competition, which would have ruined our foreign trade but for the power of aggregated capital in producing business economies in the manufacturing and marketing of our product. The business has given employment to a constantly increasing force of workmen, who obtain constant employment, sure pay, and above the average wages. Every intelligent workman has a chance to rise. Hundreds are drawing large salaries who began as ordinary employees. Employment is anxiously sought by the better class of workmen and strikes are almost unknown. Competition has not been destroyed. The amount of oil refined to-day by competitors of the trust exceeds the total quantity refined at the time the combination was formed.

Other trusts, it is claimed, have shut down manufactories and put up prices. In so doing they may have done a very wise thing, or may have been guilty of foolish, immoral and illegal acts. It all depends on circumstances. If the price of the product was so low that manufactories were losing money, it was no crime to curtail production and stop selling at a loss. Competition may be carried on until the weakest are ruined, workmen thrown out of employment and creditors unpaid, or the inevitable may be foreseen and prevented by agreements, arrangements, compromises and associations. It will be a serious day for business when such agreements, arrangements and combinations are prevented by law. If, however, trusts have attempted to extort an unjust price for products they adopt an illegal policy sure to end in loss, if not in ruin.

My anti-trust readers may say that the admission here made that combinations may be instrumental in unduly restricting production and in extorting unjust prices, even for a limited time, is a yielding of the whole question; that is what they particularly desire to prevent. I am glad to meet such a reader on common ground. Men are seldom far apart in their views of right and wrong when once the questionable subject is clearly defined. Few sane persons will assert that those combinations are either beneficial or legitimate which are formed not for the purpose of obtaining the many legitimate advantages of association; not for the purpose of avoiding the disasters which often overtake business by reason of excessive competition and over-production, but for the purpose of unduly restricting production and extorting undue prices from the public. Such combinations may take the form of a trust or any other form, and in any form are contrary to law. If our Legislatures deemed it necessary to re-enact the common law on this subject or to prescribe additional penalties, no word would be raised in opposition. The evil is specific, clear and well-defined. No circumlocution is necessary in order to reach it by prohibitory legislation. But our special wonder is excited when Congress and a score of State Legislatures gravely propose to eradicate this evil by prohibiting all business association and all agreements and arrangements in relation to prices and production. The Interstate Commerce law prohibited the charging of unjust and unreasonable prices for transportation. That is a direct, as well as an effective, mode of reaching a specific evil. It was never seriously suggested that all charges for transportation be made criminal because an unjust and unreasonable price might be extorted. Such action would, however, have been fully as wise as to prohibit all combinations because some may be for an improper purpose, and to make criminal all agreements and arrangements which influence production and prices, because agreements and arrangements may be made to extort undue prices. . . .

Part IV

Industrial Labor

11. Massachusetts Bureau of the Statistics of Labor —Reports (1878, 1881)

One of the most significant developments of the 1870's and 1880's was the creation by the leading industrial states of bureaus of labor statistics. Labor leaders were quick to recognize the need for hard factual information about wage levels, the cost of living, and working conditions if they were to make a strong case for their demands for higher wages, shorter hours, and the like. Since they did not seek the establishment of commissions with actual regulatory powers, many state legislatures acceded to their wishes. These bureaus varied in effectiveness and point of view, but as a group they performed invaluable work and at trivial cost. The most affluent operated on budgets of from five to six thousand dollars a year.

By far the most influential of the bureaus was that of Massachusetts, which was headed after 1873 by Carroll D. Wright. Typical of the studies carried out under Wright's direction were the investigation of workingmen's attitudes, conducted by the questionnaire method in 1878, and the more elaborate field study of three textile towns, Fall River, Lowell, and Lawrence, in 1881. Reports such as these made Wright the leading expert in the field, and led to his appointment as the first U.S. Commissioner of Labor in 1886. Excerpts from the reports follow.

SOURCE: A: Massachusetts Bureau of the Statistics of Labor, "Testimony of Workingmen," *Tenth Annual Report* (Boston, 1879), pp. 99-104, 116-21, 124, 126-8, 130-2, 134, 138.

SOURCE: B: *Ibid.*, "Fall River, Lowell, and Lawrence," *Thirteenth Annual Report* (Boston, 1882), pp. 195-7, 202-3, 218-20, 271-6, 282-3, 285, 301-3, 329-31, 337-43, 345-8, 360-6.

A: Testimony of Workingmen

The labor question, in a statistical sense, has two sides. The representatives of these two sides are capital and labor. In the gathering of statistics of labor, the most complete information has been secured from the statistics of capital, principally because capital manages large mercantile and manufacturing undertakings, and proper and complete business records are necessary to a full comprehension and successful carrying on of business ventures. The superintendent of a large manufacturing corporation can turn to his books, and show the numbers of persons employed, days that the establishment runs in a year, the hours per day, time lost by repairs, etc., wages paid to workmen in every branch of his business, value of goods made, and hundreds of other points necessary in making up statistics of industry. This capital does. The difficulty has been to secure from labor full and correct returns, so that both sides of the question could be understood and compared. There have always been many difficulties in the way. A manufacturing establishment may employ five thousand hands. One man, in the name of the corporation, can easily and cheaply give facts from his books relating to these five thousand employés. The task is to secure returns from the five thousand employés themselves. The representative of the corporation is easily reached by a circular letter, or by an agent. It is manifestly impossible to reach a large number of employés by personal visits from agents, without an appropriation for the services of a large number of agents, and for travelling expenses. It is also too expensive to summon a large number of workingmen from their labors to testify before the officers of this Bureau. The plan of addressing circulars to workingmen with a request for replies is manifestly the only way of reaching them. Then is found another obstacle. The manufacturers' names can be found in directories, business registers, and the corporation returns made to the Tax Commissioner. Since the census of 1875, this office has possessed the means of addressing manufacturers in every line of business without trouble or expense; but, when it is proposed to send circulars to workingmen, the difficulty arises as to whom to address. Although our past experience, and that of our predecessors, had been against the idea that circular letters to the workingmen would be answered fully and freely, as we possessed, upon the family census returns, the names and addresses of every working man and woman in the State upon May 1, 1875, we determined to again try the plan of sending circular letters with inquiries to workingmen. . . .

. . . The questions were asked in all seriousness and careful consideration and conscientious replies were expected. Those to whom the circulars were sent were assured that there would be no mention of their names or residences in the report. They were asked to speak their minds freely, in the hope that, by the facts gathered from all quarters of the State, from workers in all our productive industries, something to direct benefit to them and their brother workmen might result.

Few of the questions required calculations, or reference to account books. Those who could not, or did not wish to, answer all the questions, were requested to reply to such as they could, or felt inclined to. Extended answers to questions were solicited to be written upon a blank page supplied for "Remarks," or upon extra sheets, if they were necessary. In order that the nature of the inquiries may be understood, we present them in full.

INQUIRIES

1. Occupation?
2. *a.* How long have you been engaged in your present occupation? *b.* How long by your present employer?
3. How many different trades, or kinds of business, have you been engaged in since you were twenty-one years of age?
4. *a.* How many hours a day do you work? *b.* How many hours do you work on Saturday? *c.* Do you consider yourself overworked? *d.* What reduction in daily working time do you think should be made in your business?
5. *a.* Is your business dangerous or unhealthy? *b.* If so, in what respects?
6. How many days have *you* lost by sickness during the year ending Aug. 1, 1878?
7. What has been the *combined* outlay and loss of pay, on account of sickness, in your *whole* family during the year ending Aug. 1, 1878?
8. *a.* How many days have you been unemployed in your regular business during the year ending Aug. 1, 1878? *b.* Allowing for such other work as you may have been engaged in, what has been your money loss in wages for the time unemployed?
9. *a.* Do you live as well as you did five years ago? *b.* If, not, in what respect are you worse off than then? *c.* Have you been obliged to reduce your outlay for rent, food, clothing, and other necessities? or

have you only been forced to deprive yourself of what might properly be called "extras," or luxuries?

10. *a.* What way, if any, have you thought of by which you think you could be paid more fairly and equitably for your labor than you are now? *b.* In what way, if any, do you consider your employer unfairly profits by your labor? *c.* How much yearly do you consider yourself underpaid?

11. *a.* Have you been obliged to run in debt for the necessities of life during the past year? *b.* Are you ever obliged to take merchandise in payment for wages due you? *c.* Do you take such goods at cost prices, a *little* above or *much* above the market rates?

12. *a.* At what intervals are you paid? (Weekly, fortnightly, or monthly?) *b.* Could you buy cheaper if paid oftener?

13. During the past five years how much wages legally due you have you been unable to collect from your employers?

14. *a.* Are your children receiving a proper education to enable them to earn their own living? *b.* Have you or they decided upon their future employment? *c.* Is it the same business as your own?

15. *a.* Are your future prospects good? In other words, will you be able to comfortably support yourself and family until your children arrive at the proper age to look out for themselves, wholly or in part? *b.* Do you anticipate being able to lay by enough to support you in your old age,—say, after sixty-five?

Before proceeding to send out the blanks to the individual workingmen, a circular was mailed to the editors of nearly all the daily and weekly papers in the State, numbering 227. It is impossible for us to tell how many papers printed the notice as requested; but, from report, we know that many did: and some of the Boston papers, in addition, published the inquiries. Following is a copy of the newspaper notice in question:—

The Massachusetts Bureau of Statistics of Labor is at present conducting a very extended inquiry into the condition, wants, and prospects of the workingmen of the State. Any working man or woman who is desirous of answering the questions asked by the Bureau should send name and address on a postal card to the Bureau of Statistics of Labor, 33 Pemberton Square, Boston. The blanks and instructions for answering will then be sent by the Bureau; and workingmen will be desired to express their minds freely, in order that the truth may be arrived at. They will be doing a patriotic service to the State, and rendering their brother workingmen a valuable service, by giving these questions careful consideration and prompt and reliable answers, so that their accumulated testimony may be presented to the legislature of 1879 in the Tenth Annual Report of the Bureau.

Our next step was to prepare a "notice to working men and women," containing substantially the same points that were given in the newspaper notice. Our object was to enable every working man and woman to receive a blank who desired to answer the questions, or to express their opinions upon the question of labor. They were requested to send name and address on a postal card to us, we agreeing to send the blank by return mail, and also a postage-paid addressed envelope, in which they could return replies. We sent several copies of this notice to each address, so the parties could distribute them among friends. We also solicited lists of names and addresses, so we could forward the blanks. Five thousand of these "notices" were sent to working men and women throughout the State, especial care being taken to select workers in the different cities and towns, and in the various branches of industry.

The result of the publication of the item in the newspapers, and the sending out of the 5,000 notices to workingmen, was the receipt of 638 requests, either in person or by mail, for the inquiry blank. These orders were promptly filled; and in every case a stamped and addressed envelope was given or enclosed to the applicant, in which to return the reply. It will be noticed that signatures were not requested; and mention of names or residence, it was distinctly promised, would not be made. Several manufacturers made application for the blanks to distribute among their workingmen: but they were only supplied on the understanding that they should be returned by the workingmen themselves by mail, and not pass through the hands of the manufacturer after being answered; our aim being to render the investigation in every way free and outspoken on the part of the workingmen.

We have stated the number of inquiry blanks sent out as 638. Of this number, 272 were returned. Of the number sent back, 20 were unfilled, and 22 so imperfectly filled as to render them useless for our purpose, making the total of available answers 230.

It is almost needless to say that we are disappointed with the meagre returns, and that we believe it is impossible to secure, by means of correspondence, an adequate number of answers to give labor a proper representation statistically, in comparison with the statistical returns so freely supplied by capital. Although the number of answers (230) renders it impossible for us to formulate therefrom any conclusions applicable to the whole State, they are, in themselves, so valuable in matters of information and suggestion, that we propose to take up each inquiry in order, and present the replies in the most condensed form. . . .

About 160, out of 230 answering, expressed themselves at length upon some phase of the labor question. These opinions and suggestions are from actual workingmen: they are not the ideas of mere theorists. Each workingman writes at length upon that subject in which he is most interested, which has struck him forcibly during his own experience, which has some practical application to himself or fellow-workingmen; and he writes earnestly and often forcibly, supporting arguments with facts. . . .

HOURS OF LABOR.—*From a Carpet-Mill Operative.*—I am satisfied with sixty hours a week: it is plenty time for any man, although there are some employed in the same place over that time, and get nothing extra for it. I know of one young man under age who was absent two Saturday afternoons, and his overseer gave him his bill on Monday morning when he went in. If there is any inspector of the ten-hour law, he would do well to call round, and see for himself.

From a Shoemaker.—I think there ought to be an eight-hour law all over the country. There is not enough work to last the year round, and work over eight hours a day, or forty-eight hours a week. There can be only about so much work to do any way: and, when that is done, business has got to stop, or keep dragging the year round, so that a man has to work for almost any price offered; when, if there was an eight-hour law, things would be more even, and a man could get what his labor was worth, according to the price of living, and there would be plenty of work for all, and business would be good the year round. I think every State ought to submit to the United States to decide how many hours people should work all over the country. Just so long as there is an over-production, business will drag the year round: and the only way to stop over-production is to work less hours; for business never will be good when we work more hours than the demand calls for.

From a Carpenter.—I think that eight hours a day is enough for a man to work at his trade. Then I think there would be more work; and he would have time to make his house and garden look more tidy, if he has one, or to study and improve the mind. I think that a man would do more work at home when he is at work than he would when unemployed; for he is down-hearted, and does not feel like working at home. I find too, that, the lower wages are, the more work they expect a man to do.

From a Furniture Varnisher and Polisher.—I have noticed in different shops where I have been employed, that the men (both day and piece workers) would earn and do as much work short days as they would long days. I have also noticed that the men who worked eight hours, instead of ten, were, as a general rule, more contented and happy than those who were obliged to work ten. I believe there would be as much work done, and as well, in eight hours as there is now in ten. . . .

From a Carpenter.—In regard to the number of hours a day's work should consist of, I think ten hours is a fair day's work, and do not think an eight-hour law would be any help to the laboring class. There are some who would make good use of their spare time; and there are others who would not. This same class would want pay for ten hours, and would strike if they could not get it. I for one never could see where the laboring class gains any lasting good by a strike. I think a man should make the best terms possible with his boss; and, if he cannot get as much as he wants, he should try other places. He cannot expect to have every thing as he did in good times. If he gets enough to eat, and plain clothes to wear, he should be content for the present. Better times will come soon. I believe that hard money is the money for all, the poor as well as the rich. I believe in the poor making friends with the rich; and, in so doing, they will be gainers. . . .

OVERWORK.—*From a Harness-Maker.*—In answer to the question, "Do you consider yourself overworked?" I answered, "Yes"; and it is my honest and firm conviction that I am, by at least two hours a day. With the great increase in machinery within the last fifteen or twenty years, I think, in justice, there ought to be some reduction in the hours of labor. Unless the hours of labor are shortened in proportion to the increase of machinery, I consider machinery an injury rather than a benefit to humanity. I tell you that ten hours a day, hard, steady work, is more than any man can stand for any length of time without injuring his health, and therefore shortening his life. For my own part, although my work is not very laborious, when I stop work in the evening, I feel completely played out. I would like to study some; but I am too fatigued. In fact it is as much as I can do to look over the evening paper; and I am almost certain that this is the condition of a majority of workingmen.

From a Shoe-Finisher.—The laboring class, perhaps, are not overworked if they could take time for recreation when needed, but oftentimes are out of work for months when they would work; so that, when they get work, they feel obliged to follow it closely: for in gangs, where one's work affects others, they work when not able, as they may lose their place if absent even by sickness. Some piece hands work more than ten hours. Under these circumstances, I consider that, in boot and shoe towns, the laboring classes are overworked, having no time for social enjoyment or self-culture, or for acquiring information. If they get the time, they are unfit for it after ten hours' hard labor.

From a Quarryman.—In filling this blank, there are a good many questions which I did not answer relative to men with families; but, however, I would say, on behalf of married men in this locality, that they are poorly situated, working hard eleven and a half hours a day for $1.25 in summer, and 80 cents a day in winter, and obliged to purchase merchandise in company stores, and pay enormous rents for tenements. Merchandise being thirty per cent above market price, and being paid monthly, they are obliged to purchase at supply store; if not, they will be discharged, and starvation is the result. It is ridiculous in a free country that the laws are not more stringent, whereby the capitalist cannot rule and ruin his white slaves. I would draw your attention carefully to this matter, and I lay before you all truth, not hearsay, but from experience. I am a single man, and I would not be so if times were better than they are now. I do not want to have any more tramps or paupers in the country than there are now. Excuse me if I have deviated from my course altogether. We send representatives each year to General Court; and this matter of long hours in this locality is never thought of by them, because they are controlled and ruled by capitalists in this section. If there is any place that needs reform, it is this place. It would be better for the legislature to make laws and enact them, so that no individual or corporation can override them, than to have men striking for ten hours, and losing money which would be required otherwise. Give this your attention, and relieve a class of honest laborers from their present state.

From a Machinist.—In reply to your question concerning over-work, I wish to say, that, in employment requiring close applica-tion of mind or body, to be successful, the diligent and conscien-tious workman often, I might say always, finds his energy exhausted long before his ten hours are up. Then he is obliged to keep up an appearance to get the pay for his day's work, which he might do in eight hours as well as ten. If we are to have our pay by the hour, I should not advocate the eight-hour system. I think the employer would be the gainer, and the employé the loser. In the shop I work a little less than ten hours. To do that I have to leave home at 5:30 A.M., and arrive home again at 7 P.M.; so you see it makes a pretty long day. I travel not less than thirty-four miles daily, and pay $28.50 per quarter for car-fare. If I want to have a garden, I must do the work nights, or hire it done. I do not think I should be able to follow up work in this way until the age of sixty-five. Hope to find some way to avoid some of the long hours and some of the heavy work before then. I do not mean to complain; but it does seem as if the burdens and the pleasures of this world were very unequally divided. It is a hard matter to say what is right in every case. If my answers and statements should be of any service in improving the condition, prospects, or possi-bilities of the toiling thousands in our State, I shall be well paid for the same. . . .

THE USE OF MACHINERY.—*From a Carpenter.*—Less hours of labor will enable the man to procure more days of labor, stop the ruinous competition in the labor market, enable the producers to purchase more, give them time to study the great problems of this life without infringing upon the necessary hours of rest; in fine, make more intelligent the masses who must rule this and other countries. Under the present system of distribution of the prod-ucts of labor, we are fast drifting to that condition of society which has preceded the downfall of Sparta, Macedonia, Athens, and Rome, where a few were very rich, and the many very poor. If the institutions of this country are to be preserved, it must be by an intelligent, well-to-do yeomanry, not by a moneyed aristocracy, composed of the few, while the masses are in abject poverty.

From a Carpenter.—If machinery must be used, it should have a high rate of tax put on it by the United States, and the tax on tobacco, matches, and the like, taken off. I think, if such a move as this could be made, it would help the laboring class in this country.

From a Boot and Shoe Cutter.—Tax machinery. Bring it in common with hand labor, so a man can have twelve months' work in a year, instead of six or eight months. Protect hand labor, same as we protect trade from Europe, by tax or tariff.

From a Machinist.—Machinery and the swarms of cheap foreign labor are fast rendering trades useless, and compelling the better class of mechanics to change their occupation, or go to farming. . . .

SUPPLY STORES.—*From a Stone-Cutter.*—All incorporated companies here have stores, and many have tenement houses. Men are often discharged for not trading with them. I know from experience that their prices are fully ten per cent more than cash prices elsewhere. It also perpetuates the credit system, and leads to improvidence. Most workmen would live more prudently by cash payments and no trust. The companies have not reduced their rents, although wages have fallen one-half.

From a Quarryman.—There are eight companies in the stone business here, only four of which are running at present; and, running or loafing, they have a store apiece. All their employés must trade in their stores; if not, "get work where you trade. We keep as good articles here as you can get elsewhere, and sell as cheap, too." And that is all the satisfaction you will get for your complaint. I have had to pay $1.35 for a pair of children's shoes that I could buy outside for 50 cents, and so on with every thing else, to $2 on a barrel of flour; and everybody else must do likewise, i.e., those who work on stone. And that is not all either: some of them have tenement houses, and they must be kept full; and those who live in them are in a complete state of vassalage. And that is not all: no matter how frugally you live, you never can get any thing ahead; and those having helpless families scarcely ever receive a dollar. They are closely watched on the books, lest they might overrun their wages; and consequently they will get nothing, only as they earn it. Such is the atrocious system here; and this is a part of free, enlightened Massachusetts! I suppose, if the workingmen protested against this state of affairs, they'd be dubbed "communists;" but no: their manhood is completely gone. They dare not murmur at it even; and is it any wonder? They have no means to better their condition; and it is, to say the least, deplorable. A workingman has a boy; and that child is on the quarry, lugging tools, or, with himself, pounding on granite, at the age of ten years. He cannot afford to send him to school only a few months in winter. All summer the child must work hard for his living. Consequently, before he is twenty years old, in seven out of ten cases, he is broken down, and a sorry-looking specimen of manhood, without education or any thing else, and totally unfit to work at any other kind of laboring work. This is a very sorry-looking picture, Mr. Chief; and the worst feature in it is, that it is true. . . .

HABITS OF INDUSTRY.—*From a Clerk in a Country Store.*— Business is not very brisk, and there is not a large amount of money circulating in this vicinity; yet I do believe that, if a person enjoys good health, and is willing to work, he may earn an honest living, and perhaps lay aside a few dollars for future wants. A large portion of our poor people have poor ways: they will sit around the corner groceries and saloons, chew and smoke tobacco, swear and curse those who seem to be prospering, complain of the hard times and their hard luck,—nothing to do, nothing to do,—when it is a fact that their overworked wives are holding a child in one arm, and trying to cut firewood with the other to cook a scanty meal for their lazy husband's dinner.

From a Sole-Leather Cutter.—When the employé shall have fully comprehended the fact that labor and capital are not antagonistic, but allies, neither of which can well exist alone; that ignorance and dissipation do not, on the whole, advance a man's position in life; that the only true way to gain a position is by becoming morally and intellectually fitted for it; in short, when he shall have learned to live more in accordance with the maxim of Pythagoras, "Of all things, reverence thyself,"—then, and not until then, may we expect any permanent improvement in the condition of the laborer. Legislation is powerless to a great degree, as business must invariably be governed by the great law of demand and supply. Employers really desirous of elevating the laborer can contribute greatly to that result by giving preference of employment to such as are seen to be striving to rise, and not act on the principle of a manufacturer, who once told me in sub-stance, "I care little what a man *is*, so long as he does his work well."

From a machinist.—The great need now of the laboring man is honesty and contentment. I mean, being willing to do an honest day's work, and contented with the wages his labor will bring in the market. The idea that a man can get rich, without hard work of some kind, must be given up. Thirty-three years of hard work, and yet far from being rich, is my condition.

From a Shoe-Cutter.—There is no way I think I could be paid more fairly than I now am. I do not consider that my employers profit unfairly by my labor. My labor is in the market for sale. My employers buy it just as they buy a side of leather, and expect, and I think are willing to pay, a fair market price for it. The miller who makes a grade of flour up to the very highest point in excel-lence will command the highest price for it in the market. The workingman who makes his labor of the most value will generally command the highest market price for it, and sharp business men are quick to discover its value. I consider all legislation in regard to any thing connected with labor as injurious. All trades-unions and combinations I also consider as injurious to the mass of work-ing-people. A few profit by these associations, and the many pay the bills. If working-people would drop the use of beer, tobacco, and every thing else that is not of real benefit, and let such men as————and a host of others earn their own living, they would have far more money for the general expenses of a family than they now have. I live in a village of about two thousand inhabitants; and I do not know of a family in destitute circum-stances which has let alone vicious expenditures, and been indus-trious. It is the idle, unthrifty, beer-drinking, don't-care sort of people, who are out at the elbows, and waiting for some sort of legislation to help them. The sooner working-people get rid of the idea that somebody or something is going to help them, the better it will be for them. In this country, as a general thing, every man has an equal chance to rise. In our village there are a number of successful business men, and all began in the world without any thing but their hands and a will to succeed. The best way for working-people to get help is to help themselves. . . .

DUTIES OF GOVERNMENT.—*From a Paving-Stone Cutter.*— Remedy, in my opinion, must come from Congress; and it is a very simple matter. Pass a bill aiding the industrious idle poor to a home on the public lands, thereby making them producers instead of consumers,—take them from the squalor and filth, and consequent debasement, in the crowded centres of the East, to the broad acres of the West, all of which a patriotic Congress could do,—also adjust the tariff, so as to be tantamount to prohibition, on all imported articles that can be produced and manufactured here, the raw material which we possess (this measure would stimulate labor and all the industries of the nation), and no tax on articles, necessaries in particular, such as tea, coffee, spices, etc., which we do not and cannot produce here, to which may be added a government currency in substitution for bank notes, etc., making the same legal tender, absolute money for all debts, public and private, in the United States. . . .

From a Steam and Gas Fitter.—The war created a class of money aristocrats, who, with old manufacturing men, are bound to keep the poorer class and laboring men down, not giving them any encouragement or help. If they start for themselves, they do all in their power to make their efforts a failure. Fifteen years ago a man could start a successful business with from one hundred to three hundred dollars; while it now requires one to three or more thousand, thereby making a poor man's chances poorer every year. In fifteen years this country will be worse off than the old countries of Europe and Asia. The rich will be very rich, the poor very poor, and the government will be controlled by the moneyed class; and the cause is, in my opinion, due wholly to the fact,—minor offices with large salaries and little work. Commissions and committees are allowed to settle government business, which should be settled directly by the State legislature, or the national Senate and House of Representatives. It now means only to vote to pay a man so much money per day when the people elect him to represent their interest in any legislative body. Continual change is all that will make American office-holders honest. A party in power more than eight continuous years, will, of necessity, be corrupt. . . .

From a Cabinet-Maker.—Abolition of the present unjust political and social conditions. Discontinuance of all class rule and privileges. Abolition of the workingman's dependence upon the capitalist, by the introduction of co-operative labor in place of the wage system, so that every laborer will get the full value of his work. Abolition of all monopolies. Manufacturing to be carried on by free-labor societies, under the guaranty of the people, with government credit. Prohibition of children's labor for industrial purposes. Equalization of women's wages with those of men. As the contract system leads invariably to corruption, bribery, and felony, I demand its abolition by the State, and that all work for the general and municipal governments shall be by day-wages, according to the eight-hour system prescribed by law; also, introduction of the eight-hour system for all workingmen. . . .

From a Custom Shoemaker.—The best thing the government (national) can do for workingmen is to let them alone. The wise and the prudent need no help; for the unwise and imprudent nothing effectual can be done. Forethought and economy, carefully practised in early life as well as age, would banish poverty; and nothing else ever will.

From a Comb-Maker.—I do not know of any legislation that will help the workingman, and not affect the successful employer. He has the capital; and, if he cannot employ it so as to make it pay more than in other investments, he would not be likely to employ many workingmen at very high prices. . . .

From a Mill-Operative.— . . . The public schools are only a sham, at least so far as the children of the poor are concerned. We will suppose a man getting ten cents an hour: he works ten hours a day, or sixty hours a week, thereby earning six dollars a week. If he has to do all of this out of six dollars a week now, can it be possibly expected that that man can keep his children to school as long as he would wish to? We know, also, that mothers are often seen in the mills, the counting-rooms, and rooms in general throughout the mills, seeking for the overseers, to beg and crave at their hands work for their young and tender offspring. It is not wanting in natural feeling for their children that compels them to resort to these measures: it is necessity, and downright necessity at that,—necessity that compels them to lie on account of the age of their children in order that they may more easily obtain work. The overseers are, or at least some of them are, men of feeling, and will give heed to the sorrowful wail of these poor people, even at their own risk. I believe in agricultural, mechanical, and commercial schools being connected with the primary schools, and dispense with the Greek, Latin, music, and other showy matter.

From a Tallow-Renderer.—My future prospects are gloomy. I

have six children: my oldest is fourteen years old, my youngest two years old. Last year three of my children were promoted, and I was notified to furnish different books. I wrote a note to the school committee, stating that I was not able to do so; that I had been out of employment for some time; and that I never had called on the town before, and was sorry to do it then, but necessity compelled me to do so at that time. I then received a note, stating that, unless I furnished the books called for, I must keep my children at home. I then had to reduce the bread for my children and family, in order to get the required books to keep them at school. Every cent of my earnings is consumed in my family; and yet I have not been able to have a piece of meat on my table twice a month for the last eight months.

B: *Fall River, Lowell, and Lawrence*

In April, 1881, we received a letter from a member of the Massachusetts House of Representatives from which we make the following extract:—

"I have seen the following question directed to you by a Worcester paper: 'Why is it that the working people of Fall River are in constant turmoil, when at Lowell and Lawrence they are quiet?'" The letter also expressed the desire of the writer for an answer to the inquiry given above. Answers to this question in regard to Fall River have also been requested by numerous correspondents of the Bureau, as well as by parties visiting the office.

The matter seemed to be worth careful investigation; and after thorough research to see if the question had ever been fully considered by others, we began an investigation in the cities of Fall River, Lowell, and Lawrence, in June, 1881, and kept our agents in the field until late in November.

The pre-eminence of the textile industry in the cities named necessarily made the investigation one principally devoted to the condition of the mill operatives, they forming the great majority of the "working people."

If the reason or reasons for the discontent presumed to exist in Fall River, or the comparative state of contentment said to be found among the operatives in Lowell and Lawrence, had been canvassed by the press, the newspapers would have enlightened the public. The matter had been discussed in the columns of Boston, Lowell, and Lawrence papers, and perhaps in those of Fall River also; but such articles as had come to our attention reflected personal opinions rather than stated facts. To supply the necessary facts to answer the question under consideration, we endeavored to learn the direct and related causes that have produced the labor convulsions in Fall River in past years, while at the same time in Lowell and Lawrence there was an equilibrium of the interests of labor and capital.

It was our intention from the first to make the investigation exhaustive; to seek every avenue of information in the three cities, and to take testimony as long as valuable information could be seecured. . . .

The operatives were visited first at their homes, in the evening, by our agents; they were asked in general terms to give their reasons for being discontented, or for being contented, as the case might be. No uniform questions were asked, each operative being left free to choose his own topics. As soon as the alleged reasons for discontent became known to us, they were arranged in the form of inquiries, to be made of the manufacturers who were next visited by our agents. Parties known to be conversant with the industrial life of the respective cities were visited, whether they were private individuals, or connected with the city government, associations, or other organizations. A careful inspection was made of the corporation boarding-houses and tenements; a member of the board of health in each city accompanying our agents. After the personal investigation was concluded, with a view of giving others who were in condition to know an opportunity to express their opinions, and supply facts, a circular was prepared and sent to leading citizens, in all callings, in the three cities. . . .

From this large array of informants, a mass of testimony was secured aggregating seven hundred manuscript pages, of which about four hundred were from operatives and manufacturers, one hundred and fifty from citizens, and the balance were devoted to statistics. In editing the testimony, as far as possible the exact language of our informants has been retained; but similarity, both in ideas and expression, has caused the statements of many to be condensed and given as if they were the testimony of one person, thereby avoiding duplication. . . .

Women and Children in the Mills.—"Mill life," said a Fall River operative, "has a most demoralizing effect on women and children, especially on girls who have no parents in the mill to watch over them. I will not permit my girls to work in any other mill than the one I am in, and where I can keep my eye on them; not that I fear they will do any thing wrong, but the influences of a mill are very bad. If a child of a certain age goes to work in the mill, constantly breathing a temperature of 90° both winter and summer, it is sure to grow up puny, and die early. I get so exhausted that I can scarcely drag myself home when night comes." Another operative said that he had seen children in the mill who claimed to be fourteen years of age, but who were very small for their age. He said that children put into the mills at this early age often become useless when they reach their twentieth year; and young girls from fourteen and upwards learn more wickedness in one year than they would in five years out of the mill. He thought that the effect on women was equally bad. Another operative said that mill-work tended to afflict women with diseases peculiar to their sex, and corrupt children both morally and physically. It was asserted that many parents took a false oath in order to get their children into the mill, and thus make more money. "In this they are willingly aided by the manufacturers, who are willing to employ children; this is especially true of the shore mills over the line in Rhode Island, where they employ young people to do adults' work." An operative of Lawrence said that there were a number of children working in the mills who are under age, the parents being obliged to do this to earn sufficient for the maintenance of their family. One of the Lawrence weavers said, "One of the evils existing in this city is the gradual extinction of the male operative. The female operative has the preference. . . . I know of a number of men who are compelled to stay at home, do the housework, and attend to the children, because they can get nothing to do. This must be the rule in all of the mills, else the men who are good workmen could get something to do in the other mills. Within a radius of two squares in which I am living, I know of a score of young men who are supported by their sisters and their mothers, because there is no work in the mills for them. Owing to this unreasonable demand for women, a man out of employment can stand but little chance of securing any. Some of these young men are in jail; they have tried to obtain work to do, and failing, have become discouraged and finally got to loafing, then to stealing and intemperance, and then in prison; and when they are released all they seem to care about is revenge; all ambition has fled. . . .

CLASSIFICATION	CITIES			Aggregates
	Fall River	Lowell	Lawrence	
1880				
Number of open accounts	18,694	32,029	13,728	64,451
Number of accounts exceeding $300 at any time during the year	951	1,659	758	3,368
Deposits	$7,705,584 46	$10,404,330 67	$4,179,256 49	$22,289,171 63
Assets	$8,079,554 55	$10,983,776 33	$4,385,617 00	$23,448,947 88
Loans on real estate	$2,983,697 06	$ 3,922,595 07	$1,636,518 77	$ 8,542,810 90
Loans on personal security	$2,511,296 46	$ 503,630 11	$ 486,891 84	$ 3,501,818 41
1881				
Deposits in 1881	$7,832,629 61	$11,043,240 08	$4,619,372 27	$23,495,241 96
Excess of deposits in 1881 over 1880	$ 127,045 15	$ 638,909 41	$ 440,115 78	$ 1,206,070 34
Assets in 1881	$8,198,204 07	$11,646,212 99	$4,821,766 33	$24,666,183 39
Excess of assets in 1881 over 1880	$ 118,649 52	$ 662,436 66	$ 436,149 33	$ 1,217,235 51

Condition and Appearance of the Operative Population in the Three Cities.—The welfare of the operatives is a secondary consideration in Fall River if all that operatives, manufacturers, and others say is true; certainly the condition of the city does not tend to create a feeling that cleanliness is one of its paramount virtues. The poor quarters of the city are very uncleanly. . . .

The conduct and condition of the operatives of Lowell was most excellent. They dressed well, especially the females. There were no disturbances while the agent was there, and the city was quiet at nine o'clock. A person connected with the corporations said that the one great difference between Lowell and Fall River was the absence of the family and Union influences. He thought that the majority of the Fall River population was composed of the worst elements of English and Irish. He cited a case of a Fall River agitator who came to Lowell for the purpose of creating disorder. He started a Spinners' Union, and gained a large number of converts, despite the fact that when the operatives were employed they were obliged to sign a paper in which they promised not to join any trade unions. The seeds of discontent that this agitator sowed ripened into a full-blown strike, and then their leader deserted them and went to Lawrence to work. "If we have any troublesome people they are told to go to the office, collect their money, and get out. Our agents will not submit to any dictation on the part of the operatives." An operative said, "In Fall River a girl comes out of the mill with bare feet, and a shawl thrown over her head, and all she cares for is a loaf of bread and a mug of beer. Here, our girls dress well, and I have no doubt save considerable money. Some of them hire a room for $1.60 a week, and board at the corporation houses for $1.70; the men pay $2.65 a week for board."

The operatives met by the agents in Lawrence were quiet, orderly people, and seemed to be good workmen and intelligent citizens. On the streets the people were well behaved, and the women neatly dressed. By half-past nine the streets were almost deserted, and the city quiet. The operatives, as they came from the mills, were a fine-looking, intelligent set. The men appeared strong and hearty, and the women and girls cheerful and well dressed; everybody seemed contented and happy. None of the operatives complained of abject poverty, or continual discontent; and spoke in the warmest terms of their overseers, who were pleasant and agreeable, and were as contented as the operatives themselves. One operative stated, "Take Fall River with all its rough, tyrannical despotisms, turn it over and make black white, and you have a good picture of Lawrence. Here we are paid well, but no better, work easily, live well, do not hurry, and are contented." . . .

Tenements.—In their visits to the tenement houses in Fall River, Lowell, and Lawrence, our agents were always accompanied by members of the local boards of health, who did all in their power to aid the investigation. They were asked to point out the "worst" tenement houses, and they cheerfully complied. The power of right of entrance possessed by members of the boards enabled our agents to make more thorough examinations than would otherwise have been possible. In seeking information from the mill officials, the first question asked was, "Are your tenements in as good condition as you would like to have them?" and comparatively few expressed themselves as being entirely satisfied.

In discussing this part of our subject, we shall refer to each city separately.

FALL RIVER.—One of the questions asked the operatives was, "What is the condition of the working classes in their homes?" To judge by their remarks the fitness of the houses as dwellings was certainly questionable. A great many asserted that many of the mill people did not have a respectable place of abode, especially those who lived in the tenements that belonged to the mills. There was much complaint about the sanitary condition, as well as the fact that many of the tenements were not supplied with running water. The vaults of the privies received unstinted condemnation, many of them said to emit foul odors, which on warm summer nights, when all the windows of the tenements were open, charged the atmosphere with noxious gases, and made it stifling and nauseating. One weaver visited spoke unreservedly of the so-called tenement house nuisance, though his apartments were in good condition, clean, and had a generally tidy appearance; but, as a rule, the surroundings were more complained of than the dwellings themselves.

A spinner, who was employed in one of the mills that bore the reputation about town of having some of the worst houses, said, in substance, "The tenements throughout the city are in a very poor condition. The reason why I live in this one is because I am compelled to. Compulsion is used by this mill, and whether the manufacturers have the legal or the moral right to keep us in their houses I do not know; but I think it is wrong. The sink is in the corner of this room, which we use as our living-room, dining-room, and kitchen. The closets in the yard are very bad, and their odor is the reverse of pleasant. There is a hydrant in the yard to which we all have to go for drinking water, having none in the house that is fit to drink. Shortly after six o'clock any night you can see a line of men, women, girls and boys, waiting their turn, laden with pails, to get the water to use for drinking and cooking. . . ."

. . . One operative, a spinner, used strong language when speaking of the mill tenements. He had a kitchen, two bedrooms, and a wash-room; and he spoke bitterly of the fact that such close quarters had a demoralizing effect on the young of his family, it being necessary for himself and wife, owing to the smallness of their sleeping-rooms, to dress in the kitchen before their children, one boy sleeping in the kitchen, while the two younger children, boy and girl, slept in the smaller bedroom. . . .

A spinner in one of the central mills, who had a very neat looking tenement, thought that nearly all of the mill tenements were unfit to live in. "But," said he, "you take whole families, like mine, who work in the mills, and what benefit do they derive from a home? They are only there at night to sleep, and on Sunday, and to such, one kind of a house is as good as another. . . ."

The manufacturers, as a rule, spoke strongly in favor of their houses. One said, "Our tenements are very good indeed: they were built ten or twelve years ago, and must be in good condition. We try to keep them so, at all events. The help take fair care of them; of course there are exceptions. The intemperate do not: they do not care; they get intoxicated, and use their rooms as though they were bar-rooms." Another said, "They are not as good as we would like to have them, but good enough for the operatives." This remark was repeated by another, a treasurer, who stated that the help do not appreciate clean homes. Another, while acknowledging that their tenements were not as good nor as clean as they would like to have them, thought that, as a class, the operatives show no regard for clean rooms; that they destroy rather than build up. All agreed on this, as well as on the fact that they were fixing them up continually. One president said, "Our first mill was built in 1866. I built four cottage houses on our land for some of our help; but the operatives proved to be very dirty: many of them kept poultry in the cellars. They do not show much appreciation of a clean house. The French Canadians in our employ are not neat." . . .

A resident of Fall River, who formerly worked in one of the mills, stated, ". . . There are no gardens about these houses, and I know of a place where there is but one water-faucet to nearly fifty families, while the privies are exposed to everybody. Dead rats and chickens and other refuse lie about, regardless of any of the common laws of health. Into these tenements families come and go, and the best of care is consequently unknown. When a man is employed by the mill he is compelled to move into their tenements. Their breakfast depends on their moving in, and their life on their moving out. . . ."

LOWELL.—There are not many tenements in Lowell that are owned by the corporations: those that they do let out to families are called the small boarding houses, and are, as a rule, occupied by the heads of the various departments. A section hand who occupied a corporation dwelling house said, "Another thing in favor of Lowell is our tenements. I have a tenement of nine rooms, for which I pay $6.68 per month, and it is a very good house. For that sum you might rent a place to stay in in Fall River, but not a respectable abode. In our boarding houses, which are rented to private individuals, the average cost of board, lodging, and washing, is $7.40 a month. In what other maufacturing city can you find as low a price as this? . . ."

"Little Canada."—This is a settlement of French Canadians in Lowell, on the bank of the Merrimack River. It is situated, for the most part, on made ground, from eight to fifteen feet in depth, and which was formerly a swamp. The material used in filling this section is composed of the refuse of the city and mills, among which could be distinguished tin cans, bottles, swill, ash-barrels, general household refuse, and a quantity of wool and cotton waste, which the agent of the local board of health said would rot and breed disease. Three blocks of tenements, named, respectively, Norombega, Arcadian, and Austin, were occupied by French Canadians, with a sprinkling of the Irish element. They are owned by a prominent physician. In one house, No. 32 of the Arcadian Block, a family was visited which paid $4 per month for two rooms, one used as a kitchen and living-room, and the other a dark room, used as a bedroom. The size of the former was 14.2 feet long, 15 feet wide, and 8 feet high; the bedroom was 14.2 feet long, 8.2 feet wide, and 8 feet high. There were two windows in the large room, and one in the small, the latter opening on the back of a privy. There was no way of securing thorough ventilation save by having a draught, and the only light that was attainable was by the means of two windows which opened immediately on the rear of the Norombega Block and on the privy before mentioned, the foul air of which entered into this room, there being no opportunity for it to be carried away, for the space between these two blocks was about one and a half feet. The cellars were dark and gloomy, and partitioned to give each family one apartment which was littered with chips and refuse, though no decaying vegetable matter could be discovered. The cellar walls had no appearance of ever having been whitewashed, and the general appearance was forbidding. The inhabitants in the Norombega Block have to carry their refuse of all kinds and human excrement, save when they throw it between the two blocks, around between the Arcadian and Austin Blocks, into what is called Austin Avenue, for deposit. . . .

LAWRENCE.—The boarding house system is not so expensive in Lawrence as in Lowell; more of the operatives in the mills here owning their own houses. The tenements of the laboring classes are in a fairly good condition, the corporation houses coming second, and those owned by operatives ranking first. Those houses that are owned by the corporations are clean and healthy, as a rule, and are thoroughly overhauled every spring, and painted once in two years. One of the operatives stated: "In their homes the Arlington Mill operatives are better off than many others. Some of our help own their own houses, and these are kept in good repair, and always look neat and attractive. In the private tenements and boarding houses (the Arlington Mill has but one boarding house) , the families and single people do all they can to make their rooms look bright and cheerful. The sanitary condition is good, and the light and ventilation afforded by a large number of windows add greatly to the healthy appearance of the help." . . .

Working Time; Ten-Hour Law, etc.—There was considerable fault found in Fall River because the ten-hour law was not thoroughly enforced. It was asserted, that, upon the arrival of a State detective in the city, all of the mills were telephoned and informed of the fact, and then strict time was kept. . . . A spinner said, "Really, the ten-hour law has been of no practical benefit to our operatives. The manufacturers have counteracted the good by

an increase of speed, and the work is much more tiresome."
Another said that he was supposed to begin work at 6:30 A.M., but
is really required to commence at 6:15, and his dinner hour is frequently absorbed in cleaning his machinery. He noted several
times that the mill opposite him would not stop until after theirs,
and would begin work before they did. One operative stated that
a universal strike was prevented, a short time ago, by the fining of
a number of overseers for violating the ten-hour law. Another
operative said, "We are three miles from the City Hall, and can
do about as we please, and if the superintendent takes ten minutes
in the morning, fifteen at noon, and five at night, it is nobody's
business, and the operative ought to be thankful that he has got a
place to work in, and not grumble about a little thing like half an
hour; and then, do they not have that much more time in which
to earn more money? If they do not appreciate the kindness of the
manufacturers, all they have to do is to complain, and get out.
Speed is an absolute science in Fall River, and what the superintendents and overseers do not know about it, you may rest assured
is not worth knowing. We are running at a greater speed than we
were six months ago. Help being slack, the manufacturers desire
to get off as much as they can in order to keep up to the average.
We were speeded up three teeth, but that was found to be too
much, so one was taken off. The manufacturer says to his operative, 'Why should you complain? Are you not able to earn more
money by extra speed?' But the question is, whether the extra
drive and exhaustion necessary to do more work compensates for
the small amount of extra money earned." From the testimony of
the operatives it will be seen that the mills are charged with
"stealing on time," as it is called. The time so gained is said to be
from six to sixteen minutes a day. The custom at present is to
start at 6.22 A.M., and shut down at 12 M.; start again at 12:52
P.M., and shut down at six,—the eight minutes before 7 A.M. and
the eight minutes before 1 P.M. being the time said to be stolen.

The agents and superintendents claim that it is simply done to
get the machinery running, and that the help is not required to
begin work until one o'clock; the testimony of all of the operatives is that they must be in their places ready to begin work when
the wheel starts. . . .

The ten-hour law seems to be observed strictly in Lowell. A
visit to the Merrimack Mills at the noon hour showed that all the

mills run on the same time; for at these mills an electric gong was struck which connected with every mill in the city, and they all started up at the same time, and stopped at the same time.

A former Lowell operative, now in Fall River in other business, said, "In Lowell the gates to the mill yards are opened on the stroke of a gong, which strikes simultaneously in all of the mills, and every operative is expected to be out of the mill immediately after. Five minutes after the gong sounds, the watchmen go through the rooms and order out every operative unless they are there by permission of the overseers, who are the last out of their rooms."

In Lawrence there was only one complaint made in regard to overtime. . . .

Wages.—The operatives in Fall River made many complaints about wages, claiming that they were not paid as much as they ought to be; that their work was of a character that demanded a much larger recompense. One operative said, "Our wages are not so high as they are in Lawrence, perhaps higher than in Rhode Island, but extra speed produces this result. My father used to support his family of six off of the product of one hand-loom, in England; with the improvements of machinery it takes eight looms (average pay $9 per week) to support two persons in this city. The benefits of improved machinery do not reach as far as Fall River." Another operative said, "Whenever the market is dull, and the mill is not making money, the operatives have to be reduced, and, as a rule, they swallow the fact, and accept the situation; but now, when the mills are making money, the manufacturers do not increase the pay. Every mill in the city is making money; they are crowded with orders, and are erecting new mills, and the recent dividends have been most generous; but the operatives travel in the same old path,—sickness, suffering, and small pay." Another operative said, "When any one goes to the manufacturers to investigate as to the pay of the operatives, they are shown the pay-roll with the amount set against each operative's name. It looks all right in the books; but, when a man loses one month out of six, that paybook does not show any change, but the pocket-book of the operative does." . . .

The operatives of Lawrence expressed no absolute dissatisfaction as to their pay, nor did the operatives of Lowell, but they all agreed that they would like more. A former operative in Lawrence said, "The smallest amount paid is ninety cents per day, and the largest is $1.15. Some of the operatives, after mill hours, try to earn a little more money by peddling tea and other articles. Some make it pay, and others do not." . . .

Complaints of Operatives.—When the general question was put to the operatives in Fall River, "Are there any special causes for content or discontent existing in this city?" the nature of the replies involved so many subjects that it was deemed best, for a proper presentation of the results of the investigation, to classify them under sub-heads, as has been done. The answers in the abstract were as thoroughly interesting as those that dwelt on only one item of discontent, and these we shall now present.

One of the operatives summarized the feeling throughout the city, in the following: "Bad cotton, stealing time, and a constant and steady 'grind,' constitute the three greatest complaints in Fall River to-day." Another, commenting on the above mentioned causes, could think of none others of moment, and thought that the agent would not find many who could; "for," said he, "they only speak of that which hurts them just before they go home to supper." Many comparisons were made between the treatment of the operatives by American and English overseers, some being of the opinion that the American did not know how to tyrannize, and others thinking they did. One of the latter said, "They are more tyrannical here in Fall River than they are in England. I always thought they were tyrants at home, but found out differently when I came here. We could always make a complaint of any grievance there; but here, if we dare to do such a thing, we are told that if we don't like it we can get out." This final remark we found was adopted by nearly every operative visited; for though he might be unusually conservative on other points, when it came to the question of entering a complaint, they agreed that the answer invariably given was, "There is no redress here, and no appeal. The by-word is 'If you don't like it, get out!' " Another operative said, "The former feeling of bitterness between the North and South is but an example of the feeling 'twixt employed and employer in Fall River." . . .

One of the operatives, and there were many like him, spoke in a very intelligent manner, recognizing that in dealing with a large class of help one must expect to find bad as well as good characters. He said, "When you ask what is the cause for discontent, you open a subject that is full of talk, and one which I am somewhat acquainted with, having been in Fall River for ten years or more. I can assure you that things have changed; and, if the ignorant operatives can be only made to understand it, Fall River will soon become settled. But they must get rid of the turbulent agitators, who really cause a great deal of trouble. Now, I am not particularly contented; but I am contented when I look back and see how we were treated years ago, and how we are treated now. The majority of the spinners and weavers will tell you that they are the ones who brought about this improvement in the existing state of affairs, by their determined strikes and resistance to arbitrary measures. Well, perhaps they are right; but public opinion has done a great deal more, I can assure you. To prove their claim, the operatives will say, that, without their striking, public opinion could not have been aroused; but no intelligent man needs to be assured of the nonsense of that statement. A great many of the strikes were brought about by despicable actions on the part of the manufacturers, and were, perhaps, necessary. I thought so once, because I was brought up in England, where a strike was natural as a day's rest on Sunday. But the more I think of it the more confident I am that if the operatives, in the very first instance, had adopted the petition and spirit of arbitration that seems to be a part and parcel of American institutions, they would have been better off in the first place, and, of course, better off now. But they could not do this; in fact, they did not understand how to do it. The manufacturers brought to Fall River, from England, whole cargoes of English, Scotch, and Irish, all men of family, who were put into the mills. They were a power in those days; that is both conceded and regretted; and, knowing only the English method of obtaining what they wanted, began striking whenever any thing displeased them. What was the result? The manufacturers being short of help, and only having secured the shipment of the number necessary to run their mills, were compelled to give way, but with a mental reservation that one day they would repay the operatives in their own coin; and they have done it effectually. This is what I believe to be the only just solution of the present attitude of the masters toward the men."

A resident of Fall River, who was formerly an operative, when asked if he could throw any light on the reasons for discontent said, "A good deal of the trouble in this city is caused by outside agitators who breed dissensions among the operatives. Fall River is a filter; the good go away never to return, while the bad always remain. Operatives came here from England with their Old Country notions and prejudices, which are out of place here." Another resident, who also had been an operative, said, "The trouble is caused by the overseers and superintendents, who are, as a rule, burly Englishmen or Irishmen, without a particle of good breeding, and who will use oaths and violent language when addressing a woman or girl, just as readily as when speaking to a man. The American overseer does not do this, for he likes to be treated well himself, and therefore treats others well. You never hear the operatives in Lowell or Lawrence complaining of their overseers and superintendents."

When the manufacturers were visited, the question was asked, in regard to the existing state of affairs, "Why is it that the operatives of Lowell and Lawrence are apparently so well contented, and those of Fall River apparently so discontented?" . . .

[One official said,] "The discontent among the Fall River operatives is the outgrowth of the abnormal increase of the mills in 1871. We have the scum of the English and Irish in our midst; they brought their antagonistic notions with them. We never employ a man who belongs to a trades union if we know it; we root them out whenever we find them. We manage more help in Fall River than they do in any other city. Two years ago the operatives went out on a strike; the trouble was, that we discharged an obnoxious spinner. Look at the Spinners' Union; its officers are all blacklisted men, and cannot get work in any of the mills. Its secretary gets $15 a week to look out for the interests of the Union and to stir up trouble. He is a good enough fellow, and we understand him and he us. The president and treasurer after being blacklisted received grants of $100 each from the Union's treasury, and started rum shops, and the spinners patronize them." . . .

From the operatives questioned in Lowell the oft repeated answer came, "I am contented, and do not know why the other operatives should be discontented." One added that he could see no reason why any one should complain, "for we are better treated than anywhere else, and I think you can search the city through, and not find a discontented man." Another said, "We are the best paid and the best treated class of help in Massachusetts, as well as being a better class of operatives than you will find in Fall River." . . .

Of all the operatives visited in the city of Lawrence, none referred to any general complaint, and, in the main, they all appeared satisfied with their lot. A resident of the city, one of the leading men in political, social, and business circles, stated that, "The cause for contentment among our working people consists in the fact that they are treated better than anywhere else, and the general disposition of the corporations is to do for their operatives as much as private individuals will do for their help. The mills are mostly owned and run by Boston men of large means, who give their agents considerable latitude in regard to their help, and consult them rather than themselves when a question of pay comes up. The Fall River men live on the ground, and are among their employés grinding them down so as to make every dollar count; if they are asked for an increase in pay, they will not grant the request, because they do not want to part with the money already made; while here, the agents usually have the preference, and if they think the help deserve more pay, the corporations are perfectly willing to grant it." Judging by the statement of the operatives, the above was borne out by them, one saying that as far as he was concerned, he could see no reason why the operatives should complain. He rents one of the corporation houses, pays his rent, gets plenty to eat and drink, and does not pay an extravagant price for it. He also said, "I work sixty hours per week, earn what I get, save what I please, do what I like, attend to my own business, and do not meddle with the affairs of others that in no way concern me." . . .

The Black List.—Nearly all of the Fall River operatives visited by the agent seemed to fear the possibility of the manufacturers discovering that they had given any information. One of them, and his statement will cover those made by several others, said, "You will find that very few of the operatives will say any thing unless you can assure them that their names will never be known. If it was known that I was giving you any information, I would be discharged at once, so you see that I am reposing considerable faith in you. My bread is at stake, and, were I asked if I had given you any information, I should deny it from the beginning." Under these circumstances it was necessary to proceed with caution, but in the majority of cases the mere promise that no names would be mentioned was sufficient to gain the desired information.

All agreed that the "black list" was an abominable institution, one that embodied all that was pernicious in the system of spying. . . .

Naturally there was a difference of opinion on the part of the manufacturers and the operatives in regard to the black list: the former, as a rule, were as reticent in regard to it as the latter were communicative. Many acknowledged its usefulness *if* it were necessary to use it. One manufacturer said, "No, there is nothing of the kind practised here; and if there was it would only be a just retaliation for what they do themselves. . . ."

Other manufacturers granted that the black list was in existence, and stated that its use was necessary to guard against strikes; one saying, "If we wanted to blacklist a man, we would undoubtedly do so." Another stated that there was such a thing as a "black list." Another said, "This [blacklisting] is done by a committee of the Manufacturers' Board of Trade. A man's name is sent to this committee, and they examine the list and take action on it. The black list is directed mostly toward the members of the Mule-Spinners' Union, for they cause us the most trouble. For our own protection we started a secret service, and it has accomplished much good, as it gave us the names and occupations of the most prominent in agitating strikes. There have been twenty-six mule-spinners blacklisted since last fall." . . .

No complaints were made in Lowell or Lawrence about blacklisting, which is conclusive proof that the manufacturers rarely or carefully exercise a power that they possess, and which in effect, if not in name, is the same, or could be made the same, as blacklisting in Fall River. We refer to the discharge paper given an operative when he leaves a Lowell or Lawrence mill, and which he is called upon to present when he goes to another mill in the same city. The refusal to grant an "honorable" discharge to an operative would have the same effect as entering his name on a blacklist. . . .

Trades Unions; Strikes.—One of the Fall River operatives, when questioned in regard to strikes and trades unions, said, "I am a union man on principle, for I believe that we have as much right to have a union to consider matters of vital interest to us as the manufacturers have to organize a board of trade to consider their interests. . . . I do not, however, believe in strikes, nor can I ever convince myself that the end justifies the means. A strike is but the result of a bitter, turbulent spirit, that works itself much harm in the end. The fault of strikes consists in the begging that attends them. When the operatives strike, and pass around the hat begging for help and support, the manufacturers, having the most money, hold out the longest. Every body of men will lose when they attempt to fight capital by striking, especially when they are unprepared for a long vacation." Another operative, who believed thoroughly in unions, said, "I believe that while labor has its obligations it also has its privileges. We came here to make money for ourselves, but the manufacturers imported us to make money for them." Nearly all of the operatives believed in a union in the abstract, but did not believe in them as they were being conducted in Fall River, where it was claimed they were simply vehicles for the fomentation of incipient riots and disorderly conduct. The universal opinion was that the Fall River method of striking gained neither an advance nor friends, one operative saying, "I never saw a strike yet that was not a failure before it took place." It was thought that the true province of a union was to encourage improvement in the ranks of the members; to discuss measures of reform, such as a uniform ten-hour law, that would result in general good to the working classes. . . .

There seemed to be no indications of trades unions in Lowell; but a section hand stated, "I do not believe in strikes or unions. They think they have killed the Mule-Spinners' Union of Lowell, but they have not. Business is not carried on so openly as before, but the Union still lives. Instead of striking when I am dissatisfied, I go to my agent, and tell him I want more money; if he cannot give it to me, some one else may. He is not compelled to keep or pay me, and I am not obliged to remain in his employ any longer than I choose. The remedy is in my own hands, as it is in the hands of every operative. The agent is the man with the money, and I am the man with the ability; he can do as he pleases with his money, and I can turn my ability to any honorable purpose that I choose. I do not see, under these circumstances, why strikes are necessary. Looking at these later strikes, I find that they are growing worse; pistols, stones, and fire are now being resorted to, instead of respectable arguments. It is no wonder that manufacturers object to employ union men, or men who are known to be agitators."

There are no trades unions in Lawrence connected with the mill operatives, and no strikes are necessary, according to the operatives. They all agree in saying that if they have a request to make they are permitted to do so, and if they want an increase of pay they can get it without striking about it, if the market will allow. . . .

Delegations; Conferences.—As will be premised from a reading of the foregoing pages of this report, the lack of a proper feeling in regard to delegations and conferences in Fall River was a feature of the trouble in that city that was sincerely regretted, as it prevented the adjustment of troubles in a fair and mutually satisfactory manner. The operatives united in saying that complaints were not listened to by the manufacturers, though they were of the opinion that, if a deputation of the operatives were permitted to be heard, the chances were that one-half of the trouble would cease. It was asserted that if the manufacturers would meet the operatives when an advance was asked, talk with them, and if impossible to grant the request say so, and convince them why it was impossible, the probabilities were that there was not an operative in the mills but would gladly continue as they were. It would certainly mark a new era in industrial conciliation in this city. An operative said, "The manufacturers will not meet a deputation of the operatives, and settle disputes amicably by arbitration. It is done elsewhere: why can it not be done here? But no, the manufacturers have repeatedly said, 'We are the masters, and we have the money: you must do as we say, or get out;' and when a man has a wife and children to take care of, as I have, he is apt to swallow the affront, and bide his time for a softening of the masters' hearts." . . .

Some of the superintendents and treasurers knew of no delegations lately, and some thought they would receive them if they came, while others said they would refuse to listen to them at all. One asserted that he had never been able to settle any thing by conference, and during their late strike they held no conference, nor would they permit any to be held. . . . A president of one of the mills said, "We always endeavor to receive the delegations that wait upon us, politely, and listen to the story of their grievances. We sometimes receive a circular signed, 'The workmen in your employ,' but very few of our men know any thing about it. These circulars are gotten up by outside parties for the purposes of disturbance; and they always address the operatives as 'fellow-workmen,' when they are in reality discharged operatives, and only workingmen so far as they are rumsellers and are working for the operatives' money. In the spring of 1880 we made two advances in wages. The second was to go into effect the first day of May; but before the time arrived a drop occurred in the price of goods, but we made the advance. As far as arbitration is concerned, we will not agree to that. Our money built these mills, and we propose to secure whatever benefits may be derived from the business." . . .

12. Illinois Bureau of Labor Statistics— Report (1884)

The Illinois Bureau of Labor Statistics rivaled the Massachusetts bureau in influence, and by the 1880's excelled it in the sophistication of its social and economic research. Its 1884 study of the condition of workingmen in Illinois offers an incomparable, indeed a unique, record of how men lived and labored in that era. As the following selection shows, this pioneering study compares favorably in technique with the most modern sociological investigations.

In Part I of this report there are presented tables deduced from statements made by the manufacturers of the State, to agents of the general government, showing the rates of wages paid to employés, and the relation those wages sustain to the estimated profit or loss realized upon the product of the labor of those employés. That showing is supplemented in the following pages by tabulations of statements made by individual workmen throughout the State to agents of this Bureau, as to their actual earnings during the year preceding April, 1884, and the relation those earnings sustained to the amounts actually expended for the support of their families.

SOURCE: Illinois Bureau of Labor Statistics, "Earnings, Expenses and Conditions of Workingmen and Their Families," *Third Biennial Report* (Springfield, Ill., 1884), pp. 135-7, 164, 267-71, 357-62, 365, 369-70, 373, 375, 383-5, 390-3, 395, 401-2, 404, 406-7, 410.

The enquiry of the general government, through its census officials, as to manufactures was directed to every establishment in the State, the value of whose annual product was $500 or more. Those schedules therefore present the exact facts for the State at large as to the specific points embraced in the enquiry, and the results arrived at are actual and final. The investigation entered upon by this Bureau with its limited resources, could not of course reach every workingman in the State, and has necessarily been confined to those who, so far as possible, were representatives of the various occupations in the various localities. The results obtained, consequently, only approximate the actual condition of the classes considered in proportion as the individuals taken truly represent their respective classes. With this consideration in view the investigation was made as general as the facilities at the command of the Bureau permitted, and as discriminating as possible. Many thousands of families in the principal industrial centers of the State were visited, by the representatives of the Bureau, for the purpose of obtaining detailed information of their condition; and notwithstanding the indifference of some, and the indisposition of others, the number of those who responded to our interrogatories were greater than at first anticipated. It was made the duty of the canvasser to visit all classes of people who were working for wages, both in skilled and unskilled employments, and those illustrating all degrees of prosperity and adversity; to explain the purposes of the Bureau, and, if necessary, assist in making up a correct statement of the facts elicited; also to make memoranda based upon personal observations as to the general condition and apparent sanitary and social surroundings of each family. In many instances it was found, as expected, that an exact record of receipts and expenditures was not preserved and from some of these no available data whatever could be procured. In other cases partial accounts were kept, or could be referred to, upon which a very close estimate could be fairly established. As was also anticipated more or less prejudice was encountered, and reluctance on the part of some, especially the more prosperous, to furnish facts of which they were possessed, owing to imperfect or erroneous ideas as to the use to be made of them. Notwithstanding obstacles of this character, however, there were everywhere found intelligent men and women ready to cooperate with and assist the Bureau in prosecuting this work, and from such are the details herein presented principally derived.

This work was undertaken in the principal cities and towns, or mining or manufacturing centers, and although failure was encountered in some localities, either through inability to secure suitable agents, or their lack of adaptability for this particular work, the returns have been on the whole gratifying both in number and character. After excluding doubtful and imperfect statements, we are able to present herewith a picture more or less complete of the real and relative condition of 2,129 families of workingmen in Illinois. These families embrace a total of 9,834 persons, living in 51 different cities, towns and villages, engaged in 163 different occupations, and representing 16 different nationalities.

From so large a number of individual cases, covering so great a diversity of condition and surroundings, we should be able to determine with some degree of exactness very just averages on a variety of subjects, notwithstanding the investigation is less comprehensive than that of a general census.

So far as is known, this enquiry embraces a very much larger number and variety of working people than any of a similar character which has preceded it in this country; and as the presumption in favor of any deductions made, increases with the number of individual cases brought under consideration, provided they are fairly representative, the results of the investigation should possess an unusual interest and value.

We have designed to make this investigation not only so comprehensive as to give the impress of truth to such conclusions as might be reached, but at the same time to make it wholly impartial and unprejudiced. The instructions to our agents were general in their character, and directed solely to the purpose of procuring facts, without reference to preconceived opinions. . . .

. . . Representatives of the Bureau consulted with workingmen and their wives at their homes, and, when necessary, assisted them in making up memoranda of their various receipts and disbursements. In some instances access was had to the pay-rolls of employers in order to verify the items of earnings; and where "company stores" were maintained in connection with mines, or other industries, the monthly account current rendered to each employé was readily referred to, both for earnings and the greater part of expenditures. There was, notwithstanding, much patient and careful enquiry required, in order to arrive at the closest possible approximation to the exact facts. It would hardly be justifiable to assume that there was any general tendency on the part of families either in the direction of over-estimation or underestimation in making up their accounts. The disposition on the part of some to exaggerate their annual balances was offset by that of those inclined to the other extreme, and it was the delicate duty of the canvasser to check this tendency in both. In view, therefore, of the caution exercised in this respect, and the subsequent scrutiny all statements received in this office in the effort to eliminate inconsistent and doubtful returns, we feel justified in expressing confidence in the general integrity of the representations made, and in the deductions made therefrom. There can be no question as to the many advantages this plan of procuring statistics has over that of issuing circulars through the mails, and depending upon such voluntary replies as may be made. As compared with returns of that character, these may justly claim to possess a maximum as against a minimum of accuracy and value. With these remarks we present the following extended synopsis of the economic condition of a large body of workingmen in Illinois. . . .

From the foregoing we reach the following general conclusions:

1. That 24+ per cent. of the workingmen of Illinois fail to make a living.

2. That the earnings in 80 occupations average more than $600 per annum, and in 83 the average is less than $600.

3. That in 19 localities the average earnings for all trades is less than $600 per annum, and in 15 the average is $600 or more.

4. That 34+ per cent. of our workmen own the houses in which they live. . . .

Among workingmen of all classes, there are found those who require the assistance of wives and children in order to maintain themselves in the unequal struggle against want. This is in a measure true in all communities. It was declared in the House of Commons in 1873, that 184,000 mothers in England were daily away from their homes at work in the mills. Statistics on the same subject have also been compiled in the State of Massachusetts, showing that 64+ per cent. of the workingmen of that State rely upon the assistance of wives or children for the family support.

Our own returns permit us to show to what extent such assist-ance is required by the workingmen of Illinois. . . . While the results in this respect will be found gratifying as compared with conditions elsewhere, it is not the less deplorable that the neces-sity should ever arise for resorting to this alternative.

The employment of wives otherwise than in their domestic duties, and the placing at labor of children of school age, must be subversive of the best interests of the family, as well as of doubtful expediency as a measure of economy. The first obligation to the child is manifestly to give it such physical and mental develop-ment as best to prepare it for the duties and responsibilities of maturity; and the most effective assistance the wife can render the family is in the care of her children, and the practice of those small domestic economies which contribute more in the end to the permanent prosperity of the family, than any mere earnings she might obtain through the neglect of them. Yet when we con-sider the meager earnings of many heads of families, and realize that it devolves upon them not only to maintain and educate their families, but equally to make provision for those declining years when the ability to labor shall fail, it is not strange that, when the opportunity offers, they call upon those who are naturally their dependents and make them contributors to as well as consumers of the family resources. Happily the number in our State upon whom such necessity is imposed is not large. . . .

We find here that there are only 24 + per cent. of the families given who receive aid in the shape of earnings from wives and children, and that 75 + per cent. of the heads of families are able, by their individual earnings, to supply the needs of those depend-ent upon them. In Massachusetts, whose extensive mills afford unusual opportunities for the employment of women and chil-dren,the percentage of families thus assisted is 64 +, affording a very wide contrast with our 24 + per cent. . . .

In respect to the nationality of families, it is observed that Americans, as a class, are more successful in providing for their own by their individual efforts than any of the races with corre-sponding numerical representation, and that the Germans are next to them in this respect. On the other hand, the natives of Great Britain receive most assistance from their families.

In tracing the influence of occupation upon families in this regard, we find that the metal workers and those pursuing in-door occupations require least assistance from their wives and children, while coal miners and out-door workers require the most. . . .

In order to present a closer view of the manner of living, the surroundings, habits, tastes and daily diet of the Illinois working-man of to-day, under various circumstances and conditions, and to afford a more definite impression as to the details of his environment than can be obtained from the mere contemplation of columns of figures, we transcribe, for a limited number of representative families, their entire record, as procured by our agents, together with the notes of observation, made at the time of the visit. It would be manifestly impracticable to reprint those details in regard to the whole 2,129 families, and we therefore confine the exhibit to 167 families, selecting them with special reference to their representative character, from various places, occupations and walks in life. We, however, give prominence to reports from Chicago, because of the greater interest which will naturally attach to the phases of life shown in that populous metropolis. . . .

This minute catalogue of the details governing the life of each family portrays more vividly than any mere array of figures can the common current of daily life among the people. The extremes of condition and the average types are alike presented, and it may be seen, not only what manner of life ordinarily prevails with a given income, but also how some families, by thrift, temperance and prudence, save money and increase their store, upon earnings which other families find insufficient for their support.

The rewards which some of the skilled trades offer to those who succeed in them appear in contrast with the disabilities which accompany other occupations, and it will be seen how workmen in the same trades both prosper and suffer, as men will in all walks of life, with apparently equal opportunities. . . .

CHICAGO

. . .

No. 2   **BAKER**   *Pole*

EARNINGS—Of father $450

CONDITION—Family numbers 5—parents and three children, all girls, aged one month, eighteen months and four years. Rent a house containing three rooms, for which they pay a rental of $8 per month. Family are very ignorant, dirty and unkempt. The street is narrow and filthy: no pavement: mud knee-deep: no vaults or sewerage. Father works fifty weeks per year, and for a winter day's work he is employed twelve hours, and in summer fourteen. He receives $1.50 for each day's labor. His house is situated so far from his place of work that he cannot go home at noon. Carries no life insurance, and belongs to no unions.

FOOD—*Breakfast*—Coffee, bread and crackers.
　　　Dinner—Soup, meat and potatoes.
　　　Supper—What is left from dinner.

COST OF LIVING—

Rent	$96	
Fuel	15	
Meat and groceries	165	
Clothing, boots and shoes and dry goods	70	
Books, papers, etc.	3	
Sickness	40	
Sundries	65	
Total		$454

. . .

No. 4　　　　　　　　　BAKER　　　　　　　　　*German*

EARNINGS—Of father　　　　　　　　$450
　　　　　　Of son, aged sixteen　　150
　　　　　　Total　　　　　　　　　　$600

CONDITION—Family numbers 5—father, mother and three children, all boys, aged sixteen, eleven and thirteen years. Two of them attend public school. They live in three small rooms in rear part of a large house, which are very dark and dirty, and for which they pay $11 per month. The whole family seem to be very ignorant, and are unable to speak any English. Father works fifty weeks in the year, at an average of $1.50 per day. He does not belong to any union and carries no life insurance. If it were not for the assistance rendered by the oldest son, their expenses would exceed their earnings.

FOOD—*Breakfast*—Bread, coffee and crackers.
　　　Dinner—Soup, meat and potatoes.

COST OF LIVING—

Rent	$132	
Fuel	15	
Meat and groceries	300	
Clothing, boots and shoes and dry goods	100	
Books, papers, etc.	3	
Sickness	20	
Sundries	10	
Total		$580

. . .

No. 5　　　　　　　BLACKSMITH　　　　　　　*American*

EARNINGS—Of father　　　　　　　　　　$864

CONDITION—Family numbers 5—parents and three girls aged twelve, nine and five years, and all three attend the public schools. They rent a pleasant house containing six rooms, in healthy locality, for which they pay $15 per month. House is neatly kept and nicely furnished and carpeted. Have piano and sewing machine. Family neatly dressed and members of the church. They were fortunate in not having any sickness whatever in the family during the past year. Father secures work forty-eight weeks in the year, at $3 per day.

FOOD—*Breakfast*—Bread, meat, sundries and coffee.
   Dinner—Meat, bread, vegetables, pie, tea, etc.
   Supper—Bread, cold meat, pie and tea.

COST OF LIVING—

Rent	$180	
Fuel	36	
Meat and groceries	345	
Clothing, boots and shoes and dry goods	210	
Books, papers, etc.	15	
Sundries	10	
Total		$796

. . .

No. 6	BLACKSMITH	*German*

EARNINGS—Of father $450

CONDITION—Family numbers 7—parents and five children; three boys and two girls, aged from one to seven years. Two of them go to school. Occupy 4 rooms in tenement block, and pay $12 per month for same. The surroundings are only fair. The rooms are carpeted, and family appear comparatively comfortable, but are not satisfied with their condition. Father belongs to the Labor organization and considers himself somewhat benefited thereby. He, however, is only able to secure work twenty-five weeks in the year, and receives $3 per day for his work.

FOOD—*Breakfast*—Bread, meat, butter and coffee.
   Dinner—Lunch at work; family at home, bread, tea, etc.
   Supper—Bread, butter, meat and coffee or tea.

COST OF LIVING—

Rent	$144	
Fuel	40	
Meat and groceries	160	
Clothing, boots, shoes and dry goods	80	
Books, papers, etc.	10	
Trades unions	5	
Sickness	10	
Sundries	25	
Total		$474

. . .

No. 9	BRICKLAYER	*Irish*

EARNINGS—Of father $800

CONDITION—Family numbers 8— parents and six children, five girls and one boy, aged from one to twelve years. Three of them go to school regularly. The house they live in contains 4 rooms, and they pay

$10 per month for it. They would like to have more room, but the owners of the tenement do not wish to rent to families having many children. Father says he is satisfied with the general condition, if wages remain as good as they are at present. He belongs to trades union, but carries no life insurance. He works about 30 weeks in the year, and receives on an average $4.00 per day for his services.

FOOD—Breakfast—Good common food.
   Dinner—Good common food.
   Supper—Good common food.

COST OF LIVING—

Rent	$120	
Fuel	40	
Meat	100	
Groceries	325	
Clothing	50	
Boots and shoes	40	
Dry goods	100	
Books, papers, etc.	2	
Trades unions	3	
Sickness	4	
Sundries	20	
Total		$804

. . .

No. 12	BRICKLAYER	American

EARNINGS—Of father $1,050

CONDITION—Family numbers 7—parents and five children, three boys and two girls, aged from two to eleven years. Two of them attend school. The house they occupy contains 4 rooms, for which they pay rental of $12 per month. Father says they would like to better themselves as regards the neighborhood, but if he moves farther from the center of the city he would be compelled to pay out too much money for car fare. He is a pressed-brick layer, which branch of the business requires greater skill, and therefore he receives $1 per day more money than the regular bricklayer. He works thirty-five weeks in the year, at $5 per day. The trades union is in first-class condition, but is overrun by apprentices. For ordinary living he uses all he makes.

FOOD—Breakfast—Beefsteak, bread, butter and coffee.
   Dinner—Meat and vegetables.
   Supper—Bread, butter, tea and fruit.

COST OF LIVING—

Rent	$144
Fuel	50
Meat	156
Groceries	350
Clothing	100
Boots and shoes	50
Dry goods	50

Books, papers, etc.	15	
Trades unions	3	
Sickness	10	
Sundries	122	
Total		$1,050

• • •

No. 21   CIGAR MAKER   *Bohemian*

EARNINGS—Of father	$480	
Of son	750	
Of son	600	
Total		$1,830

CONDITION—Family numbers 7—four boys and one girl. The boys pay for their board to their parents, clothe themselves, and otherwise aid in the support of the family. They occupy a house containing 6 rooms, for which they pay $12 per month rent. The father is a member of the trades union, and considers himself and family benefited thereby. House is in healthy location, fairly furnished, with 3 of the rooms carpeted. With the assistance of the boys they are enabled to save a little money each year.

FOOD—*Breakfast*—Meat, coffee, bread, butter and potatoes.
  Dinner—Meat, vegetables, soup, etc.
  Supper—Cold meat, tea, bread and butter.

COST OF LIVING—

Rent	$144	Dry goods	$200	
Fuel	80	Books, papers, etc.	20	
Meat	100	Trades uions	12	
Groceries	300	Sickness	75	
Clothing	200	Sundries	100	
Boots and shoes	60	Total		$1,291

• • •

No. 22   CIGAR MAKER   *German*

EARNINGS—Of father	$240	
Of son, aged sixteen	200	
Total		$440

CONDITION—Family numbers 8—parents and six children, four boys, aged sixteen, fifteen, nine and six, and two girls, thirteen and two. Occupy house of 3 rooms, for which rent is paid at the rate of $20 per month. House is scantily and poorly furnished, no carpets, and the furniture being of the cheapest kind. Wife attends to news stand and candy store, and, with the proceeds of this business added to what earnings father and son make, they manage barely to keep out of debt. House is in an unhealthy location and kept in a filthy condition, consequently children are sick at all times. Three children attending school. Father belongs to trades union, and says he is unable to procure steady work, and only works at "piece-work."

FOOD—*Breakfast*—Bread and plain coffee.
  Dinner—Lunch.
  Supper—Bread, meat and potato soup.

COST OF LIVING—

Rent	$240	
Fuel	20	
Meat and groceries	364	
Clothing, boots and shoes and dry goods	150	
Trades unions	11	
Sickness	100	
Sundries	300	
Total		$1,185

. . .

No. 35   LABORER   *Italian*

EARNINGS—Of father $270

CONDITION—Family numbers 5—parents and three children, all boys, aged one, three and five. Live in one room, for which they pay $4 per month rent. A very dirty and unhealthy place, everything perfectly filthy. There are about fifteen other families living in the same house. They buy the cheapest kind of meat from the neighboring slaughter houses and the children pick up fuel on the streets and rotten eatables from the commission houses. Children do not attend school. They are all ignorant in the full sense of the word. Father could not write his name.

FOOD—*Breakfast*—Coffee and bread.
       Dinner—Soups.
       Supper—Coffee and bread.

COST OF LIVING—

Rent	$48	
Fuel	5	
Meat and groceries	100	
Clothing, boots and shoes and dry goods	15	
Sickness	5	
Total		$173

. . .

No. 36   LABORER   *Bohemian*

EARNINGS—Of father	$480	
Of son, aged twenty-three	384	
Of son, aged seventeen	250	
Total		$1,114

CONDITION—Family numbers 6—parents and four boys, aged twenty-three, seventeen, fourteen and twelve. Father works 52 weeks per year; owns comfortable house of 4 rooms. The boys help support the family. House is comfortably furnished. Their expenditures equal their income.

FOOD—*Breakfast*—Bread, butter and coffee.
       Dinner—Lunches.
       Supper—Meat, vegetables, bread and coffee.

COST OF LIVING—

Fuel	$30	
Meat and groceries	600	
Clothing	150	
Boots and shoes	20	
Dry goods	30	
Books, papers, etc	20	
Trades unions	11	
Sundries	253	
Total	———	$1,114

• • •

No. 46   LABORER   *American*

EARNINGS—Of father $360
        Of wife   100
          Total   ——— $460

CONDITION—Family numbers 7—parents and five children, aged from six months to eight years. They live in a house which they rent, and pay rental of $10 per month. Two of the children attend school. House is situated in good, respectable neighborhood. The furniture and carpets are poor in quality, but substantial. The father is not a member of a labor organization, but subscribes for the labor papers. Their living expenses exceed their income.

FOOD—*Breakfast*—Salt meat, bread, butter and coffee.
        Dinner—Bread, meat and vegetables.
        Supper—Bread, coffee, etc.

COST OF LIVING—

Rent	$120	
Fuel, meat and groceries	225	
Clothing, boots and shoes and dry goods	85	
Books, papers, etc.	2	
Sundries	75	
Total	———	$507

• • •

No. 47   LABORER   *Irish*

EARNINGS—Of father $343

CONDITION—Family numbers 5—parents and three children, two girls, aged seven and five, and boy, aged eight. They occupy a rented house of 4 rooms, and pay a rental, monthly of $7. Two of the children attend school. Father complains of the wages he receives, being but $1.10 per day, and says it is extremely difficult for him to support his family upon that amount. His work consists in cleaning yards, basements, out-buildings, etc., and is, in fact, a regular scavenger. He also complains of the work as being very unhealthy, but it seems he can procure no other work.

FOOD—*Breakfast*—Black coffee, bread and potatoes.
        Dinner—Corned beef, cabbage and potatoes.
        Supper—Bread, coffee and potatoes.

COST OF LIVING—

Rent	$84	
Fuel	15	
Meat and groceries	180	
Clothing, boots and shoes and dry goods	40	
Sundries	20	
Total		$339

. . .

No. 51   MACHINIST   *American*

EARNINGS—

Of father	$540	
Of mother	255	
Of son, aged sixteen	255	
Total		$1,050

CONDITION—Family numbers 10—parents and eight children, five girls and three boys, aged from two to sixteen. Four of the children attend school. Father works only 30 weeks in the year, receives $3 per day for his services. They live in a comfortably furnished house, of 7 rooms, have a piano, take an interest in society and domestic affairs, are intelligent, but do not dress very well. Their expenditures are equal, but do not exceed their income. Father belongs to trades union, and is interested and benefited by and in it.

FOOD—*Breakfast*—Bread, meat and coffee.
    Dinner—Bread, meat, vegetables and tea.
    Supper—Bread, meat, vegetables and coffee.

COST OF LIVING—

Rent	$300	
Fuel	50	
Meat	100	
Groceries	200	
Clothing	160	
Boots and shoes	50	
Dry goods	25	
Books, papers, etc.	15	
Trades unions	10	
Sickness	50	
Sundries	90	
Total		$1,050

. . .

No. 75   STEEL WORKER   *Irish*

EARNINGS—Of father $760

CONDITION—Family numbers 3—husband, wife and one male child nearly two years of age. He owns a nice cottage, containing 4 rooms, which are well furnished; wife has a fine piano. They live very well indeed. Father belongs to trades union. His trade pays him $5 per day, but owing to the rolling mill, in which he was employed, not working but about 20 weeks during the year, his earnings are comparatively small, but he has hopes of work for the entire year, and strong hopes for the future.

FOOD—*Breakfast*—Bread, butter, steak and coffee.
  Dinner—Bread, butter, corned beef and cabbage.
  Supper—Bread, butter, cold meat and coffee.

COST OF LIVING—

Fuel	$30	
Meat and groceries	190	
Clothing, boots and shoes, dry goods	210	
Books, papers, etc.	10	
Trades unions	30	
Sundries	250	
Total		$720

. . .

No. 79   STREET-CAR CONDUCTOR   *American*

EARNINGS—Of father $780

CONDITION—Family numbers 6—father and five children, three girls and two boys, aged four to fifteen years. Three children attend public school. Family live in a house containing 5 rooms, for which they pay a rental of $18 per month. House situated in good location and well furnished. Father works fifteen hours per day during fifty-two weeks of the year. The mother being dead, the older children keep house and take care of the younger child. When asked what they usually had for their meals, the father declined to inform the canvasser. They manage to save $100 per annum.

COST OF LIVING—

Rent	$216	
Fuel	45	
Meat and groceries	215	
Clothing, boots and shoes and dry goods	175	
Trades unions	4	
Sickness	5	
Sundries	20	
Total		$680

. . .

No. 80   STREET-CAR CONDUCTOR   *German*

EARNINGS—Of father $728

CONDITION—Family numbers 7—parents and five children, three girls, aged one, two and three years, and two boys, five and eight. Four of the children attend school. Live in a house containing 4 rooms, and pay rent for same at the rate of $12 per month. House is in unhealthy location, and furnished poorly. Father says he was compelled to run in debt, and that fact keeps him behind in his expenses. He works sixteen hours every day in the year; never gets time to read the papers. Says the company is grinding him and all the others down to the starvation point. The only time he has when not at work is occupied in sleeping.

FOOD—*Breakfast*—Coffee, bread, butter and cakes.
  Dinner—Lunches.
  Supper—Bread, butter, tea, steak, etc.

COST OF LIVING—

Rent	$144
Fuel	22
Meat	70
Groceries	190
Clothing, boots and shoes, dry goods, books, papers, etc	150
Sickness	30
Sundries	150
Total	$756

• • •

No. 81   STREET-CAR CONDUCTOR   *Irish*

EARNINGS—Of father $672

CONDITION—Family numbers 9—parents and seven children, five girls and two boys. The girls are one, two, three, five and six years of age. The boys are eight-year old twins. Family live in tenement containing 4 rooms, for which they pay $17 per month. Four of the children attend school regularly. The father works fifteen hours per day in winter, and sixteen in summer. Father seems to be intelligent, but is afraid of his employers. Did not seem disposed to give truthful answers to questions propounded, and when asked what food they had for their different meals, declined to say.

COST OF LIVING—

Rent	$204
Fuel	20
Meat and groceries	400
Clothing, boots and shoes and dry goods	50
Sickness	10
Total	$684

• • •

No. 97   UPHOLSTERER   *Pole*

EARNINGS—Of father $360

CONDITION—Family numbers 4—parents and two children, two boys, aged five and nine years, and one of them attends school. They rent a house containing 3 rooms for $5 per month, which is dirty and in an unhealthy location, consequently had considerable sickness during the past year. The children pick up coal on railway track, and while doing so, one of them was run over by the cars, thereby losing a leg. He now blacks boots and sells newspapers, but his earnings are not taken into consideration. Father carries no life insurance, and does not belong to trade union.

FOOD—*Breakfast*—Coffee, bread and lard.
　　　　Dinner—Meat, soup and potatoes.
　　　　Supper—Coffee and bread.

COST OF LIVING—

Rent	$60
Fuel	10

Meat and groceries	175
Clothing and boots and shoes	50
Dry goods	10
Sickness	50
Sundries	5
Total	$360

. . .

No. 100   **UPHOLSTERER**   *Bohemian*

EARNINGS—Of father   **$420**

CONDITION—Family numbers 8—husband, wife and six children, four girls and two boys, the former aged, respectively, one month, one and a half, three and nine years, the latter five and seven. One of the children attends school; the rest of them, that are old enough, pick up coal, and go to the fruit warehouses and collect decayed fruit and other spoiled food. The family eat poor and spoiled meats, and live miserably, but seem to grow fat on it, and have but very little sickness. House contains three rooms, into which the eight persons are huddled. They pay $6 per month for the house. Family is dirty and ignorant in the extreme. The stench from the rooms is as bad as that from the stock yards.

FOOD—*Breakfast*—Coffee and bread.
     Dinner—Soup and potatoes.
     Supper—Coffee and bread.

COST OF LIVING

Rent	$72	
Fuel	8	
Meat and groceries	240	
Clothing, boots and shoes	80	
Dry goods	10	
Sickness	10	
Total		$420

FAMILIES OUTSIDE OF CHICAGO

In Various Cities and Towns

No. 101   **BAGGAGE-MASTER**   *American*

EARNINGS—Of husband	$720	
Of wife	$280	
Total		$1,000

CONDITION—Family numbers 3—husband and wife, and a relative. They rent a house of 6 rooms, and pay per month for it $17. House is comfortable and fairly furnished—carpets on the floors, and own a sewing machine. Tenement is situated on good-sized lot, in healthy and pleasant locality. Most of the lot is neatly cultivated as a garden, with strawberries and other small fruits. Surroundings kept neat and attractive. Flowers cultivated. Wife gives meals to two or three men, and makes some money besides. Family cheerful and happy. Surplus money put in bank for future contingencies. Husband carries some life insurance.

FOOD—*Breakfast*—Beefsteak, bread, butter, potatoes and coffee.
　　　Dinner—Boiled meats, bread, butter, potatoes, pastries and tea.
　　　Supper—Cold meats, bread, butter, potatoes, jellies, fruits and
　　　　　tea.

COST OF LIVING—

Rent	$204	
Fuel	40	
Meat	146	
Groceries	180	
Clothing	25	
Boots and shoes	35	
Dry goods	25	
Books, papers, etc.	7	
Life insurance	33	
Sickness	25	
Total		$725

．．．

No. 105	BRAKEMAN	*Irish*

EARNINGS—Of father　　　　　　　　　　　$360

CONDITION—Family numbers 10—parents and eight children, six girls and two boys, aged one year to fifteen. Four of them attend public school. Family occupy a house of 3 rooms, for which they pay $5 per month rental. The house presents a most wretched appearance. Clothes ragged, children half dressed and dirty. They all sleep in one room regardless of sex. The house is devoid of furniture, and the entire concern is as wretched as could well be imagined. Father is shiftless and does not keep any one place for any length of time. Wife is without ambition or industry.

FOOD—*Breakfast*—Bread, coffee and syrup.
　　　Dinner—Potatoes, soup and bread, occasionally meat.
　　　Supper—Bread, syrup and coffee.

COST OF LIVING—

Rent	$60	
Fuel	25	
Meat	20	
Groceries	360	
Clothing	50	
Boots and shoes	15	
Dry goods	30	
Books, papers, etc.	20	
Sickness	5	
Total		$585

．．．

No. 112   COAL MINER   *American*

EARNINGS—Of father $250

CONDITION—Family numbers 7—husband, wife, and five children, three girls and two boys, aged from three to nineteen years. Three of them go to the public school. Family live in 2 rooms tenement, in healthy locality, for which they pay $6 per month rent. The house is scantily furnished, without carpets, but is kept neat and clean. They are compelled to live very economically, and every cent they earn is used to the best advantage. Father had only thirty weeks work during the past year. He belongs to trades union. The figures for cost of living are actual and there is no doubt the family lived on the amount specified.

FOOD—*Breakfast*—Bread, coffee and salt meat.
         Dinner—Meat, bread, coffee and butter.
         Supper—Sausage, bread and coffee.

COST OF LIVING—

Rent	$72	Dry goods	20	
Fuel	20	Trades union	3	
Meat	20	Sickness	10	
Groceries	60	Sundries	5	
Clothing	28	Total		$252
Boots and shoes	15			

. . .

No. 130   COAL MINER   *Irish*

EARNINGS—Of father $420
         Of son, twenty-one years of age   420
         Of son, eighteen years of age   420
         Of son, sixteen years of age   150
         Total $1,410

CONDITION—Family numbers 6—parents and four children, three boys and one girl. The girl attends school, and the three boys are working in the mine. Father owns a house of six rooms, which is clean and very comfortably furnished. Family temperate, and members of a church, which they attend with regularity. They have an acre of ground, which they work in summer, and raise vegetables for their consumption. They have their house about paid for, payments being made in installments of $240 per year. Father belongs to mutual assessment association and to trades union.

FOOD—*Breakfast*—Steak, bread, butter, potatoes, bacon and coffee.
         Dinner—Bread, butter, meat, cheese, pie and tea.
         Supper—Meat, potatoes, bread, butter, puddings, pie and coffee.

COST OF LIVING—

Rent	$240	Books, papers, etc.	$15	
Fuel	10	Life insurance	18	
Meat	200	Trades unions	3	
Groceries	700	Sickness	4	
Clothing	80	Sundries	75	
Boots, shoes		Total		$1,415
and dry goods	70			

. . .

No. 131   COAL MINER   *German*

EARNINGS—Of father $200

CONDITION—Family numbers 6—parents and four children, two boys and two girls, aged two, four, nine and eleven years. Two of them attend school. Family occupy a house containing 3 rooms, for which they pay $60 per annum. Father works all he can, and only receives $1 per day for his labor. He has only been in this country two and one half years and is anxious to get back to Germany. The house is miserably furnished, and is a wretched affair in itself. They have a few broken chairs and benches and a bedstead. Father is a shoemaker by trade, and does some cobbling which helps a little toward supporting his family. He receives the lowest wages in the shaft.

FOOD—*Breakfast*—Bread and coffee.
       Dinner—Bread, meat and coffee.
       Supper—Bread, meat, potatoes and coffee.

COST OF LIVING—

Rent	$60	
Meat	36	
Groceries	84	
Clothing	12	
Boots and shoes and dry goods	15	
Sickness	1	
Sundries	20	
Total		$228

. . .

No. 137   IRON AND STEEL WORKER   *English*

EARNINGS—Of father $1,420
      Of son, aged fourteen   300
   Total $1,720

CONDITION—Family numbers 6—parents and four children; two boys and two girls, aged from seven to sixteen years. Three of them attend school, and the other works in the shop with his father. Family occupy their own house, containing 9 well-furnished rooms, in a pleasant and healthy locality. They have a good vegetable and flower garden. They live well, but not extravagantly, and are saving about a thousand dollars per year. Father receives an average of $7 per day of twelve hours, for his labor, and works about thirty-four weeks of the year. Belongs to trades union, but carries no life insurance. Had but little sickness during the year.

FOOD—*Breakfast*—Bread, butter, meat, eggs, and sometimes oysters.
       Dinner—Potatoes, bread, butter, meat, pie, cake or pudding.
       Supper—Bread, butter, meat, rice or sauce, and tea or coffee.

COST OF LIVING—

Fuel	$55
Meat	100

Groceries	300	
Clothing	75	
Boots and shoes	50	
Dry goods	50	
Books, papers, etc.	10	
Trades unions	6	
Sickness	12	
Sundries	50	
Total		$708

. . .

No. 145   LABORER   *American*

EARNINGS—Of father $50
    Of son, fourteen years of age   25
        Total $75

CONDITION—Family numbers 6—parents and four children, two boys and two girls, aged respectively six and fourteen, and girl twins of ten years. Father works only at odd jobs, from two to eight hours in summer. Is not able to do hard work and does not work during the cold months of the year. They live in a two room house, which is owned by friends of the family, and for which no rent is charged them. The house is in good locality. Two of the children attend school, and one of the boys earns a little money in different ways. Their expenses, amounting to about $150, is mostly furnished by charity.

FOOD—*Breakfast*—Corned beef and potatoes, occasionally coffee.
    Dinner—Bread, sometimes meat and fruit.
    Supper—Corn bread and salt, and oftener nothing.

COST OF LIVING—
Fuel	$20	
Meat and groceries	100	
Clothing, boots and shoes and dry goods	30	
Total		$150

. . .

No. 146   LABORER   *French*

EARNINGS—Of father $505
    Of son, nineteen years old   200
    Of son, fourteen years old   100
        Total $805

CONDITION—Family numbers 10—parents and eight children, three boys and five girls, aged from four to nineteen. Four of them attend school, and two of the boys at work. Family live in their own house, which contains 5 rooms, with down stairs floors carpeted. The entire family present a comfortable appearance; own a sewing machine; children clean and bright looking; mother industrious and economical. They all go to church, and children attend Sunday school. They keep a cow and raise pigs, which they put up for winter meat. They have to struggle hard to keep within their income.

FOOD—*Breakfast*—Bread and coffee, occasionally meat.
    Dinner—Potatoes, bread, meat and tea.
    Supper—Bread, tea and corn meal mush.

COST OF LIVING—

Fuel	$25	
Meat	120	
Groceries	360	
Clothing	100	
Boots and shoes	50	
Dry goods	75	
Books, papers, etc.	25	
Sickness	30	
Sundries	20	
Total		$805

. . .

No. 156   PLASTERER   *Irish*

EARNINGS—Of husband $731

CONDITION—Family numbers 2—husband and wife. They live in their own house, which contains 8 rooms. The husband receives an average of $3.25 per day for his work, which is above the general average of wages received by plasterers. He sometimes employs from three to four men during the busy season. He estimates his time worked during the year at 225 days, which is also above the average of men at his trade, which varies in this climate from 155 days in a dull and late season, to 260 in an early and lively season. The work is difficult, and requires unusual skill. He says the majority of the better plasterers are foreigners. Few men of this trade continue at the business after the age of fifty years, especially in the west, on contract work, as the foreman is usually an expert, and requires his men to work rapidly and well. They are generally paid according to their ability to keep up in their work with an unusually good young workman, and those nearing the age of fifty years are compelled to drop out and give room for the younger class of workmen. Apprentices are few, probably for two reasons, viz., the laws of this State do not protect the master, and the majority of young and intelligent men prefer office work to mechanical employment. Those applying for apprenticeships are, as a rule, foreigners, or sons of foreigners. He considers that a good apprentice law, that would protect both the apprentice and the master, would be of great benefit to all concerned. Few, if any of the men who have learned trades in the past few years, are as good workmen as those they learned from, and he thinks the tendency in all trades is to a subdivision of labor, which in the building trade develops an inferior lot of workmen. He also thinks men could and would be better protected in their trades if there was a State or county system of licensing good men who should be obliged to prove that they were masters of their trades. He believes that sooner or later some practice of this kind will have to be adopted. He belongs to no trades union, but is a member of a friendly society, and he carries no life insurance. Both husband and wife belong to the church.

FOOD—*Breakfast*—Summer:Buckwheat cakes, potatoes, coffee and meat.
"   Winter: Bread, butter, coffee, vegetables, ham and
        eggs or fish.
    Dinner—Summer: Roast or boiled meat, soup, coffee and
        vegetables.
"   Winter: Beefsteak or mutton, vegetables, tea or coffee.
    Supper—Bread, butter, eggs, fruit in season, cake or pastry.

COST OF LIVING—

Fuel	$30	
Meat and fish	90	
Groceries	248	
Clothing	60	
Boots and shoes	18	
Dry goods	40	
Books, papers, etc.	28	
Church	20	
Society	12	
Sickness	35	
Sundries	50	
Total		$631

. . .

No. 159   ROLLER BAR MILL   *American*

EARNINGS—Of father $2,200

CONDITION—Family numbers 5—parents and three children, two boys
and one girl, aged four, six and eight years. Do not attend school.
Family occupy house containing 3 rooms, well furnished in healthy
locality, but the surroundings are not of the best. Family ordinarily
intelligent. Father works eleven hours per day for 37 weeks in the
year, and receives $10 per day for his labor; he saves about $1,400 per
year, which he deposits in the bank. Family live well, but not extravagantly.

FOOD—*Breakfast*—Bread, meat, eggs, and coffee.
    Dinner—Bread, meat, vegetables, fruits and coffee.
    Supper—Bread, fruits, coffee and meat.

COST OF LIVING—

Rent	$120	
Fuel	40	
Meat	125	
Groceries	200	
Clothing	55	
Boots and shoes	35	
Dry goods	60	
Books, papers, etc.	8	
Sickness	50	
Sundries	75	
Total		$768

13. Ohio Bureau of Labor Statistics— Report (1885)

Another fine example of the work of the state bureaus of labor statistics is provided by this report of the Ohio bureau, published in 1885. The character of mining, which frequently required corporations to construct company towns in remote areas, tempted many owners to take advantage of their employees by charging them high rents for jerry-built housing and forcing them to pay exorbitant prices for goods and supplies at company-owned stores. To keep down cash outlays, they often paid workers in scrip, which, if redeemable at all in noncompany establishments, was usually sharply discounted by merchants. The Ohio bureau repeatedly published studies of these practices, without, as the following example reveals, succeeding in eliminating them. The study reads more like an exposé than a dispassionate analysis, but it is so full of hard evidence as to make a damning indictment nonetheless.

The subject of payment of wages in scrip and store pay, commonly called truck, has been for years a vexatious one, and has in all probability been the cause of as much annoyance to the legislator as any other evil upon which he is called upon to legislate. That it is an evil, serious and far-reaching, is attested by the fact that four general assemblies have passed as many stringent acts for its suppression. To the casual observer it does not seem a hardship to be furnished with credit in a store and have the bills deducted from wages earned, and doubtless it would not be, in fact, were the charges for the articles purchased made at current market rates.

But when the market price from fifteen to twenty-five per cent. is added, the system begins to display its beauties. . . .

Many schemes have been devised to make men trade at the company stores without making the owners amenable to law, one of the most diabolical of which was brought to the notice of the commissioner by a miner during a visit to Shawnee, Perry county.

He said: "No direct compulsion is used, but nevertheless should an employe refuse or neglect to patronize the company's store, a hint is conveyed to him in a round-about way, that his prospects at the mine would be vastly improved by trading at the store of his employer. If this has not the desired effect, he is laid off for a

SOURCE: Ohio Bureau of Labor Statistics, "Scrip," *Ninth Annual Report* (Columbus, Ohio, 1885) , pp. 214-18, 220, 222-8.

few days and then the hint is renewed, with the addition, that it is
the last chance. This failing, the next move is to make the miner's
situation so unpleasant by a system of persecution that life
becomes a burden. Upon the finishing up of his room he is told
there is no more work for him." . . .

The passage of an act by the Sixty-sixth General Assembly,
better known as the Jones law, was hailed as an harbinger of
better times to the suffering families of the miners, in many parts
of the State. Its provisions were thought to be so strict that its
mere passage would give "scrip" and "truck pay" a quietus forever. A glance at the law, which we here insert, would seem to
confirm that opinion. But laws do not execute themselves.

AN ACT

To provide against the payment of wages in scrip, orders, etc., and
against selling goods or supplies to employes at excessive prices.

SEC. 7015. It shall be unlawful for any person, firm, company, or
corporation to sell, give, deliver, or in any manner issue, directly
or indirectly, to any person employed by him or it, in payment of
wages due for labor, or as advances on the wages of labor not due,
any scrip, token, check, draft, order, or other evidence of indebtedness payable or redeemable otherwise than in money; any violation of the provisions of this section shall be punishable by a fine
of not less than twenty-five, nor more than one hundred dollars,
or imprisonment of not more than thirty days, or both. . . .

We have personally and by letter caused complaints to be made
to the prosecuting attorneys in four counties of the State where
flagrant violations of this law were of almost hourly occurrence,
and with the exception of Perry county, so far as we are advised,
not one case of this kind has been made the subject of investigation by grand juries. Prosecuting attorneys take special pains in
hunting down thieves, and for this they receive, and are entitled
to, the thanks of the community. If a hungry man steals a ham
and forces a lock or pries open a door to do it, it is burglary, and a
prosecuting attorney will take special delight in having him sent
to the penitentiary for it; for the man who pays his men in
"scrip," and thus indiscriminately robs the helpless families of his
employes, prosecuting attorneys have "nought but smiles and

pleasant greetings," as though those, upon whom these men were depredating, were entitled to no protection, and wealth could do no wrong.

The man who compels his employe to take "scrip" in payment of wages, violates the statute, and is as great a criminal before the law as a burglar whose punishment is swift and sure. Both are equally criminal, and is it not a travesty on justice to see one sent to the penitentiary while the other enjoys the free air of heaven, with no one to molest him in the enjoyment of the "swag"? Were one indictment found against the violations of this law and the case prosecuted to a conviction, it would relieve prosecutors from much of the odium against them in communities suffering from this baneful system and put an end to "scrip payments" forever. . . .

Early after the passage of the law and before the General Assembly that enacted it had adjourned, it became apparent that some of those who had profited largely by running the "pluck me's" would use any effort at their command to nullify the act of the Legislature. Sharp lawyers were employed and all sorts of schemes were adopted to secure the benefits of the "scrip" without the attendant danger of an open violation of the law. . . .

The first scheme to subvert the law that was brought to the notice of the Bureau was from Salineville, Columbiana county, and was in the nature of an order to be signed by the employe before commencing work, and was as follows:

SALINEVILLE, *May*—1885

I authorize the Ohio and Pennsylvania Coal Company to pay McGary, Nixon & Co. the amount of my indebtedness to said firm and deduct the same from the amount due me from the Ohio and Pennsylvania Coal Company for this and each succeeding month.
(Signed.)

This order was to be signed by the employe before the goods were purchased or money earned. . . .

September 1, by request of business men and miners, we visited Shawnee, Perry county, and found the place flooded with "scrip" in denominations from one (1) cent to five (5) dollars. Three of the firms were issuing in open violation of law. Such as the following are samples:

NOT INTENDED AS A CIRCULATING MEDIUM.

VILAS STORE, SHAWNEE, O.

ONE | CENT.

DUE IN GOODS.

No. 4225

TEN CENTS.

Shawnee, O., May 23, 1885.

For Value Received,

ONE YEAR AFTER DATE,

We promise to pay to the Bearer,

TEN CENTS.

UPSON COAL CO.

5c   Shawnee, O., Oct. 1, 1885.   5c

Five Years after Date I promise to Pay Bearer

FIVE CENTS,

with Interest after maturity.

5c   *JOHN CHAMBERLAIN.*   5c

. . . On October 1, we submitted questions to the Attorney-General, which had relation to the situation at Shawnee, and was as follows:

STATE OF OHIO, BUREAU OF LABOR STATISTICS,
COLUMBUS, *October* 1, 1885

Hon. Jas. Lawrence, Attorney-General:

DEAR SIR: What remedy, at law, have holders of such orders as the enclosed check? How can third parties, holding such check, collect their value in money, from parties issuing them? Can an order for merchandise, in payment of wages, and marked "not transferable," be voided by transfer to third parties? Are such orders in the hands of third parties collectable?

Respectfully yours,

L. McHUGH

In reply the Attorney-General gave the following opinion:

ATTORNEY-GENERAL'S OFFICE, COLUMBUS, O., *October* 2, 1885

Hon. Larkin McHugh, Commissioner of Labor Statistics:

DEAR SIR: Your favor of the 1st inst. is received. Section 7015, Revised Statutes, as amended April 11, 1885 (82 O. L. 120), provides that the amount of any scrip, token, check, draft, order, or other evidence of indebtedness, sold, given, delivered, or in any manner issued in violation of the provisions of said section, may be received in money at the suit of any holder thereof, against the person, firm, company or corporation selling, giving, delivering, or in any manner issuing the same. The fact that scrip so issued is marked "not transferable," does not prevent the operation of the foregoing provision of the statutes. Although thus marked, such scrip may be assigned by the original holder, and the person to whom the same is assigned may bring a suit thereon in his own name, and recover a judgment in money for the amount thereof. In case of a suit by an assignee, or subsequent holder of such scrip, it will be necessary to show that the same was originally issued in violation of the statute.

Yours truly,

JAMES LAWRENCE, *Attorney-General*

. . . October 26, on complaint of a miner, we visited Justis, a small mining town on the Cleveland, Lorain and Wheeling Railroad, eight miles south of Massillon in Stark county. The system in practice at this place is unlike anything previously brought to the notice of the Bureau, but is fully as effective. After a lengthy talk with the miners, we were unable to get the exact method used in conducting the company "pluck me," but learned enough to enable us to say that a more perfect system of oppression was never devised by man.

A miner came there about one year previous to our visit, secured a job and went to work. Upon the arrival of his family he purchased an amount of supplies, valued at nearly eighty dollars, for which he paid one half cash. Being unable to read or write, he was asked to sign what was represented to him as a "chattel mortgage," to secure payment of the balance due, and to which he attached his X mark. From this time forward the owners of the mine exercised a complete guardianship over him, and so careful were they that he should not suffer in his good name, they paid his debts out of his monthly earnings, even to his doctor bills.

A monthly statement was given the miner from the company showing him how they had expended his earnings. These for the two months preceding my visit, the results of which are here given as samples, and indicate very clearly the beautiful workings of the system. The total earnings for the two months of the man and his two boys amounted to $99.21, $94.06 of which was used by the company to pay his *doctor and other bills,* and the balance, $5.15, was handed him in cash—$2.43 for the first month, and $2.72 for the latter month. Here was a family of six persons with a monthly income of $44.60 when at work, $2.57 of which they were generously permitted by their employers to use for the purchase of such of their necessaries as could not be furnished them at the company's store and to keep them from starvation during the stoppage of the mine, for, when the mine was stopped for any cause, the store was conveniently out of everything that was wanted by every miner who was not a property-owner in the town.

The attention of the commissioner was called to the prices charged for goods at this place. A six-foot extension table made of ash was shown, for which the pass book showed eight dollars was charged. This may be taken as a sample of the whole. On my return to Columbus, I ascertained by inquiry at the furniture stores that the retail price for such was sixty cents per foot, or $3.60 for this size. . . .

Under the pressure of precedent we have labored faithfully to enforce this law, but unfortunately with but limited success. Were our efforts in this regard seconded by the law officers of the State with the same vigor and determination that characterized the conduct of the United States officers, this evil would have been suppressed in thirty days. Hundreds of complaints of the oppression practiced upon the miners were filed with the Bureau, and yet not one of them had the nerve to begin suit to test the matter in court, which was the only way to put a quietus on the system forever. They seemed to be of the opinion that all they had to do was to call the attention of the commissioner to the fact that scrip was being used to pay wages and then their duty was done. They could not be made to understand that the commissioner of the Bureau had neither the power nor the means at his command to prosecute the violations of the law, and that they who suffered were the proper persons to test the question. The Attorney-general had repeatedly given opinions that any one holding pieces of scrip taken as wages, could recover its face value in money in a suit before any magistrate, and this advice was given publicly through the newspapers, orally and in writing by the Commissioner for the guidance of parties aggrieved, and yet not one person could be found, out of the hundreds of complainants, who would take the initiatory step. Individuals seemed to be inspired with a fear that the vengeance of the operators would be visited upon the head of anyone interfering with the issuing of scrip. To this fear can be attributed the non-action on the part of the men, but the conduct of business men, in this respect, is an enigma to the Bureau. While they have been very loud in their denunciations of the violators of the scrip law, and profuse in their promises to break it up, if any feasible plan was presented to enable them to do so successfully, not one was found who would stand up to their promises, when a test would have demonstrated their sincerity. . . .

We in America boast of our superiority in the freedom and democracy of our institutions and our respect for the laws made by the representatives of the people, and that all laws regularly enacted are entitled to obedience and respect until declared unconstitutional by the courts. Upon this foundation have we builded up a vast empire and expended mountains of wealth and oceans of the best blood of the nation for its maintenance. But if the manner in which the scrip law in Ohio is enforced and respected, should be taken as evidence against us, would we not have to hang our heads in shame and acknowledge that our boasted veneration for law is but a sham and a delusion, and that statutes that puts a curb on our cupidity have no binding force or effect, and were only enacted for the purpose of pandering to a sentiment. . . .

Part V

Organized Labor

14. Terrence V. Powderly— The Knights of Labor (1889)

The decade of the 1880's was for organized labor a time of transition, one of wildly fluctuating hopes, of confusion, and of conflict, both with employers and within its own ranks as well. The great phenomenon of the era was the meteoric rise and equally sudden decline of the Noble Order of the Knights of Labor. This union was in some respects amazingly forward-looking in its policies. It tried to enroll workers of every kind, not merely skilled craftsmen, to cut across barriers of race, class, and sex in order to found a "great brotherhood" of labor. Yet it was in other respects archaic in viewpoint. Its leaders, like their forebears in the Jacksonian era, sought broad social reforms only indirectly related to the practical problems produced by the growth of great industrial enterprises. They rejected practical tactics aimed at forcing employers to share the profits of production more equitably. For example, they opposed strikes and collective bargaining, and favored doing away with the wage system.

Nevertheless the Knights of Labor grew rapidly in the late 1870's and early 1880's, reaching a peak of over 700,00 members in 1886. Then, chiefly because of the inability of its leaders to provide intelligent direction for the rank and file, it suffered a swift decline. By 1890 membership was down to about 100,000 and its influence had practically disappeared.

Throughout its period of growth and decline, the Knights of Labor was headed by Terrence V. Powderly, a machinist prominent in an earlier labor organization, the Industrial Brotherhood. Powderly's memoir, *Thirty Years of Labor,* published in 1889, is a major source for the history of the Knights. The following selection from this book describes the founding of the Order and reveals something of Powderly's philosophy.

source: T. V. Powderly, *Thirty Years of Labor:* 1859 to 1889 (Columbus, Ohio, 1889), pp. 242-5, 248-9, 258-61, 264-5, 270-1.

The first committee on constitution of the order of the Knights of Labor, appointed by Mr. Stephens, consisted of representatives Robert Schilling, Chairman; Ralph Beaumont, Thomas King, T. V. Powderly, and George S. Boyle. Two members of this committee, Messrs. Schilling and Powderly, were members of the Industrial Brotherhood; and though neither one knew that the other would be present, both brought with them a sufficient supply of constitutions of the I. B. to supply the body. The adoption of the preamble was left to these two, and a glance at it will show what changes were made in the declaration of principles whose history has been traced down from year to year since it was first adopted by the National Labor Union of 1866.

The committee on constitution adopted the constitution of the Industrial Brotherhood so far as practicable. The constitution, when printed, bore the same legend on the title page as was adopted at the Rochester meeting in 1874. The following is the preamble adopted at Reading, January 3, 1878:

"When bad men combine, the good must associate, else they will fall, one by one, an unpitied sacrifice in a contemptible struggle."

Preamble

The recent alarming development and aggression of aggregated wealth, which, unless checked, will invariably lead to the pauperization and hopeless degradation of the toiling masses, render it imperative, if we desire to enjoy the blessings of life, that a check should be placed upon its power and upon unjust accumulation, and a system adopted which will secure to the laborer the fruits of his toil; and as this much-desired object can only be accomplished by the thorough unification of labor, and the united efforts of those who obey the divine injunction that "In the sweat of thy brow shalt thou eat bread," we have formed the * * * * * with a view of securing the organization and direction, by co-operative effort, of the power of the industrial classes; and we submit to the world the objects sought to be accomplished by our organization, calling upon all who believe in securing "the greatest good to the greatest number" to aid and assist us:—

I. To bring within the folds of organization every department of productive industry, making knowledge a stand-point for action, and industrial and moral worth, not wealth, the true standard of individual and national greatness.

II. To secure to the toilers a proper share of the wealth that they create; more of the leisure that rightfully belongs to them; more societary advantages; more of the benefits, privileges, and emoluments of the world; in a word, all those rights and privileges necessary to make them capable of enjoying, appreciating, defending and perpetuating the blessings of good government.

III. To arrive at the true condition of the producing masses in their educational, moral, and financial condition, by demanding from the various governments the establishment of bureaus of Labor Statistics.

IV. The establishment of co-operative institutions, productive and distributive.

V. The reserving of the public lands—the heritage of the people—for the actual settler;—not another acre for railroads or speculators.

VI. The abrogation of all laws that do not bear equally upon capital and labor, the removal of unjust technicalities, delays, and discriminations in the administration of justice, and the adopting of measures providing for the health and safety of those engaged in mining, manufacturing, or building pursuits.

VII. The enactment of laws to compel chartered corporations to pay their employes weekly, in full, for labor performed during the preceding week, in the lawful money of the country.

VIII. The enactment of laws giving mechanics and laborers a first lien on their work for their full wages.

IX. The abolishment of the contract system on national, State, and municipal work.

X. The substitution of arbitration for strikes, whenever and wherever employers and employes are willing to meet on equitable grounds.

XI. The prohibition of the employment of children in workshops, mines and factories before attaining their fourteenth year.

XII. To abolish the system of letting out by contract the labor of convicts in our prisons and reformatory institutions.

XIII. To secure for both sexes equal pay for equal work.

XIV. The reduction of the hours of labor to eight per day, so that the laborers may have more time for social enjoyment and intellectual improvement, and be enabled to reap the advantages conferred by the labor-saving machinery which their brains have created.

XV. To prevail upon governments to establish a purely national circulating medium, based upon the faith and resources of the nation, and issued directly to the people, without the intervention of any system of banking corporations, which money shall be a legal tender in payment of all debts, public or private. . . .

In accepting the preamble of the Industrial Brotherhood, the convention fully realized that for the most part the reforms which were asked for in that preamble must one day come through political agitation and action. The chief aim of those who presented the document to the convention was to place something on the front page of the constitution which, it was hoped, every working-man would in time read and ponder over. It was their hope that by keeping these measures, so fraught with interest to the people, constantly before the eye of the worker, he would become educated in the science of politics to that extent that he would know that those things that were wrong in our political system were wrong simply because he did not attend to his political duties in a proper manner; that the righting of such things as were wrong would not be done by those who had the management of political affairs up to that time, but by himself. . . .

. . . The belief was prevalent until a short time ago among workingmen, that only the man who was engaged in manual toil could be called a workingman. The man who labored at the bench or anvil; the man who held the throttle of the engine, or delved in the everlasting gloom of the coal mine, did not believe that the man who made the drawings from which he forged, turned, or dug could be classed as a worker. The draughtsman, the time-keeper, the clerk, the school teacher, the civil engineer, the editor, the reporter, or the worst paid, most abused and illy appreciated of all toilers—woman—could not be called a worker. It was essential that the mechanics of America should know who were workers. A more wide-spread knowledge of the true definition of the word labor must be arrived at, and the true relations existing between all men who labor must be more clearly defined. Narrow prejudice, born of the injustice and oppressions of the past, must be overcome, and all who interest themselves in producing for the world's good must be made to understand that their interests are identical. All the way down the centuries of time in which the man who worked was held in bondage or servitude, either wholly or partially, he was brought directly in contact with the overseer, the superintendent, or the boss. From these he seldom received a word of kindness; indeed it was the recognized rule to treat all men who toiled as if they were of inferior clay.

The conditions which surrounded the laborer of past ages denied to him the right to dress himself and family in respectable garb. The coarsest material, made in the most untidy fashion, was considered good enough for him. Not only did his employer and overseer believe that his dress, habitation, furniture, and living should be of the coarsest, cheapest material or quality, but he also shared in that belief, and took it for granted that it was ordained of heaven; that the stay of the laborer on earth was only as a matter of convenience for his master, and that he must put up with every indignity, every insult, and privation rather than violate the rules of government, which were held up to him as being as sacred as the Ten Commandments. The holy Scriptures were quoted to show to the toiler that it was said in holy writ that he should be content with his slavish lot on earth in order that he might enjoy an eternity of bliss in a future world, through the portals of which those who held him in subjection could not get a glimpse of the happiness beyond. . . .

It was necessary to teach the laborer that it was not essential for him to grovel in the dust at the feet of a master in order to win his title deed to everlasting bliss in the hereafter; and it can not be wondered at that many who strove to better the condition of the toiler lost all respect for religion when they saw that those who affected to be the most devout worshipers at the foot of the heavenly throne, were the most tyrannical of task-masters when dealing with the poor and lowly, whose unfortunate lot was cast within the shadow of their heartless supervision. . . .

. . . Knowledge for the workingman meant that he should be able to detect the difference between the real and the sham. Whenever a learned man said that which did not appear to be just to labor, he was to be questioned, publicly questioned, as to his base of actual facts. All through the centuries toilers have erected the brass and granite monuments of the world's greatness, and have thrown up on hillside and plain the material for other homes than their own. The weary feet of toil have trodden the earth, and strong hands have formed the pillars of the bondage of old. All along the blood-stained march of the years that have flown, the struggling ones have given to earth more of richness in the sweat which fell to earth from their throbbing foreheads; the grain which lifted its head for long ages of time under the care of the toiler, has been enriched by the sweat, the blood, and the flesh of the poor, plodding men of toil. While the sun kissed to warmth and life the wheat and corn which their hands nurtured and cared for, they received the husks and stalks as their recompense for labor done. Their masters took the grain for themselves, but lifted no hand in its production. . . .

To make moral worth the standard of individual and national greatness, the men of toil had to be roused to a sense of duty; they had to be taught what their rights and duties were. To do this the hollow pretenses of the political parties, which every year came before the country and on platforms of "glittering generalities" appealed for the suffrages of the people, had to be exposed and shown to the people in their true light.

Legislation for labor came through the halls of Congress and State Legislature as a bone comes through the fingers of a stingy master to a half-starved dog, with the meat picked from it. The bone was there, but it only served the hungry one as a reminder that there should be something else. When tested before a tribunal of any kind, nearly all of the legislation of that day would be declared unconstitutional to grant a whole territory to a railroad company, or to grant a valuable franchise to a corporation, but the moment the well-picked bone that was bestowed upon the hungry dog,—Labor,—was taken to the Supreme Court, it was declared to be only a bone, nothing more. A knowledge of who his friends were in each Congress, in each session of the Legislature, was to be made the standpoint for action when the time rolled round to select new legislators. Moral worth was to be established as the future standard, and why should not the laborer do his own legislating, instead of letting it out to a second party?

This was a question which was debated long and earnestly in the councils of the workingmen, and attempt after attempt was made, with little or no success, at first, to elect workingmen to serve as representatives of the people. Those who represented, and those who were to be represented, were in need of education on the questions which concerned all alike, but it was evident that parties would never educate the people. They gave out their platforms each year, and before they were understood, they were exchanged for something else without accomplishing the reforms they aimed at.

Once every four years, in national contests, questions of political economy were brought before the people on public platform and in ward meeting, but with the sound of the candidate's voice went the thought of what he said, for it was understood that he talked for himself alone. A change had to come, and with it the placing of the preamble of the Knights of Labor in every man's hand every day of the year, to be studied not one day in every four years, but every day in every year, so that those things that were pointed out in it would be carefully bedded in the mind of man or discarded as untrue, and therefore worthless. . . .

15. Adolph Strasser—
Philosophy of a Trade Unionist (1883)

In contrast to the ambitious objectives of the Knights of Labor in the 1880's stood the more limited aims of practical-minded leaders of the trade unions. Although not entirely forswearing broad reform goals, these men, faced with the task of wresting a larger share of the fruits of industrial production from powerful employers, were primarily interested in bread-and-butter issues—wages, hours, working conditions, collective bargaining. They concentrated on organizing skilled workers in particular trades and building up strong cash reserves in the form of union dues. Relying upon their control of the skills needed by manufacturers and their ability to pay benefits to tide their members over during work stoppages, they were prepared to enforce their demands by striking. The classic statement of this "pure and simple unionism" is contained in the following colloquy between Adolph Strasser, president of the Cigar Makers' Union, and members of the Senate committee investigating the relations between labor and capital in 1883. Strasser's questioners in this selection are Senators Henry W. Blair of New Hampshire, James L. Pugh of Alabama, Wilkinson Call of Florida, and James Z. George of Mississippi.

NEW YORK, *August* 21, 1883.

ADOLPH STRASSER sworn and examined.

SOURCE: United States Senate, Committee on Eudcation and Labor, *Report on the Relations Between Labor and Capital* (Washington, D.C., 1885), I, 449, 459-62, 465-6.

Sen. Pugh: Question. Please state your residence and occupation.—Answer. I reside in New York. At present I am acting president and secretary of the Cigarmakers' International Union of America, and editor of the journal of the organization. I do not work at my trade now, but am simply acting as an officer of the Cigarmakers' International Union. . . .

Sen. Blair: It occurs to me to ask you whether it is in contemplation, as one of the ultimate purposes of the trades unions, that their funds shall be accumulated so that if, in order to prevent a panic by the excess of products being thrown upon the market, they can in future lessen production by suspending labor for a time, and maintain the laborers meanwhile out of the accumulated fund. Have your trades organizations any such idea as that?—A. The trades unions try to prevent panics, but in fact they cannot prevent them, because panics are governed by influences beyond their control.

Q. Panics result, do they not, largely from overproduction?—A. The trades unions try to make their members better consumers, thereby enlarging the home market, and at the same time to make them better producers. If we can make the working people generally better consumers we shall have no panics.

Q. But if the increase of the power of production goes on by the improvement of machinery and all that, will not your efforts be counteracted in that way?—A. Then we propose a reduction of the hours of labor. That will decrease production and will increase consumption. We hold that a man who works but eight hours a day will demand a better home than a man who works longer hours; he will not be willing to live in one or two squalid rooms; he will demand better clothes, better food, more books, more newspapers, more education, more of the commodities that labor provides, more of the world's wealth, and that will bring about a better distribution of wealth and will consequently check panics to a certain extent. I do not believe that it is possible for the trades unions to do away with panics altogether, because panics depend not merely upon the condition of the industries of the United States, but upon the condition of the industries of the whole civilized world.

Q. Do you not contemplate, in the end, the participation of all labor and of all men in the benefits of the trades unions?—A. Of course we try to extend the good of the trades unions as well as we can and as far as we can.

Q. You have some hope even of the Hottentot, have you not?—A. What do you mean by that?

Q. I mean this: That although it is a great way off, still some time every man is to be an intelligent man and an enlightened man?—A. Well, our organization does not consist of idealists.

Q. But how are you to limit the progress of civilization? It goes from land to land. Races improve continually and the elements of human nature are always the same.—A. Well, we do not control the production of the world. That is controlled by the employers, and that is a matter for them.

Sen. Pugh: Q. You are seeking to improve home matters first?—A. Yes, sir; I look first to the trade I represent; I look first to cigars, to the interests of men who employ me to represent their interests.

Sen. Blair: I was only asking you in regard to your ultimate ends.

Strasser: We have no ultimate ends. We are going on from day to day. We are fighting only for immediate objects—objects that can be realized in a few years.

Sen. Call: Q. You want something better to eat and to wear, and better houses to live in?—A. Yes; we want to dress better and to live better, and become better off and better citizens generally.

Sen. Blair: I see that you are a little sensitive lest it should be thought that you are a mere theorizer. I do not look upon you in that light at all.

Strasser: Well, we say in our constitution that we are opposed to theorists, and I have to represent the organization here. We are all practical men. . . .

Sen. Pugh: Q. You have furnished us with a very valuable fund of information. Have you any further statement to make of any other facts connected with this labor question?—A. Well, I have not yet proposed any remedies.

Q. We shall be glad to hear your views on that subject.—A. Well, we propose—

1. That trades unions shall be incorporated. At present there are a great many of the States that do not protect our funds. It is simply a breach of trust to use our funds improperly and we have lost considerable money in that way. . . . Therefore, we request that the Committee on Education and Labor of the Senate report . . . a bill for the incorporation of the trades unions, giving them legal rights and allowing them to have headquarters wherever

they deem most fit or practicable. This, we hold, will give our organization more stability, and in that manner we shall be able to avoid strikes by perhaps settling with our employers, when otherwise we should be unable to do so, because when our employers know that we are to be legally recognized that will exercise such moral force upon them that they cannot avoid recognizing us themselves.

2. The next demand we make, one which we think will benefit labor, is the enforcement of the eight-hour law and its extension to the operation of all patents granted by the Government. By that I mean that if the Government grants a patent to anybody for any kind of invention, it shall be with the stipulation that the labor performed under that patent shall not be more than eight hours a day.

3. Our third demand is this: We claim that it is necessary to obtain information in regard to such questions as those which this committee is now investigating, and to that end we believe there is a necessity for a national bureau of labor statistics. . . . We hold that such a national bureau of labor statistics would give our legislators a great deal of information which will be very valuable to them as legislators, and we hold further that it would be a benefit, not only to labor, but, also, even greater benefit to capital, to have all this information compiled annually and distributed generally. . . .

Sen. George: Q. I suppose you are aware that the power of Congress to pass acts of incorporation of the kind that you desire, outside of the District of Columbia and the Territories of the United States, is a matter of dispute?—A. Well, let Congress enact the law and let somebody who is opposed to it bring the question before the judiciary, and let it be submitted to the Supreme Court of the United States, and its constitutionality decided. I hold that it is constitutional. . . .

Sen. Blair: Q. The constitution of your union I suppose is similar to that of other unions in the country?—A. The difference in our organization is that it pays these various benefits which other organizations do not, because they do not accumulate the funds. We believe in the theory of accumulating a large fund, but some of the other trades do not. They have not had the experience that we have had.

Q. Capital is necessary to a successful strike, is it not?—A.

Undoubtedly it is. You have to be equally as strong as the employers in order to be successful; you have to have means to hold out. . . .

Sen. George: Q. What is the feeling on the part of wage receivers generally towards their employers; is it a feeling of amity and confidence or is it a feeling of distrust?—A. In places where men receive good wages there is general good feeling; where they receive poor wages—starvation wages—there is generally bad feeling. The feeling between labor and capital depends largely on the employers. If they treat their men well and pay them fair wages, there is generally good feeling. If the employers treat their men badly and pay starvation wages, there is generally bad feeling. It depends wholly upon the employer. He has the power to encourage good feeling or the reverse.

Q. Mr. Lenz, the editor of a paper called Capital and Labor, expressed an opinion here that there was a growing socialistic feeling among the members of the trades unions; what is your observation in regard to that?—A. It is not so in the Cigar Makers' International Union. That organization does not inquire into the private opinions of a member; it takes in Democrats and Republicans, or anybody else so long as they are workers at the trade; that organization aims at practical measures, and will not allow any vague theories to be foisted upon it.

Q. Then you deny Mr. Lenz's statement so far as it relates to your organization?—A. As regards the Cigar Makers' International Union, I positively deny it. The members of that organization are simply practical men, going for practical objects that can be accomplished in a few years. . . .

16. Origins of
the American Federation of Labor (1886)

Conflict between the Knights of Labor and the trade unions, chronic during the late 1870's and early 1880's, came to a head in 1886. First a group of trade unionists, including Strasser of the Cigar Makers' and Peter J. Maguire of the Brotherhood of Carpenters, offered to sign a "treaty" with the Knights which was in effect a demand that the latter

SOURCE: N. J. Ware, *The Labor Movement in the United States:* 1860–1895 (New York, 1929), pp. 283-4, 294-7.

group stop trying to organize skilled craftsmen. When the Knights refused, the trade union leaders summoned a national conference and founded the American Federation of Labor. The treaty, the call of the trade unionists, and the resolution establishing the A.F.L. are reproduced below.

In our capacity as a committee of six selected by the conference of the chief officers of the National and International trade unions held in Philadelphia, Pa., May 18, 1886, beg leave to submit for your consideration and with hope of approval the following terms with a view to secure complete harmony of action and fraternity of purpose among all the various branches of organized labor:

Treaty

1st. That in any branch of labor having a National or International Trade Union, the Knights of Labor shall not initiate any person or form any assembly of persons following a trade or calling organized under such National or International Union without the consent of the nearest Local Union of the National or International Union affected.

2d. No person shall be admitted to membership in the Knights of Labor who works for less than the regular scale of wages fixed by the trade union of his craft or calling, and none shall be admitted into the Knights of Labor who have ever been convicted of "scabbing," "ratting," embezzlement or any other offense against the union of his trade or calling until exonerated by said union.

3d. The charter of any Knights of Labor Assembly of any trade having a National or International Union shall be revoked, and the members of the same be requested to join a mixed Assembly or form a local union under the jurisdiction of their National or International Trade Union.

4th. That any organizer of the Knights of Labor who endeavors to induce trade unions to disband or tampers with their growth or privileges, shall have his commission forthwith revoked.

5th. That wherever a strike of any trade union is in progress, no Assembly or District Assembly of the Knights of Labor shall interfere until settled to the satisfaction of the trade union affected.

6th. That the Knights of Labor shall not establish nor issue any trade mark or label in competition with any trade mark or label now issued, or that may be hereafter issued by any National or International Trade Union. . . .

On May 18, 1886, a conference of the chief officers of the various national and international trade unions was held in Philadelphia, Pa., at which twenty national and international unions were represented and twelve more sent letters of sympathy tendering their support to the conference. This made at that time thirty-two national and international trades unions with 367,736 members in good standing.

Since then quite a number of trades union conventions have been held, at all of which the action of the trades union conference has been emphatically and fully endorsed and a desire for a closer federation or alliance of all trades unions has been generally expressed. Not only that but a great impetus has been given to the formation of national trades unions and several new national unions have recently been formed, while all the trades societies with national or international heads have increased in membership and grown stronger in every respect.

The time has now arrived to draw the bonds of unity much closer together between all the trades unions of America. We need an annual Trades Congress that shall have for its object:

1. The formation of trades unions and the encouragement of the trades union movement in America.

2. The organization of trades assemblies, trades councils or central labor unions in every city in America and the further encouragement of such bodies.

3. The founding of state trades assemblies or state labor congresses to influence state legislation in the interest of the working masses.

4. The establishment of national and international trades unions based upon the strict recognition of the autonomy of each trade, and the promotion and advancement of such bodies.

5. An American Federation or Alliance of all national and international trades unions to aid and assist each other and furthermore to secure national legislation in the interest of the working people and influence public opinion by peaceful and legal methods in favor of organized labor.

6. To aid and encourage the labor press of America and to disseminate tracts and literature on the labor movement. . . . Where-

as the Knights of Labor have persistently attempted to under-mine and disrupt the well-established trades unions [, have] organized and encouraged men who have proven untrue to their trade, false to the obligation of their union, embezzlers of moneys and expelled by many of the unions and conspiring to pull down the trades unions . . .

Resolved: That we condemn the acts above recited and call upon all workingmen to join the unions of their respective trades and urge the formation of national and international unions and the centralization of all under one head, the American Federation of Labor.

Part VI

Urbanization

17. Samuel Lane Loomis—
The Urban Problem (1887)

Ever since colonial times the population of the United States has been shifting from rural to urban areas. In a sense, of course, this trend has merely reflected the increasing population of the country, but it has been greatly accelerated by industrialization, which has required the clotting together of large masses of people. Therefore the decades following the Civil War, when industry was developing very rapidly, were years of enormous urban expansion. In 1870 only a fifth of the population lived in centers of 8,000 or more; in 1890 a third of the people did so. This swift growth of American cities brought with it many benefits, but it also exacerbated many old problems. Slums proliferated, crime rates rose, severe health and sanitation hazards developed. The documents in this section on Urbanization all deal with one or another aspect of these unpleasant phenomena.

American religious leaders were particularly alarmed by the social problems resulting from urban growth. Many of them blamed the city dwellers themselves for the evils of the day, but an increasing number placed the chief responsibility on the environment and pictured the city resident as a victim more than as a producer of bad conditions. The Reverend Samuel Lane Loomis of Brooklyn, New York, was an early advocate of the latter position. Loomis preached what became known as the Social Gospel, which urged the churches to pay more attention to the problems of the cities and to provide leadership in the fight for social reform along with moral and religious guidance of the traditional sort. The following statement of Loomis's position is taken from his book *Modern Cities and Their Religious Problems*, which was based on lectures delivered at Andover Theological Seminary in 1886.

In a great city every man finds in its highest development the side and sort of life that pleases him best. For the vicious, there

SOURCE: S. L. Loomis, *Modern Cities and Their Religious Problems* (New York, 1887), pp. 31–4, 53, 82–3, 85–8, 100–5.

are unbounded opportunities for vice; for those who love God and men, extraordinary advantages for philanthropic work and Christian fellowship. Many, with special musical, literary, or artistic talents, are quite alone in a small community with neither opportunity nor stimulus for growth in the directions toward which their tastes incline them; but upon entering a city they find the surroundings so congenial that they can never again be persuaded to quit them. With its libraries, lectures, public gatherings, book-stores, companionships, and above all, the perpetual stimulus of contact with many minds, the great city is the paradise of literary men. Hume pronounced it the only fit place of residence for a man of letters. Dr. Johnson declared that a man who was tired of London was tired of his own existence. . . .

Great cities have a special fascination for young men. They offer to the successful, high and tempting prizes. There is little in the position of leading merchant, lawyer, or physician in a country town to spur the ambition of the young; but those who hold the like positions in the cities are the princes and mighty men of the times. Ambitious fellows prefer a hard race with high stakes to one on an easier course with fewer competitors and contemptible prizes. Hence, they have flocked to the cities until a new attorney's sign has become a by-word, and a single advertisement for a book-keeper enough to bring an army about your door. Besides all these special attractions for special classes, who can measure the fascination for the masses of manhood, of the great city's unequalled facilities for instruction and amusement? The churches and the schools, the theatres and concerts, the lectures, fairs, exhibitions, and galleries—how widely on every side are the doors of life opened! Even the streets and the shops have an attraction that few can deny; the bright and costly goods displayed in the windows, the prancing horses and sparkling carriages, the roar and rumble of drays, wagons, and cars, and the mighty streams of human beings that forever flow up and down the thoroughfares, exhibiting such an infinite variety of face, feature, form, and dress, from exquisite beauty to hideous ugliness, and from the richest silks and furs to the filthiest, faded, fluttering rags. But above and beyond all this is that vague delight at being one in the midst of a great multitude of men and women, which, though it may not often be defined or expressed, is the greatest of all the causes which contribute to the cities' growth.

Such tendencies would draw the whole world into cities,—into one great city, perhaps,—were it not for the existence of certain opposite tendencies—centrifugal forces, as one may call them—which counterbalance the centripetal force and preserve the equilibrium of society. While, on the one hand, city life is richer than rural, on the other it is more costly and less healthful. It is more costly because food, fuel, and every needful product of the soil must be produced by others, and brought from afar; because competition for the land is great and rent high; because the cost of living being great, personal service is correspondingly costly. City life is less healthful than the rural, because of the difficulty in getting a good and sufficient supply of the four things on which life chiefly depends: food, water, air, and light. Many must go with an insufficient quantity of food because of its costliness; and that they have, being the cheapest, is often unwholesome. Water is difficult to get, and unless brought from afar at great expense, is almost sure to be tainted with impurity. In closely crowded quarters filth quickly accumulates, and cleanliness can only be secured by eternal vigilance. No art has been discovered by which the air of a great town can be kept free from the disease germs and poisonous gases that reek from noisome places. Where thousands of furnaces are pouring their foul breath out into the sky, and where hundreds of thousands of human beings are always robbing the air of its vitality, a far less wholesome atmosphere necessarily prevails than on the mountain-side or by the sea; sickness comes on more easily and is harder to throw off. All these difficulties obviously bear most heavily upon the poorer classes. The tattered fringe which hangs upon the border of the social fabric is broadest in cities. That portion of the people, comprising the poorest, the weakest, and the most helpless, which is being gradually crowded to the wall and crushed amid the strife and struggle of the strong, is found largely — in some countries almost wholly — in the towns. . . .

All efforts to arrest the progress of the cities and to check the population that continually flows into them, must be fruitless. The great social movements of the age cannot be stopped. Each successive year is certain to see a smaller place for the workers of the world in the fields and on the farms and a larger place in shops, counting-rooms, offices, banks, manufactories, and the myriad industries that make their home in the metropolis. Let it not be assumed that great cities are of necessity, what Thomas Jefferson called them: "Great sores upon the body politic." . . .

The wisest efforts of philanthropy will not be spent in the vain effort to prevent the incoming of men to them, but in the effort to make them better places for human habitation; not in checking their growth, but in quenching their iniquity. . . .

It will not be difficult to convince those who are acquainted with the life of our cities, that the Protestant churches, as a rule, have no following among the workingmen. Everybody knows it. Go into an ordinary church on Sunday morning, and you see lawyers, physicians, merchants, and business men with their families:—you see teachers, salesmen, and clerks, and a certain proportion of educated mechanics: but the workingman and his household are not there. It is doubtful if one in twenty of the average congregation in English-speaking, Protestant, city churches fairly belongs to this class; but granting the proportion to be so great as one in ten or one in five, even then you would have two-thirds of the people furnishing only one-tenth or one-fifth of the congregation. The recent experiment of an enterprising newspaper reporter in a certain American city which has the reputation of being the model Christian city of the world will not be forgotten. He donned the garb of a decent laborer, and presented himself for admission, at each in turn of the principal churches in the city. At some he was treated with positive rudeness, at others with cold politeness. Only one or two gave him a cordial, and even then a somewhat surprised welcome. The incident shows that in that city, at least, the appearance of a workingman at church on Sunday morning is not common.

The same thing is illustrated by the experience of those churches which have been so located that their former congregations have moved away from them, and in the course of the city's growth their neighborhood has been filled up by the working-classes. How few have succeeded in holding their own, not merely in financial strength, but even in the size of the congregation, under such trying circumstances. . . .

In striking contrast with this is the condition of the Roman Catholic Chruch. It may be true that she holds her people with a looser grasp here than in Europe, and that she has altogether lost her influence over very considerable numbers of them; yet it must be acknowledged, on the other hand, that there have been surprisingly few conversions from Romanism to Protestanism. Considering the fact that she has been compelled to push her system amid the full blaze of the light of modern times, in an atmosphere permeated with that spirit of freedom whose pure breath is her poison, the success of Rome in the United States appears amazing. There are, at the present time, about 7,000,000 of Roman Catholics (communicants) in the land....

The Catholic Church is emphatically the workingman's church. She rears her great edifices in the midst of the densest populations, provides them with many seats and has the seats well filled. They are the places in which you never fail to find large congregations at the appointed times of public worship, the vast majority of whom are obviously workingmen and workingwomen....

The religion of Rome is far better than none, and we may well believe that many humble souls under the leadings of the Spirit have found their way through tangled meshes of falsehood with which she has covered it, down to the eternal truths on which her venerable faith is based. The influence of the Catholic Church, on the whole, is doubtless conservative, and will, probably, become more and more so. The Romanism of America is likely to be better than that of Europe. Yet Romanism is not the religion we wish for our fellow-citizens. It conceals the fatherhood of God behind the motherhood of the Church, and the brotherhood of Christ behind the motherhood of the Virgin. It degrades the atonement by making its benefits a matter of barter; it leads to idolatry and image-worship; it snatches from the believer the great gift bought with the blood of Christ, by thrusting in a priest between him and his heavenly Father. It has kept the people from the Word of God and compelled them to accept forced and unscholarly interpretations of it. It has lowered the tone of morality. It has quenced free thought, stifled free speech, and threatens to throttle free government. It has limited the advancement of every country on which its hand has been laid. If the religion of Rome becomes ours, then a civilization like that of Italy will be ours too....

We have thus endeavored to show that the workingmen of American cities are almost wholly shut out from the direct, and largely from the indirect influences of Protestant Christianity, by their foreign birth, training, and religious traditions, and also by the peculiar nature of the relations between the laborer and the capitalist. If, now, the propositions with which the chapter opened are true; namely—that the body of Christian society cannot exist without the soul, and that so soon as Christian influence is withdrawn from even a portion of society, that portion must forthwith lapse toward barbarism at the peril of the whole—if these are true, we should expect to see tokens of such a catastrophe in the American cities to-day, and such tokens are not lacking.

Consider, for example, the matter of municpal government. There is no need of enlarging upon the well-known fact that the governments of most of our important cities have for a long time been more or less rotten, and in some cases little more than gigantic systems of fraud. It has been frequently observed that if it were not for the control of State legislation life and property would hardly be safe within them. And now that State legislatures are more and more coming under the control of the gangs from the cities it is time that sober men were awakening to the seriousness of the situation. But let us ask, what is the significance of such a state of things? What does it mean when New York aldermen are convicted of receiving bribes by the wholesale; when Chicago mayors laugh at the laws of the land and snap their fingers in the face of those who urge their execution; when Cincinnati juries refuse to bring verdicts against criminals of undoubted guilt? Does it not mean that the people by whose suffrages such officials have obtained their positions are either too ignorant or too immoral for self-government?

Or consider, again, the drunkenness of the cities. The fearful statistics of the vice need no repetition. But it should not be forgotten that, unlike the churches, the drinking-saloons find the majority of their patrons among the workingmen. A machine moulder recently said to the writer that he did not know a person in his trade who is not a drinking man. Drinking-saloons are both causes and effects of a city's degradation. They are effects; they come where poverty makes the home dingy, squalid, and unattractive. Day and night their doors are open, offering to the weary laborer retreats that, with their polished brass and stained glass, their light and warmth and cheery company, are immeasurably more attractive than his home. Apart from the drinking, the drinking-places have a strong fascination for their patrons; but the drink too is made the more enticing by the misery of the drinker. Exhausted by long hours of monotonous labor, or by a still more trying search for labor when "out of a job," the man has an irresistible craving for some stimulus which will lighten his heart and banish his sorrows for an hour. . . .

Drinking-places are also *causes* of an inestimable deal of ruin. Besides actual drunkenness and the ghastly train of disease and crime that follows it, there is a moral poison about the grog-shops whose deadly power, though less frequently recognized, is scarcely less pernicious. A hellish atmosphere pervades these places. They are full of profanity, indecency, and infidelity, the headquarters of political corruption and the hotbeds of crime. It would be very unjust to put them all on a level. Some are certainly much more respectable than others; but none of them are too good, and the tendency of all is downward. . . .

Other evidence in the same direction appears in the increase of crime that the past thirty years have witnessed. In 1850 Massachusetts had one prisoner to 804 of the population. In 1880 she had one to 487. The criminal population in proportion to the whole population had nearly doubled in thirty years. . . . Have we not here, too, ominous indications that the foundations of Christian civilization are rotting away beneath us?

The increase of poverty and pauperism is another token of the same thing. This was one of the heaviest chains that dragged old Rome down to the dust. The public statement was recently made that from one in twelve to one in fifteen of the inhabitants of Ohio received charitable aid in the course of a single winter. . . .

As a final token of the threatening dissolution of the fabric of Christian society, notice the nature of the new gospel for workingmen which many of the socialists are preaching. This is not the place for the discussion of socialism. We have no time to speak here of its wide and rapid spread in our own country and all over Europe, nor to consider how much of what is true and valuable may be mixed up with its teachings; nor can we notice the extent to which it has influenced the thinking of multitudes who have not accepted its doctrines as a whole—an influence clearly seen in recent labor troubles, in the late elections, in the formation of the Anti-Poverty Society, etc. But the thing to be observed is the tendency of the doctrines that are at present advocated by its leaders. The International Workingmen's Association, which is the principal socialistic society in this country and the world, makes it its direct purpose to promote the very thing which, as we have tried to show, is now threatening us, namely: the overthrow of the present system of society. These anarchists have most vague and varied notions of what should take the place of that which they wish to destroy. Whenever they attempt to tell how the new society should be organized, they become involved in hopeless confusion. The one plan upon which they all agree is that of destruction. Many of the leaders go so far as to advocate the abolition with private property of religion, the State, the Church, and even the family. Give such men their way, not that they are likely to get it, and they would dash the proud temple of civilization with a single blow to the ground, and leave the world in as dense a darkness of barbarism as ever enveloped our fathers of the Northland.

18. Commissioners of Labor Statistics and Economist Richard T. Ely— The Town of Pullman (1884-85)

The urban expansion of the 1880's took place largely without plan; as a result, most cities were plagued by traffic, housing, and sanitation problems and by a shortage of adequate park and recreational facilities. A shining exception was the new city of Pullman, Illinois, near Chicago. This model community was created by George Pullman to house the workers who were employed in the manufacture of his famous Pullman "Palace" cars for the railroads. It attracted a great deal of attention and discussion, mostly favorable, among persons concerned with city planning. The two following analyses of the community were written in the mid-eighties. The first is a report made by a group of commissioners of state bureaus of labor statistics, the second economist, an article written for *Harper's New Monthly Magazine* by a young economist Richard T. Ely. The commissioners, despite their pro-labor sympathies, had nothing but praise for Pullman. Ely, however, while noting the advantages provided, was disturbed by the tight controls exercised over the populace by the Pullman company. His was a minority view in the eighties; only after the great Pullman strike of 1894 had demonstrated how Pullman dominated the city did the town become notorious.

SOURCE: A: Illinois Bureau of Labor Statistics, "Industrial, Social and Economic Conditions at Pullman, Illinois," *Third Biennial Report* (Springfield, Ill., 1884), pp. 638-9, 642-3, 645-7, 649-51, 653-4.

SOURCE: B: R. T. Ely, "Pullman: A Social Study," *Harper's New Monthly Magazine*, LXX (1885), 455-7, 460-6.

*A: "Industrial, Social and Economic Conditions at
Pullman, Illinois"*

At the annual convention of the chiefs and commissioners of
the various bureaus of statistics of labor in the United States, held
at St. Louis in June, 1884, it was determined to make a full and
exhaustive investigation of the economic experiment conducted
by Pullman's Palace Car Co. on the plan projected by Mr. George
M. Pullman, the president.

In carrying out this determination the convention met at Pullman, Ill., in September following, and for three days studied all
the economic, sanitary, industrial, moral, and social conditions of
the city.

Every facility was afforded for the closest scrutiny of every feature and phase of any and all the affairs the members of the convention saw fit to examine. . . .

Four or five years ago Mr. Pullman determined to bring the
greater portion of the works of the company into one locality. To
accomplish this he must leave the great cities for many reasons,
and yet it was essential that a site should be selected where communication could be had with the whole country, and near some
metropolitan place like Chicago. He wished above all things to
remove his workmen from the close quarters of a great city, and
give them the healthful benefits of good air, good drainage, and
good water, and where they would be free, so far as it would lie in
the power of management to keep them free, from the many
seductive influences of a great town.

He was fortunate in securing about 4,000 acres of land on the
Illinois Central Road, a dozen miles to the south of Chicago. This
land was located in the town of Hyde Park, and here he built his
city. . . .

The appearance from the railroad as one approaches from Chicago is effective. The neat station; the water tower and the works
in front; the park and artificial lakes intervening; to the right a
picturesque hotel backed by pretty dwellings; the arcade containing stores, library, theatre, offices, etc.; still further to the right,
and beyond, a church which fits into the landscape with artistic
effect.

The laying out of the whole town has been under the guidance
of skilled architects aided by civil engineers and landscape garden-
ers.

The dwellings present a great variety of architecture, yet give harmonious effects. They are not built like the tenement houses of ordinary manufacturing towns where sameness kills beauty and makes the surroundings tame, but a successful effort has been made to give diversity to architectural design.

The streets are wide, well built, and wherever possible parked. The lawns are kept in order by the company; the shade trees are cared for, and all the police work is done under competent supervision.

Every care has been taken to secure convenience inside as well as outside the dwellings. The cheapest tenement is supplied with gas and water and garbage outlets. The housekeeper throws the garbage into a specified receptacle and has no more care of it.

The testimony of every woman we met was that housekeeping was rendered far more easy in Pullman than in any other place. In fact the women were in love with the place: its purity of air, cleanliness of houses and streets, and lessened household burdens, are advantages over their former residences which brought out the heartiest expressions of approval. The women of the comparatively poor bear most of the drudgery of life, enjoy the least of pleasures, and are most narrowly circumscribed, with little change in cares, scenes, or social surroundings. Pullman has really wrought a greater change for the women than for any other class of its dwellers.

All the works and shops are kept in the neatest possible order. The planning rooms are as free from dust as the street, blowers and exhaust fans taking away all shavings, dust and debris, as fast as it accumulates. One notices everywhere the endeavor to save time and space in the construction of goods. As an illustration of the science which enters into manufacture we need only cite the shops where freight cars are built. All the timber is taken in lengths at one end and is never turned around until it finds its proper place in a completed freight car, being carried constantly from one process to another in a direct line from its reception at one end to its utilization at the other.

There are 1,520 brick tenements in houses and flats. The frontage of all the buildings extends along five miles of solid paved streets, and there are fourteen miles of railroad track laid for the use of those in the shops and the town. The buildings are of brick or stone. . . .

The rentals at Pullman are a little higher for the same number of rooms than in Chicago, but in Chicago the tenement would be in a narrow street or alley, while in Pullman it is on a broad avenue where no garbage is allowed to collect, where all houses have a back street entrance, where the sewage arrives at a farm in three hours' time from its being deposited, and where beauty, order, and cleanliness prevail, and fresh air abounds.

There are no taxes to be paid other than personal, and, when all the advantages which a tenant has at Pullman are taken into consideration as compared with his disadvantages in other places, the rent rates are in reality much lower.

The tenant is under no restrictions beyond those ordinarily contained in a lease, except that he must leave his tenement at ten days' notice, or he can give the same notice and quit. This short limitation has been established in order that no liquor saloons, objectionable houses, or anything likely to disturb the *morals* of the place, can become fastened on the community.

All the houses in Pullman city are owned by the company. This policy has been considered the best in the early years of the city in order that a foundation may be securely laid for a community of good habits and good order.

The men are employed without restriction. There are no conditions laid upon their freedom; they are paid fortnightly, and they expend their wages when and where they see fit, their rent being charged against their wages. This, at first, caused some complaint, but the system is now generally liked, for when wages are paid there is no bother about rent bills, and the wife and the children know that the home is secure. Repairs, if due to the carelessness or negligence of the tenant, are made by the company at the lowest possible expense, and charged against the tenant. Of course, the company, like all landlords, expects to keep the houses in tenantable condition.

There has been some friction in this matter, but as the policy of the company becomes more generally and better understood, the complaint ceases.

The company has erected a very fine school building having fourteen commodious rooms, which now contain about 900 pupils. The schools are under the charge of the school authorities of Hyde Park. They are in a prosperous condition and well accommodate the school population.

There are two or three religious societies and the beautiful church which has been built by the company, while occupied by any sect or by anybody that wishes to hold meetings there, is awaiting the occupancy of some society that chooses to lease it at a fair rental.

In the arcade is to be found a library handsomely fitted and well stocked with books.

The company has also provided a gymnasium, an amphitheatre for games, baseball grounds, and in the arcade is one of the most aesthetic theatres in the country.

All these influences are gradually elevating the society of Pullman city, and their influence is largely felt.

There is but little crime or drunkenness in Pullman, and one policeman, an officer appointed by the authorities of Hyde Park, constitutes the police force for 8,500 people. In two years but 15 arrests have been made; there is no general beer drinking, for there are no liquor saloons in the town. The hotel provides its guests with liquors, but under orderly restrictions.

There is no pauperism; two or three families, where the head had been taken away, or where some accident or misfortune had rendered it necessary, have been aided; but pauperism, as such, does not exist at Pullman. . . .

The principle on which Pullman city is founded, and on which its success largely depends, is that in all industrial enterprises business should be so conducted and arranged as to be profitable to each of the great forces, labor and capital.

Mr. Pullman does not believe that a great manufacturing concern can meet with the highest economic and moral success where the profit is unduly large to capital, with no corresponding benefit to labor. The mutual benefit which comes from well adjusted forces is to his mind what brings the best success.

On the other hand, he has made no claim to being a philanthropist; the sentiment prevails in his city that true philanthropy is based on business principles and should net a fair return for efforts made.

Promiscuous charity has no place in the establishment of Pullman. Personally, the president of the company makes the favorable conditions, and, having made them, he then concerns himself chiefly in supplying his people with steady employment. The art interests, the moral interests, the social and human interests, with favorable conditions supplied, take most excellent care of themselves. Incidentally his competent staff have an eye to all interests.

Mr. Pullman is no dreamer; he has studied the plans of socialists and reformers and the schemes of philosophers for the benefit of humanity.

Beginning at the bottom rung of the ladder, and therefore familiar with the wants and aspirations of the workers of society, he has risen by the force of his own character and genius to his present position; he does not care to leave the world and look back upon his action and see that he has only offered a glass of water to the sufferer by the wayside, but he wishes to feel that he has furnished a desert with wells of living water that all may come and drink through all time. So he commenced with the foundation idea of furnishing his workmen with model homes, and supplying them with abundant work with good wages, feeling that simply better conditions would make better men and his city become a permanent benefaction. . . .

After very careful investigation and the study of Pullman city from the standpoint of the manager, and that of the laborer, the mechanic, the physician, the priest, and from all points of view that we could muster, the question naturally arose, as it might arise in all men's minds who examine such institutions, what are the weak points in the plan? Superficially, we could see at once that the workman had no status as an owner of his home, but we could see that in the early years of Pullman city, if he had such a status it might be the means of his ruin financially. The company owns everything, manages everything; the employes are tenants of the company. This feature will be for some time longer the chief strength of the place, but in this strength lies its weakness. This feature is its strength so long as the industries of Pullman city belong to one great branch, the manufacture of one thing, or the things auxiliary to that manufacture. Now, should the industry of car building collapse or stagnate to any degree, the tenant employe is at liberty to remove at once; he has to give but ten days' notice to vacate his tenancy. He is free to take up his abode where he chooses, without the fear or the fact of any real property going down on his hands. But Mr. Pullman and his company have contemplated this very state of affairs, and are doing all in their power to bring in a diversity of manufactures so that if one kind of goods are not produced another will be. . . .

If the workman at Pullman lives in a "gilded cage," we must congratulate him on its being so handsomely gilded; the average workman does not have his cage gilded. That there is any cage or imprisonment about it is not true, save in the sense that all men are circumscribed by the conditions with which they surround themselves, and imprisoned by the daily duties of life.

It is quite possible that the Pullman community has been organized and developed thus far on a plan as comprehensive as commercial prudence permits, but when the experiment as now fairly outlined shall have become an established success, it would be gratifying to see certain additional features considered, and if feasible introduced for practical test.

To make Pullman the ideal establishment of the theorists, in addition to the option of purchasing homes and the strength which must come from diversified industry, one would naturally expect that when the enterprise shall have survived adversity as well as prosperity, and the wise and beneficent policy now being tested shall have borne its fruit in a permanent community of intelligent and prosperous workingmen, it may then be found possible to advance them to a share of the profits of the business itself. However this may be, we think we are justified in the belief that, as long as the present management, or the spirit of that management exists, the beneficent features of this most progressive industrial establishment will be extended as rapidly as circumstances may ripen for them.

Let the model manufactory and the industrial community of Pullman city be commended as they deserve for whatever they are or what they promise to be. Let them be held up to the manufacturers and employers of men throughout the country as worthy of their emulation. Let Mr. Pullman and his coadjutors be assured of the good wishes of all those who seek the advancement of their kind.

B: R. T. Ely, "Pullman: A Social Study"

... Much could be said of Pullman as a manufacturing centre, but the purpose of this article is to treat it as an attempt to furnish laborers with the best homes under the most healthful conditions and with the most favorable surroundings in every respect, for Pullman aims to be a forerunner of better things for the laboring classes.

The questions to be answered are these: Is Pullman a success from a social standpoint? Is it worthy of imitation? Is it likely to inaugurate a new era in society? If only a partial success, what are its bright features and what its dark features? . . .

Very gratifying is the impression of the visitor who passes hurriedly through Pullman and observes only the splendid provision for the present material comforts of its residents. What is seen in a walk or drive through the streets is so pleasing to the eye that a woman's first exclamation is certain to be, "Perfectly lovely!" It is indeed a sight as rare as it is delightful. What might have been taken for a wealthy suburban town is given up to busy workers, who literally earn their bread in the sweat of their brow. No favorable sites are set apart for drones living on past accumulations, and if a few short stretches are reserved for residences which can be rented only by those whose earnings are large, this is an exception; and it is not necessary to remain long in the place to notice that clergymen, officers of the company, and mechanics live in adjoining dwellings.

One of the most striking peculiarities of this place is the all-pervading air of thrift and providence. The most pleasing impression of general well-being is at once produced. Contrary to what is seen ordinarily in laborers' quarters, not a dilapidated door-step nor a broken window, stuffed perhaps with old clothing, is to be found in the city. The streets of Pullman, always kept in perfect condition are wide and finely macadamized, and young shade trees on each side now ornament the town, and will in a few years afford refreshing protection from the rays of the summer sun.

Unity of design and an unexpected variety charm us as we saunter through the town. Lawns always of the same width separate the houses from the street, but they are so green and neatly trimmed that one can overlook this regularity of form. Although the houses are built in groups of two or more, and even in blocks, with the exception of a few large buildings of cheap flats, they bear no resemblance to barracks; and one is not likely to make the mistake, so frequent in New York blocks of "brown-stone fronts," of getting into the wrong house by mistake. . . . The streets cross each other at right angles, yet here again skill has avoided the frightful monotony of New York, which must sometimes tempt a nervous person to scream for relief. A public square, arcade, hotel, market, or some large building is often set across a street so ingeniously as to break the regular line, yet without inconvenience to traffic. Then at the termination of long streets a pleasing view greets and relieves the eye—a bit of water, a stretch of meadow, a clump of trees, or even one of the large but neat workshops. All this grows upon the visitor day by day. No other feature of Pullman can receive praise needing so little qualification as its architecture. Desirable houses have been provided for a large laboring population at so small a cost that they can be rented at rates within their means and yet yield a handsome return on the capital invested. . . .

. . . The entire town was built under the direction of a single architect, Mr. S. S. Beman, an ambitious young man whose frequently expressed desire for an opportunity to do a "big thing" was here gratified. This is probably the first time a single architect has ever constructed a whole town systematically upon scientific principles, and the success of the work entitles him to personal mention. The plans were drawn for a large city at the start, and these have been followed without break in the unity of design. Pullman illustrates and proves in many ways both the advantages of enterprises on a vast scale and the benefits of unified and intelligent municipal administration. . . .

The Pullman companies retain everything. No private individual owns to-day a square rod of ground or a single structure in the entire town. No organization, not even a church, can occupy any other than rented quarters. With the exception of the management of the public school, every municipal act is here the act of a private corporation. What this means will be perceived when it is remembered that it includes such matters as the location, repairs, and cleaning of streets and sidewalks, the maintenance of the fire department, and the taking of the local census whenever desired. When the writer was in Pullman a census was taken. A superior officer of the company said to an inferior, "I want a census," and told what kind of a census was desired. That was the whole matter. The people of the place had no more to say about it than a resident of Kamtchatka. . . .

One of Mr. Pullman's fundamental ideas is the *commercial value of beauty*, and this he has endeavored to carry out as faithfully in the town which bears his name as in the Pullman drawing-room and sleeping cars. He is one of the few men who have thought it a paying investment to expend millions for the purpose of surrounding laborers with objects of beauty and comfort. In a hundred ways one sees in Pullman to-day evidences of its founder's sagacious foresight. One of the most interesting is the fact that the company finds it pays them in dollars and cents to keep the streets sprinkled with water and the lawns well trimmed, the saving in paint and kalsomine more than repaying the outlay. Less dust and dirt are carried and blown into houses, and the injury done to walls and wood-work is diminished. For the rest, the neat exterior is a constant example, which is sure sooner or later to exert its proper effect on housewives, stimulating them to exertion in behalf of cleanliness and order.

It should be constantly borne in mind that all investments and outlays in Pullman are intended to yield financial returns satisfactory from a purely business point of view. . . .

The great majority at Pullman are skilled artisans, and nearly all with whom the writer conversed expressed themselves as fairly well satisfied with their earnings, and many of them took pains to point out the advantages of the steady employment and prompt pay they always found there. The authorities even go out of their way to "make work" for one who has proved himself efficient and faithful. . . .

There are a thousand and one little ways in which the residents of Pullman are benefited, and in many cases without cost to the company. Considerable care is taken to find suitable employment for those who in any way become incapacitated for their ordinary work. A watchman with a missing arm was seen, and a position as janitor was found for a man who had become partially paralyzed. These are but examples. Men temporarily injured receive full pay, save in cases of gross carelessness, when one dollar a day is allowed. Employes are paid with checks on the "Pullman Loan and Savings Bank," to accustom them to its use and encourage them to make deposits.

Encouraging words from superiors are helpful. One warm-hearted official, to whom the welfare of the laboring classes appears to be a matter of momentous concern, wrote a note of thanks to the occupant of a cottage which was particularly well kept and ornamented with growing flowers. In another case he was so well pleased with the appearance of a cottage that he ordered a couple of plants in pots sent from the greenery to the lady of the house, with his compliments. The effect of systematic persistence in little acts of kind thoughtfulness like these is seen in the diffusion of a spirit of mutual helpfulness, and in frequent attempts to give practical, even if imperfect, expression to the truth of the brotherhood of man. . . .

But admirable as are the peculiarities of Pullman which have been described, certain unpleasant features of social life in that place are soon noticed by the careful observer, which moderate the enthusiasm one is at first inclined to feel upon an inspection of the external, plainly visible facts, and the picture must be completed before judgment can be pronounced upon it.

One just cause of complaint is what in government affairs would be called a bad civil service, that is, a bad administration in respect to the employment, retention, and promotion of employes. Change is constant in men and officers, and each new superior appears to have his own friends, whom he appoints to desirable positions. Favoritism and nepotism, out of place as they are in an ideal society, are oft-repeated and apparently well-substantiated charges.

The resulting evil is very naturally dissatisfaction, a painful prevalence of petty jealousies, a discouragement of superior excellence, frequent change in the residents, and an all-pervading feeling of insecurity. Nobody regards Pullman as a real home, and, in fact, it can scarcely be said that there are more than temporary residents at Pullman. . . . The power of Bismarck in Germany is utterly insignificant when compared with the power of the ruling authority of the Pullman Palace Car Company in Pullman. Whether the power be exercised rightfully or wrongfully, it is there all the same, and every man, woman, and child in the town is completely at its mercy, and it can be avoided only by emigration. It is impossible within the realm of Pullman to escape from the overshadowing influence of the company, and every resident feels this, and "monopoly" is a word which constantly falls on the ear of the visitor. Large as the place is, it supports no newspaper, through which complaints might find utterance, and one whose official position in the town qualified him to speak with knowledge declared positively that no publication would be allowed which was not under the direct influence of the Pullman Company. A Baptist clergyman, who had built up quite a congregation, once ventured to espouse the cause of a poor family ejected from their house, and gave rather public expression to his feelings. Shortly after his support began to fall away, one member after another leaving, and it has since never been possible to sustain a Baptist organization in Pullman. It is indeed a sad spectacle. Here is a population of eight thousand souls where not one single resident dare speak out openly his opinion about the town in which he lives. . . .

. . . It required recourse to some ingenuity to ascertain the real opinion of the people about their own city. While the writer does not feel at liberty to narrate his own experience, it can do no harm to mention a strange coincidence. While in the city the buttons on his wife's boots kept tearing off in the most remarkable manner, and it was necessary to try different shoemakers, and no one could avoid free discussion with a man who came on so harmless an errand as to have the buttons sewed on his wife's boots. This was only one of the devices employed. The men believe they are watched by the "company's spotter," and to let one of them know that information was desired about Pullman for publication was to close his lips to the honest expression of opinion. . . .

In looking over all the facts of the case the conclusion is unavoidable that the idea of Pullman is un-American. It is a nearer approach than anything the writer has seen to what appears to be the ideal of the great German Chancellor. It is not the American ideal. It is benevolent, well-wishing feudalism, which desires the happiness of the people, but in such way as shall please the authorities. . . .

. . . Not a few have ventured to express the hope that Pullman might be widely imitated, and thus inaugurate a new era in the history of labor. But if this signifies approval of a scheme which would immesh our laborers in a net-work of communities owned and managed by industrial superiors, then let every patriotic American cry, God forbid! What would this mean? The establishment of the most absolute power of capital, and the repression of all freedom. It matters not that they are well-meaning capitalists; all capitalists are not devoted heart and soul to the interests of their employes, and the history of the world has long ago demonstrated that no class of men are fit to be intrusted with unlimited power. In the hour of temptation and pressure it is abused, and the real nature of the abuse may for a time be concealed even from him guilty of it; but it degrades the dependent, corrupts the morals of the superior, and finally that is done unblushingly in the light which was once scarcely allowed in a dark corner. . . .

19. Robert Treat Paine, Jr.— Improving the Slums (1881)

How to provide a decent way of life for the urban poor was a problem that occupied the minds of many persons of charitable bent in the 1870's and 1880's. Some went into tenement districts and tried to help the poor by moral exhortation, supplemented by material aid. Work of this type is described by Robert Treat Paine, Jr., in his paper "Homes for the People," read before a meeting of the American Social Science Association in 1881. Paine, a Boston philanthropist, was president of the Associated Charities of Boston, the motto of which organization was "Not Alms but a Friend."

Old houses sink into decay, where neglect by tenants as well as by landlords, makes them often too foul for human life. Charitable workers everywhere discover that foul homes are a source of crime and degradation, which it is hopeless to contend with. . . .

A paper on this subject some years ago, gave an account of the work in Boston of taking charge of the biggest and worst tenement barrack there, cleansing it and subjecting it to the good influences of a kind agent under interested gentlemen and ladies, and of the gratifying results upon the character of its occupants. Another like effort has come under my knowledge this past year, conducted by a wise and benevolent lady, with marked success, not only as a business, which is always important, but also in gaining and exerting a wonderful influence over tenants, of the lowest classes, degraded in all the relations of life.

I have here the report of a lady placed in charge of some large tenement house properties, in the worst section of New York, belonging to a Society, which takes them with the benevolent aim, not only to renovate them, but to prove how much may be done to help even drunken and degraded tenants to a better life. This also, is a successful business operation. A few extracts will show

SOURCE: R. T. Paine, Jr., "Homes for the People," *Journal of Social Science,* XV (1882), 104-8.

the missionary spirit in which Mrs. Miles has taken up this work, and what she has achieved:

Extracts from Letters of Mrs. N. Miles to R. Fulton Cutting,
March 11th, 1880

Mr. Cutting and a friend visited the "court" with me, yesterday. Mr. Cutting was thoroughly disappointed, and so was I (but agreeably so), there was really so little left of the "Gotham court," as you and I had seen it, a month ago. In house "B," you will remember the shattered windows on the first floor, and the dreadful room, in which Mrs. Burke was, also, Mrs. Moore, Mrs. Sullivan, and the woman McGuire,—Mrs. Burke, who had not been sober for six weeks when you saw her, on the day of her baby's funeral; you will also recollect a curious bundle in the corner of the room, which, upon investigation, proved to be Mrs. Burke, who is since dead. She promised the priest and myself, upon our visit, that she would drink no more; the poor thing was faithful to her promise, and went to the hospital, where, doubtless, the sudden total abstinence hastened her death. The neighbors say, "God's blessing will be upon me, because I was the means of her dying *sober.*"

That the people have been lifted and morally elevated in the course of the year, there can be no doubt. Your remark upon the occasion of your visit, "Where are the poor people?" was to me the most satisfactory proof that this result had been obtained. That they have never grown restless under the constant supervision, my knowledge that on several occasions my people had been offered rooms at *less money,* but preferred remaining where they were, and the fact that Mulberry street (where the rule is *more* stringent) has now never a vacant apartment, are all proofs positive to me, that these people do appreciate this movement in their behalf. As a missionary, I have at all times been a welcome visitor, and they are always ready and glad to hear "the word;" and, when trouble comes to them, I am the first one to whom they apply. When I consider that I have the oversight of 176 families, and from fifty to sixty mothers of my nursery children, 100 children in our Harlem Mission School, from thirty-five to forty in my gospel meetings, I am perfectly surprised at the *very small* amount of temporal aid for which I am asked; this is to me another proof that the result of our work is a good one. . . .

Extracts from Report of Mrs. N. Miles, to R. Fulton Cutting,
November 4, 1880

. . . When last Mr. Cutting went with me through the court, he remarked, the appearance of the people seemed changed; the improvement is much more perceptible now; we have not had a fight of any kind for three weeks, and very little unseemly or loud talking. This improvement, I think, is attributable to several causes: 1st. An answer to earnest and constant prayer. 2d. The influence of summer excursions. 3rd. Their appreciation of medical attention and comfort when necessary. 4th. The prohibition to the children bringing stimulants, and, 5th. Constant personal influence and intercourse with them. Our laundries have been of incalculable benefit; there had never before been so much bedding washed as during the past summer; the mothers and children were allowed the free use of the tubs for bathing purposes, which privilege they gladly accepted. I conscientiously believe there is *no lower* class of people than some of those with whom I have been in contact in Gotham court; notwithstanding, it is quite noticeable that the tenants generally are much more cleanly in their habits (although there is, of course, still great room for improvement). We shall open an Industrial School in the court on Saturday, 13th. . . .

20. Jane Addams—Hull House

To some reformers, merely visiting the poor in their dreadful environment in order to perform good works was not enough. Following the example of British social workers, a number of Americans, mostly young women fresh from colleges like Smith and Vassar, founded settlement houses in the slums. A settlement house was a combination of residence, school, and clubhouse. Settlement house workers believed that by living in a slum neighborhood they could stimulate a mutually beneficial exchange of ideas with local people, supplying them with guidance and training along with moral support, and at the same time gaining for themselves a broader understanding both of social problems and of life itself. The first and by far the best known of the American settlements was Hull House in Chicago, founded by Jane Addams and Ellen Gates Starr in 1889. In the following article, Miss Addams described Hull House and its objectives.

SOURCE: Jane Addams, "Hull House, Chicago: An Effort Toward Social Democracy," *The Forum*, XIV (1893), 226-9, 236-41.

Hull House, Chicago's first Social Settlement, was established in September, 1889. It represented no association, but was opened by two women, supported by many friends, in the belief that the mere foothold of a house, easily accessible, ample in space, hospitable and tolerant in spirit, situated in the midst of the large foreign colonies which so easily isolate themselves in American cities, would be in itself a serviceable thing for Chicago. It represents an attempt to make social intercourse express the growing sense of the economic unity of society, to add the social function to democracy. It was opened in the theory that the dependence of classes on each other is reciprocal, and that "as the social relation is essentially a reciprocal relation, it gives a form of expression that has peculiar value."

Hull House stands on South Halsted Street, next door to the corner of Polk. . . . Between Halsted Street and the river live about ten thousand Italians: Neapolitans, Sicilians, and Calabrians, with an occasional Lombard or Venetian. To the south on Twelfth Street are many Germans, and side streets are given over almost entirely to Polish and Russian Jews. Further south, these Jewish colonies merge into a huge Bohemian colony, so vast that Chicago ranks as the third Bohemian city in the world. To the northwest are many Canadian-French, clannish in spite of their long residence in America, and to the north are many Irish and first-generation Americans. On the streets directly west and farther north are well-to-do English-speaking families, many of whom own their houses and have lived in the neighborhood for years. I know one man who is still living in his old farm-house. This corner of Polk and Halsted Streets is in the fourteenth precinct of the nineteenth ward. This ward has a population of about fifty thousand, and at the last presidential election registered 7,072 voters. It has had no unusual political scandal connected with it, but its aldermen are generally saloon-keepers and its political manipulations are those to be found in the crowded wards where the activities of the petty politician are unchecked.

The policy of the public authorities of never taking an initiative and always waiting to be urged to do their duty is fatal in a ward where there is no initiative among the citizens. The idea underlying our self-government breaks down in such a ward. The streets are inexpressibly dirty, the number of schools inadequate, factory legislation unenforced, the street-lighting bad, the paving miserable and altogether lacking in the alleys and smaller streets, and the stables defy all laws of sanitation. Hundreds of houses are unconnected with the street sewer. The older and richer inhabitants seem anxious to move away as rapidly as they can afford it. They make room for newly arrived emigrants who are densely ignorant of civic duties. This substitution of the older inhabitants is accomplished also industrially in the south and east quarters of the ward. The Hebrews and Italians do the finishing for the great clothing-manufacturers formerly done by Americans, Irish, and Germans, who refused to submit to the extremely low prices to which the sweating system has reduced their successors. As the design of the sweating system is the elimination of rent from the manufacture of clothing, the "outside work" is begun after the clothing leaves the cutter. For this work no basement is too dark, no stable loft too foul, no rear shanty too provisional, no tenement room too small, as these conditions imply low rental. Hence these shops abound in the worst of the foreign districts, where the sweater easily finds his cheap basement and his home finishers. There is a constant tendency to employ schoolchildren, as much of the home and shop work can easily be done by children.

This site for a Settlement was selected in the first instance because of its diversity and the variety of activity for which it presented an opportunity. It has been the aim of the residents to respond to all sides of the neighborhood life: not to the poor people alone, nor to the well-to-do, nor to the young in contradistinction to the old, but to the neighborhood as a whole, "men, women, and children taken in families as the Lord mixes them." The activities of Hull House divide themselves into four, possibly more lines. They are not formally or consciously thus divided, but broadly separate according to the receptivity of the neighbors. They might be designated as the social, educational, and humanitarian. I have added civic—if indeed a settlement of women can be said to perform civic duties. These activities spring from no preconceived notion of what a Social Settlement should be, but have increased gradually on demand. . . .

. . . Perhaps the chief value of a Settlement to its neighborhood, certainly to the newly arrived foreigner, is its office as an information and interpretation bureau. It sometimes seems as if the business of the settlement were that of a commission merchant. Without endowment and without capital itself, it constantly acts between the various institutions of the city and the people for whose benefit these institutions were erected. The hospitals, the county agencies, and State asylums, are often but vague rumors to the people who need them most. This commission work, as I take it, is of value not only to the recipient, but to the institutions themselves. Each institution is obliged to determine upon the line of its activity, to accept its endowment for that end and do the best it can. But each time this is accomplished it is apt to lace itself up in certain formulas, is in danger of forgetting the mystery and complexity of life, of repressing the promptings that spring from growing insight.

The residents of a Social Settlement have an opportunity of seeing institutions from the recipient's standpoint, of catching the spirit of the original impulse which founded them. This experience ought to have a certain value and ultimately find expression in the institutional management. One of the residents of Hull House received this winter an appointment from the Cook County agent as a county visitor. She reported at the agency each morning, and all the cases within a radius of several blocks from Hull House were given to her for investigation. This gave her a legitimate opportunity for knowing the poorest people in the neighborhood. In no cases were her recommendations refused or her judgments reversed by the men in charge of the office. From the very nature of our existence and purpose we are bound to keep on good terms with every beneficent institution in the city. . . .

The more definite humanitarian effect of Hull House has taken shape in a day nursery, which was started during the second year of our residence on Halsted Street. A frame cottage of six rooms across our yard has been fitted up as a *crèche*. At present we receive from thirty to forty children daily. A young lady who has had kindergarten training is in charge; she has the assistance of an older woman, and a kindergarten by a professional teacher is held each morning in the play-room. This nursery is not merely a convenience in the neighborhood; it is, to a certain extent, a neighborhood affair. Similar in spirit is the Hull House Diet Kitchen, in a little cottage directly back of the nursery. Food is prepared for invalids and orders are taken from physicians and visiting nurses of the district. . . . We sometimes have visions of a kitchen similar in purpose to the New England Kitchen of Boston, but on a more co-operative plan, managed by the Hull House Woman's Club. This club meets one afternoon a week. It is composed of the most able women of the neighborhood, who enjoy the formal addresses and many informal discussions. The economics of food and fuel are often discussed. The Hull House household expenses are frankly compared with those of other households. I have always felt that "friendly visiting," while of great value, was one-sided. To be complete the "friendly visitor" should also be the friendly visited. It is quite possible that looking over her expense book with that of her "case" would be beneficial to her. The residents at Hull House find in themselves a constantly increasing tendency to consult their neighbors on the advisability of each new undertaking. . . .

Hull House has had, I hope, a certain value to the women's trades unions of Chicago. It seems to me of great importance that as trades unions of women are being formed they should be kept, if possible, from falling into the self-same pits the men's unions have fallen into. Women possessing no votes and therefore having little political value will be both of advantage and disadvantage to their unions. Four women's unions meet regularly at Hull House: the book-binders', the shoemakers', the shirtmakers', and the cloakmakers'. The last two were organized at Hull House. It has seemed to us that the sewing trades are most in need of help. They are thoroughly disorganized, Russian and Polish tailors competing against English-speaking tailors, young girls and Italian women competing against both. An efficient union which should combine all these elements seems very difficult, unless it grow strong enough to offer a label and receive unexpected aid from the manufacturers. In that case there would be the hope of co-operation on the part of the consumers, as the fear of contagion from ready-made clothing has at last seized the imagination of the public.

That the trades unions themselves care for what we have done for them is shown by the fact that when the committee of investigation for the sweating system was appointed by the Trades and Labor Assembly, consisting of five delegates from the unions and five from other citizens, two of the latter were residents of Hull House. It is logical that a Settlement should have a certain value in labor complications, having from its very position sympathies entangled on both sides. . . .

I am always sorry to have Hull House regarded as philanthropy, although it doubtless has strong philanthropic tendencies and has several distinct charitable departments which are conscientiously carried on. It is unfair, however, to apply the word philanthropic to the activities of the House as a whole. Charles Booth in his brilliant chapter on "The Unemployed" expresses regret that the problems of the working class are so often confounded with the problems of the inefficient, the idle, and distressed. To confound thus two problems is to render the solution of both impossible. Hull House, while endeavoring to fulfil its obligations to neighbors of varying needs, will do great harm if it confounds distinct problems. Working people live in the same streets with those in need of charity, but they themselves require and want none of it. As one of their number has said, they require only that their aspirations be recognized and stimulated and the means of attaining them put at their disposal. Hull House makes a constant effort to secure these means, but to call that effort philanthropy is to use the word unfairly and to underestimate the duties of good citizenship.

21. Alfred T. White—Model Tenements (1885)

Another approach to the urban housing problem was that of building model tenements. Adopting a plan first developed by English philanthropists, a number of well-to-do Americans built small apartment buildings and rented the flats at rates which, while within the reach of workingmen, afforded the owners modest returns on their investments. They sought thereby to demonstrate that commercial builders could improve the quality of tenements and still make a profit. Alfred T. White of Brooklyn, New York, was a leader of the movement. Between 1876 and 1890 he financed the construction of several projects in his native city, providing housing for more than 2,000 persons. The following essay, "Better Homes for Workingmen," was written by White in 1885.

The condition of the homes of the poor and the manner of life thereby forced on the working classes of our largest cities, if unrestrained, grow worse as a city grows larger.

SOURCE: A. T. White, *Better Homes for Workingmen* (Washington, D.C., 1885), pp. 1-4, 6-7, 10-11.

It is not yet fifty years since, in 1838, the first tenement house in New York was erected in Cherry street. There were on January 1st, 1885, 26,859 such houses, containing much over half the entire population of the city. During 1884 above 1013 such houses (costing under $15,000 each) were built. . . .

There will be no dispute that every workingman should own his own home, if possible, or, next to that, should hire and live in a separate house. These possibilities now exist in all but a few of our cities.

In Philadelphia the Building Societies have accomplished a work, in enabling the average workingman to own his home, which commands the attention of the world. They work on the knowledge that many a workingman can lay aside a few dollars every month and so become in a dozen years owner of his house free of debt, who would never have the self-denial to lay up $1,000 to buy a house outright.

In Boston, Brooklyn, and elsewhere, efforts have been made to provide single small houses, but the dearness of land and of brick place such houses (which cost from $1,000 upwards exclusive of land) out of the reach of average wage earners and within the possible grasp only of men able to pay at least $15 per month, if in the outskirts, or $18 and upward in the cities; while on New York Island the charge for the same accommodations would be raised of necessity to $25 and above, per month. . . .

Can decent and healthy houses be furnished to the laboring classes in all our cities at rentals not greater than they already pay for improper and unhealthy apartments? Unquestionably, YES. . . .

. . . It is easily possible to furnish two rooms and scullery with separate sink, closet, &c., in a new, well-aired, well lighted, healthy edifice—*a home*, entirely in the control of the occupants and complete in itself—for from $1.50 per week upwards, and this sum is within the ability of the poorest paid class of able-bodied breadwinners, when employed regularly, or of a better paid class employed spasmodically.

There is, of course, a class of people who prefer squalor and darkness to decency and light, who need moral reformation, before they can properly be moved into better surroundings. While these squalor-loving classes form a large part of the poor population of London, they are a small minority of the laboring classes in this country, for ambition to do better is the first and

moving impulse of every immigrant to our shores, and this ambition once aroused, would grow here continually were it not over-
borne by conditions so hostile as to annihilate it, and often to
create torpor or despair. . . .

In all efforts to promote the much-needed reforms in the living
conditions of the poor, it must be kept in mind that any ventures
which do not yield a fair return on the money invested are likely
to be cited as arguments *against* efforts to secure legislative action
seeking to impose healthful restrictions on existing or future
buildings. Until "Philanthropy and five per cent." happily joined
hands in Sir Sidney Waterlow's Improved Dwellings in London,
remedial legislation in England was difficult, if not impossible.

The possibility of the provision of such homes has been abun-
dantly proven in New York, Boston and elsewhere. . . .

In Brooklyn the enterprise initiated in 1876 continues to
render complete and equal satisfaction to tenants and owners.
The five blocks of tenements are built with fireproof stairs and
open balconies sunk in the front of the building. Every family has
its own separate scullery, containing water-closet, sink, wash-tub
and ash-shoot. In the last four blocks each apartment is entered
from a short private hall. No bed-rooms open into each other or
into the living-rooms, thus securing complete family privacy. . . .

To those who incline to erect improved dwellings for working
men the following hints may be of service:

Location.—Choose a district where tenement houses *are being
built* by speculative builders; these watch the drift of population
closely. You can afford to pay as much for land as they can, and
high cost is no detriment, *provided* the value is made by the pressure of people seeking residence there. Choose preferably the
border land of the tenement district to the heart of it, unless your
undertaking is a very large one.

Size of Plot.—The larger the better, for a large plot allows superior arrangements for light, air, play-grounds, and also permits the
engagement of the whole time of a competent man or woman as
agent and superintendent of the buildings.

Accommodations.—Three rooms and a scullery are the accommodation sought by most working men; but two rooms and a scullery suffice for small families of two or three people. Learn what
rents are paid by the average working man in the locality selected
and plan building so that your rents average the same, giving the

tenant as many conveniences as this average rental will allow while returning a fair interest on the investment. In determining this it is well to remember that the governing considerations should be: *first*, domestic privacy, the foundation of morality; *second*, sanitary condition, the mainspring of health; *third*, comfort, convenience, attractiveness. . . .

. . . Private owners always oppose all efforts to make or enforce improved building laws, on the ground that such buildings cannot be made to pay. The only argument that weighs with the law makers in answer, is the submission of proof that all that is demanded has been, and therefore can be, given to tenants while not interfering with a fair return on the investment. Just so fast as it can be shown that further restrictions can be put on new or old tenement houses without lowering the income below what other property returns, with fair allowances for deterioration and trouble, so fast legislation can be had, and nothing short of a visitation of cholera or yellow fever is likely to advance it faster than that.

But far more than the comforts of the tenants themselves is involved in the increased overcrowding of the poor, though that alone should be more than enough to stir any legislative body to vigorous action.

Crowded, ill-constructed tenement houses propagate' diseases and send them out by a thousand channels to work upon the well-to-do and rich a sure retribution for their neglect of their poorer neighbors. The stern necessity of acting for self-preservation may ultimately enforce that attention which, as a pleasant duty to our less fortunate brothers, is now neglected. Millions of money may rebuild unwholesome buildings or pay for their destruction, but who will value the thousands of lives yet to be sacrificed and the ten thousands whose physical and moral strength is yet to be weakened every year that such conditions endure as exist to-day in many of our cities?

In many cities there is no need to wait for State Legislative action, the local authorities often have authority to make or amend building and health ordinance or laws. In no way can a little work do more good than by pressing this idea on the Government of every city. No city can act too early. The ounce of prevention is both better and cheaper than the pound of cure. New York should take warning from London and Glasgow, and every other city from New York. If overcrowding is not prevented its remedy is difficult and costly in the extreme, and the longer delayed the more costly and difficult. . . .

22. Jacob Riis—
Life on New York's Lower East Side (1890)

The failure of housing reformers to influence the general character of slum life appreciably is dramatically illustrated by Jacob Riis's book, *How the Other Half Lives* (1890). Riis emigrated to the United States from Denmark in 1870 and became a New York newspaper reporter. His work soon gave him an intimate knowledge of New York's dreadful tenement districts. He was appalled by what he saw. After becoming acquainted with Alfred T. White, whose model houses convinced him that slum tenements were not a necessary evil, he decided to write *How the Other Half Lives*. The book created a sensation, its impact heightened by graphic photographs taken by the author.

Although his indignation at the horrifying conditions he observed in the slums was genuine, Riis had only a limited grasp of the causes of these conditions. He was not above prejudice, as the following selection shows, and believed that in the last analysis the immigrants who inhabited the slums were at least partly responsible for their own degradation.

Down below Chatham Square, in the old Fourth Ward, where the cradle of the tenement stood, we shall find New York's Other Half at home, receiving such as care to call and are not afraid. . . . Leaving the Elevated Railroad where it dives under the Brooklyn Bridge at Franklin Square, scarce a dozen steps will take us where we wish to go. With its rush and roar echoing yet in our ears, we have turned the corner from prosperity to poverty. We stand upon the domain of the tenement. . . .

. . . This one, with its shabby front and poorly patched roof, what glowing firesides, what happy children may it once have owned? Heavy feet, too often with unsteady step, for the pot-house is next door—where is it not next door in these slums?—have worn away the brown-stone steps since; the broken columns at the door have rotted away at the base. Of the handsome cornice barely a trace is left. Dirt and desolation reign in the wide hallway, and danger lurks on the stairs. Rough pine boards fence off the roomy fire-places—where coal is bought by the pail at the rate of twelve

SOURCE: Jacob Riis, *How the Other Half Lives* (New York, 1890), pp. 28-30, 32-3, 40-2.

dollars a ton these have no place. The arched gateway leads no longer to a shady bower on the banks of the rushing stream, inviting to day-dreams with its gentle repose, but to a dark and nameless alley, shut in by high brick walls, cheerless as the lives of those they shelter. The wolf knocks loudly at the gate in the troubled dreams that come to this alley, echoes of the day's cares. A horde of dirty children play about the dripping hydrant, the only thing in the alley that thinks enough of its chance to make the most of it: it is the best it can do. These are the children of the tenements, the growing generation of the slums; this their home. . . .

Some idea of what is meant by a sanitary "cleaning up" in these slums may be gained from the account of a mishap I met with once, in taking a flash-light picture of a group of blind beggars in one of the tenements down here. With unpractised hands I managed to set fire to the house. When the blinding effect of the flash had passed away and I could see once more, I discovered that a lot of paper and rags that hung on the wall were ablaze. There were six of us, five blind men and women who knew nothing of their danger, and myself, in an attic room with a dozen crooked, rickety stairs between us and the street, and as many households as helpless as the one whose guest I was all about us. The thought: how were they ever to be got out? made my blood run cold as I saw the flames creeping up the wall, and my first impulse was to bolt for the street and shout for help. The next was to smother the fire myself, and I did, with a vast deal of trouble. Afterward, when I came down to the street I told a friendly policeman of my trouble. For some reason he thought it rather a good joke, and laughed immoderately at my concern lest even then sparks should be burrowing in the rotten wall that might yet break out in flame and destroy the house with all that were in it. He told me why, when he found time to draw breath. "Why, don't you know," he said, "that house is the Dirty Spoon? It caught fire six times last winter, but it wouldn't burn. The dirt was so thick on the walls, it smothered the fire!" . . .

. . . As we stroll from one narrow street to another the odd contrast between the low, old-looking houses in front and the towering tenements in the back yards grows even more striking, perhaps because we expect and are looking for it. Nobody who was not would suspect the presence of the rear houses, though they have been there long enough. Here is one seven stories high behind one with only three floors. Take a look into this Roosevelt Street alley; just about one step wide, with a five-story house on one side that gets its light and air—God help us for pitiful mockery!— from this slit between brick walls. There are no windows in the wall on the other side; it is perfectly blank. The fire-escapes of the long tenement fairly touch it; but the rays of the sun, rising, setting, or at high noon, never do. It never shone into the alley from the day the devil planned and man built it. . . .

. . . Here, as we stroll along Madison Street, workmen are busy putting the finishing touches to the brown-stone front of a tall new tenement. This one will probably be called an apartment house. They are carving satyrs' heads in the stone, with a crowd of gaping youngsters looking on in admiring wonder. Next door are two other tenements, likewise with brown-stone fronts, fair to look at. The youngest of the children in the group is not too young to remember how their army of tenants was turned out by the health officers because the houses had been condemned as unfit for human beings to live in. The owner was a wealthy builder who "stood high in the community." Is it only in our fancy that the sardonic leer on the stone faces seems to list that way? Or is it an introspective grin? We will not ask if the new house belongs to the same builder. He too may have reformed.

We have crossed the boundary of the Seventh Ward. Penitentiary Row, suggestive name for a block of Cherry Street tenements, is behind us. Within recent days it has become peopled wholly with Hebrews, the overflow from Jewtown adjoining, pedlars and tailors, all of them. It is odd to read this legend from other days over the door: "No pedlars allowed in this house." These thrifty people are not only crowding into the tenements of this once exclusive district—they are buying them. The Jew runs to real estate as soon as he can save up enough for a deposit to clinch the bargain. As fast as the old houses are torn down, towering structures go up in their place, and Hebrews are found to be the builders. Here is a whole alley nicknamed after the intruder, Jews' Alley. But abuse and ridicule are not weapons to fight the Israelite with. He pockets them quietly with the rent and bides his time. He knows from experience, both sweet and bitter, that all things come to those who wait, including the houses and lands of their persecutors. . . .

Part VII

The Political Test

23. James Bryce—
The American Presidency (1888)

With the possible exception of Alexis de Tocqueville, the most insightful and best-known foreign commentator on American civilization was Scotsman James Bryce, whose book *The American Commonwealth* has been recognized ever since its publication in 1888 as a classic. Bryce understood the United States well, having traveled extensively throughout the country and gotten to know hundreds of its citizens. He was, in addition, a first-rate scholar, well versed in the history of the nation and its complex political institutions. He approached the task of writing about the United States from the point of view of an enlightened conservative. Dsepite the magisterial tone of his work—he seemed to be examining the country the way a scientist studies a strange tissue under a microscope—Bryce was somehow able to criticize and at the same time project a feeling of sympathy. He had a keen eye for the foibles and inadequacies of the American people, but unlike so many foreign observers he was never patronizing or carping in his judgments. As a result, his work was not only respected but also admired by a host of American readers.

Although *The American Commonwealth* deals broadly with nearly every aspect of life in the United States, it is primarily a study of the political system. The section reproduced below, one of the most famous in the book, analyzes the office of the President.

Although the President has been, not that independent good citizen whom the framers of the Constitution contemplated, but, at least during the last sixty years, a party man, seldom much above the average in character or abilities, the office has attained the main objects for which it was created. Such mistakes as have been made in foreign policy, or in the conduct of the administra-

SOURCE: James Bryce, *The American Commonwealth* (New York, 1897), I, 70-4, 76-84.

tive departments, have been rarely owing to the constitution of the office or to the errors of its holder. This is more than one who should review the history of Europe during the last hundred years could say of any European monarchy. Nevertheless, the faults chargeable on hereditary kingship, faults more serious than Englishmen, who have watched with admiration the wisdom of the Crown during the present reign, usually realize, must not make us overlook certain defects incidental to the American presidency, perhaps to any plan of vesting the headship of the State in a person elected for a limited period.

In a country where there is no hereditary throne nor hereditary aristocracy, an office raised far above all other offices offers too great a stimulus to ambition. This glittering prize, always dangling before the eyes of prominent statesmen, has a power stronger than any dignity under a European crown to lure them (as it lured Clay and Webster) from the path of straightforward consistency. One who aims at the presidency—and all prominent politicians do aim at it—has the strongest possible motives to avoid making enemies. Now a great statesman ought to be prepared to make enemies. It is one thing to try to be popular—an unpopular man will be uninfluential—it is another to seek popularity by courting every section of your party. This is the temptation of presidential aspirants.

A second defect is that the presidential election, occurring once in four years, throws the country for several months into a state of turmoil, for which there may be no occasion. . . .

Again, these regularly recurring elections produce a discontinuity of policy. Even when the new President belongs to the same party as his predecessor, he usually nominates a new cabinet, having to reward his especial supporters. Many of the inferior offices are changed; men who have learned their work make way for others who have everything to learn. If the new President belongs to the opposite party, the change of officials is far more sweeping, and involves larger changes of policy. The evil would be more serious were it not that in foreign policy, where the need for continuity is greatest, the United States has little to do, and that the co-operation of the Senate in this department qualifies the divergence of the ideas of one President from those of another.

Fourthly. The fact that he is re-eligible once, but (practically) only once, operates unfavourably on the President. He is tempted to play for a re-nomination by so pandering to active sections of his own party, or so using his patronage to conciliate influential politicians, as to make them put him forward at the next election. On the other hand, if he is in his second term of office, he has no longer much motive to regard the interests of the nation at large, because he sees that his own political death is near. . . .

. . . Even when we allow for the defects last enumerated, the presidential office, if not one of the best features of the American Constitution, is nowise to be deemed a failure. The problem of constructing a stable executive in a democratic country is indeed so immensely difficult that anything short of a failure deserves to be called a success. Now the President has, during ninety-nine years, carried on the internal administrative business of the nation with due efficiency. Once or twice, as when Jefferson purchased Louisiana, and Lincoln emancipated the slaves in the revolted States, he has courageously ventured on stretches of authority, held at the time to be doubtfully constitutional, yet necessary, and approved by the judgment of posterity. He has kept the machinery working quietly and steadily when Congress has been distracted by party strife, or paralyzed by the dissensions of the two Houses, or enfeebled by the want of first-rate leaders. The executive has been able, at moments of peril, to rise almost to a dictatorship, as during the War of Secession, and when peace returned, to sink back into its proper constitutional position. It has shown no tendency so to dwarf the other authorities of the State as to pave the way for a monarchy.

Europeans are struck by the faults of a plan which plunges the nation into a whirlpool of excitement once every four years, and commits the headship of the State to a party leader chosen for a short period. But there is another aspect in which the presidential election may be regarded, and one whose importance is better appreciated in America than in Europe. The election is a solemn periodical appeal to the nation to review its condition, the way in which its business has been carried on, the conduct of the two great parties. It stirs and rouses the nation as nothing else does, forces every one not merely to think about public affairs but to decide how he judges the parties. It is a direct expression of the will of twelve millions of voters, a force before which everything must bow. It refreshes the sense of national duty; and at great crises it intensifies national patriotism. . . .

To a European observer, weary of the slavish obsequiousness

and lip-deep adulation with which the members of reigning families are treated on the eastern side of the Atlantic, fawned on in public and carped at in private, the social relations of an American President to his people are eminently refreshing. There is a great respect for the office, and a corresponding respect for the man as the holder of the office, if he has done nothing to degrade it. There is no servility, no fictitious self-abasement on the part of the citizens, but a simple and hearty deference to one who represents the majesty of the nation, the sort of respect which the proudest Roman paid to the consulship, even if the particular consul was, like Cicero, a "new man." The curiosity of the visitors who throng the White House on reception days is sometimes too familiar; but this fault tends to disappear, and Presidents have now more reason to complain of the persecutions they endure from an incessantly observant journalism. After oscillating between the ceremonious state of George Washington, who drove to open Congress in his coach and six, with outriders and footmen in livery, and the ostentatious plainness of Citizen Jefferson, who would ride up alone and hitch his horse to the post at the gate, the President has settled down into an attitude between that of the mayor of a great English town on a public occasion, and that of a European cabinet minister on a political tour. . . .

Europeans often ask, and Americans do not always explain, how it happens that this great office, the greatest in the world, unless we except the Papacy, to which any one can rise by his own merits, is not more frequently filled by great and striking men. In America, which is beyond all other countries the country of a "career open to talents," a country, moreover, in which political life is unusually keen and political ambition widely diffused, it might be expected that the highest place would always be won by a man of brilliant gifts. But since the heroes of the Revolution died out with Jefferson and Adams and Madison some sixty years ago, no person except General Grant has reached the chair whose name would have been remembered had he not been President, and no President except Abraham Lincoln has displayed rare or striking qualities in the chair. Who now knows or cares to know anything about the personality of James K. Polk or Franklin Pierce? The only thing remarkable about them is that being so commonplace they should have climbed so high.

Several reasons may be suggested for the fact, which Americans are themselves the first to admit.

One is that the proportion of first-rate ability drawn into politics is smaller in America than in most European countries. . . . In France and Italy, where half-revolutionary conditions have made public life exciting and accessible; in Germany, where an admirably-organized civil service cultivates and develops statecraft with unusual success; in England, where many persons of wealth and leisure seek to enter the political arena, while burning questions touch the interests of all classes and make men eager observers of the combatants, the total quantity of talent devoted to parliamentary or administrative work is larger, relatively to the population, than in America, where much of the best ability, both for thought and for action, for planning and for executing, rushes into a field which is comparatively narrow in Europe, the business of developing the material resources of the country.

Another is that the methods and habits of Congress, and indeed of political life generally, give fewer opportunities for personal distinction, fewer modes in which a man may commend himself to his countrymen by eminent capacity in thought, in speech, or in administration, than is the case in the free countries of Europe. . . .

A third reason is that eminent men make more enemies, and give those enemies more assailable points, than obscure men do. They are therefore in so far less desirable candidates. It is true that the eminent man has also made more friends, that his name is more widely known, and may be greeted with louder cheers. Other things being equal, the famous man is preferable. But other things never are equal. The famous man has probably attacked some leaders in his own party, has supplanted others, has expressed his dislike to the crotchet of some active section, has perhaps committed errors which are capable of being magnified into offences. No man stands long before the public and bears a part in great affairs without giving openings to censorious criticism. Fiercer far than the light which beats upon a throne is the light which beats upon a presidential candidate, searching out all the recesses of his past life. Hence, when the choice lies between a brilliant man and a safe man, the safe man is preferred. Party feeling, strong enough to carry in on its back a man without conspicuous positive merits, is not always strong enough to procure for-giveness for a man with positive faults.

A European finds that this phenomenon needs in its turn to be explained, for in the free countries of Europe brilliancy, be it elo-quence in speech, or some striking achievement in war or admin-istration, or the power through whatever means of somehow impressing the popular imagination, is what makes a leader trium-phant. Why should it be otherwise in America? Because in Amer-ica party loyalty and party organization have been hitherto so per-fect that any one put forward by the party will get the full party vote if his character is good and his "record," as they call it, un-stained. The safe candidate may not draw in quite so many votes from the moderate men of the other side as the brilliant one would, but he will not lose nearly so many from his own ranks. Even those who admit his mediocrity will vote straight when the moment for voting comes. Besides, the ordinary American voter does not object to mediocrity. He has a lower conception of the qualities requisite to make a statesman than those who direct public opinion in Europe have. He likes his candidate to be sen-sible, vigorous, and, above all, what he calls "magnetic," and does not value, because he sees no need for, originality or profun-dity, a fine culture or a wide knowledge. Candidates are selected to be run for nomination by knots of persons who, however expert as party tacticians, are usually commonplace men; and the choice between those selected for nomination is made by a very large body, an assembly of over eight hundred delegates from the local party organizations over the country, who are certainly no better than ordinary citizens. . . .

It must also be remembered that the merits of a President are one thing and those of a candidate another thing. An eminent American is reported to have said to friends who wished to put him forward, "Gentlemen, let there be no mistake. I should make a good President, but a very bad candidate." Now to a party it is more important that its nominee should be a good candidate than that he should turn out a good President. A nearer danger is a greater danger. As Saladin says in *The Talisman,* "A wild cat in a chamber is more dangerous than a lion in a distant desert." It will be a misfortune to the party, as well as to the country, if the can-didate elected should prove a bad President. But it is a greater misfortune to the party that it should be beaten in the impending election, for the evil of losing national patronage will have come four years sooner. "B" (so reason the leaders) , "who is one of our possible candidates, may be an abler man than A, who is the other. But we have a better chance of winning with A than with B, while X, the candidate of our opponents, is anyhow no better than A. We must therefore run A." This reasoning is all the more forcible because the previous career of the possible candidates has generally made it easier to say who will succeed as a candidate than who will succeed as a President; and because the wire-pullers with whom the choice rests are better judges of the former question than of the latter.

After all, too, a President need not be a man of brilliant intellectual gifts. His main duties are to be prompt and firm in securing the due execution of the laws and maintaining the public peace, careful and upright in the choice of the executive officials of the country. Eloquence, whose value is apt to be overrated in all free countries, imagination, profundity of thought or extent of knowledge, are all in so far a gain to him that they make him "a bigger man," and help him to gain over the nation an influence which, if he be a true patriot, he may use for its good. But they are not necessary for the due discharge in ordinary times of the duties of his post. Four-fifths of his work is the same in kind as that which devolves on the chairman of a commercial company or the manager of a railway, the work of choosing good subordinates, seeing that they attend to their business, and taking a sound practical view of such administrative questions as require his decision. Firmness, common sense, and most of all, honesty, an honesty above all suspicion of personal interest, are the qualities which the country chiefly needs in its first magistrate.

So far we have been considering personal merits. But in the selection of a candidate many considerations have to be regarded besides the personal merits, whether of a candidate, or of a possible President. The chief of these considerations is the amount of support which can be secured from different States or from different "sections" of the Union, a term by which the Americans denote groups of States with a broad community of interest. State feeling and sectional feeling are powerful factors in a presidential election. The North-west, including the States from Ohio to Dakota, is now the most populous section of the Union, and therefore counts for most in an election. It naturally conceives that its interests will be best protected by one who knows them from birth and residence. Hence *prima facie* a North-western man makes the best candidate. A large State casts a heavier vote in the election; and every State is of course more likely to be carried by one of its own children than by a stranger, because his fellow-citizens, while they feel honoured by the choice, gain also a substantial advantage, having a better prospect of such favours as the administration can bestow. Hence, *coeteris paribus,* a man from a large State is preferable as a candidate. The problem is further complicated by the fact that some States are already safe for one or other party, while others are doubtful. The North-western and New England States are most of them likely to go Republican: the Southern States are (at present) all of them certain to go Democratic. *Coeteris paribus,* a candidate from a doubtful State, such as New York and Indiana have usually been, is to be preferred.

Other minor disqualifying circumstances require less explanation. A Roman Catholic, or an avowed disbeliever in Christianity, would be an undesirable candidate. Since the close of the Civil War, any one who fought, especially if he fought with distinction, in the Northern army, has enjoyed great advantages, for the soldiers of that army, still numerous, rally to his name. The two elections of General Grant, who knew nothing of politics, and the fact that his influence survived the faults of his long administration, are evidence of the weight of this consideration.

On a railway journey in the Far West in 1883 I fell in with two newspaper men from the State of Indiana, who were taking their holiday. The conversation turned on the next presidential election. They spoke hopefully of the chances for nomination by their party of an Indiana man, a comparatively obscure person, whose name I had never heard. I expressed some surprise that he should be thought of. They observed that he had done well in State politics, that there was nothing against him, that Indiana would work for him. "But," I rejoined, "ought you not to have a man of more commanding character? There is Senator A. Everybody tells me that he is the shrewdest and most experienced man in your party, and that he has a perfectly clean record. Why not run him?" "Why, yes," they answered, "that is all true. But you see he comes from a small State, and we have got that State already. Besides, he wasn't in the war. Our man was. Indiana's vote is worth having, and if our man is run, we can carry Indiana."

"Surely the race is not to the swift, nor the battle to the strong, neither yet bread to the wise, nor yet riches to men of understanding, nor yet favour to men of skill, but time and chance happeneth to them all."

These secondary considerations do not always prevail. Intellectual ability and force of character must influence the choice of a candidate, and their influence is sometimes decisive. They count for more when times are so critical that the need for a strong man is felt. Reformers declare that their weight will go on increasing as the disgust of good citizens with the methods of professional politicians increases. But for many generations past it is not the greatest men in the Roman Church that have been chosen Popes, nor the most brilliant men in the Anglican Church that have been appointed Archbishops of Canterbury.

Although several Presidents have survived their departure from office by many years, only one, John Quincy Adams, played a part in politics after quitting the White House. It may be that the ex-President has not been a great leader before his accession to office; it may be that he does not care to exert himself after he has held and dropped the great prize, and found (one may safely add) how little of a prize it is. Something, however, must also be ascribed to other features of the political system of the country. It is often hard to find a vacancy in the representation of a given State through which to re-enter Congress; it is disagreeable to recur to the arts by which seats are secured. Past greatness is rather an encumbrance than a help to resuming a political career. Exalted power, on which the unsleeping eye of hostile critics was fixed, has probably disclosed all a President's weaknesses, and has either forced him to make enemies by disobliging adherents, or exposed him to censure for subservience to party interests. He is regarded as having had his day; he belongs already to the past, and unless, like Grant, he is endeared to the people by the memory of some splendid service, or is available to his party as a possible candidate for a further term of office, he soon sinks into the crowd or avoids neglect by retirement. Possibly he may deserve to be forgotten; but more frequently he is a man of sufficient ability and character to make the experience he has gained valuable to the country, could it be retained in a place where he might turn it to account. They managed things better at Rome, gathering into their Senate all the fame and experience, all the wisdom and skill, of those who had ruled and fought as consuls and praetors at home and abroad.

We may now answer the question from which we started. Great men are not chosen Presidents, first because great men are rare in politics; secondly, because the method of choice does not bring them to the top; thirdly, because they are not, in quiet times, absolutely needed. . . .

24. Woodrow Wilson—
The House of Representatives (1885)

Woodrow Wilson's *Congressional Government* (1885) was one of the first doctoral dissertations in political science written in the United States and it is still one of the most notable. Actually, *Congressional Government* was not so much a work of scholarship as a practical political analysis. Wilson considered himself at this period of his life a frustrated statesman; he took a Ph.D. at Johns Hopkins University because he had decided that he could never achieve political office and must satisfy his ambition by influencing politics indirectly, as a critic. A fervent admirer of the British parliamentary system, he saw the federal government of his day as being dominated by a leaderless, chaotic House of Representatives. The main thread of his argument can be observed in the following selection.

Like a vast picture thronged with figures of equal prominence and crowded with elaborate and obtrusive details, Congress is hard to see satisfactorily and appreciatively at a single view and from a single stand-point. Its complicated forms and diversified structure confuse the vision, and conceal the system which underlies its composition. It is too complex to be understood without an effort, without a careful and systematic process of analysis. Consequently, very few people do understand it, and its doors are practically shut against the comprehension of the public at large. If Congress had a few authoritative leaders whose figures were very distinct and very conspicuous to the eye of the world, and who could represent and stand for the national legislature in the thoughts of that very numerous, and withal very respectable, class of persons who must think specifically and in concrete forms when they think at all, those persons who can make something out of men but very little out of intangible generalizations, it would be quite within the region of possibilities for the majority of the nation to follow the course of legislation without any very serious confusion

SOURCE: Woodrow Wilson, *Congressional Government* (New York, 1885) pp. 58–61, 70–1, 81–2, 9–14, 97, 100, 117–18, 318, 332–3.

of thought. I suppose that almost everybody who just now gives any heed to the policy of Great Britain, with regard even to the reform of the franchise and other like strictly legislative questions, thinks of Mr. Gladstone and his colleagues rather than of the House of Commons, whose servants they are. The question is not, What will Parliament do? but, What will Mr. Gladstone do? And there is even less doubt that it is easier and more natural to look upon the legislative designs of Germany as locked up behind Bismarck's heavy brows than to think of them as dependent upon the determinations of the Reichstag, although as a matter of fact its consent is indispensable even to the plans of the imperious and domineering Chancellor.

But there is no great minister or ministry to represent the will and being of Congress in the common thought. The Speaker of the House of Representatives stands as near to leadership as any one; but his will does not run as a formative and imperative power in legislation much beyond the appointment of the committees who are to lead the House and do its work for it, and it is, therefore, not entirely satisfactory to the public mind to trace all legislation to him. He may have a controlling hand in starting it; but he sits too still in his chair, and is too evidently not on the floor of the body over which he presides, to make it seem probable to the ordinary judgment that he has much immediate concern in legislation after it is once set afoot. Everybody knows that he is a staunch and avowed partisan, and that he likes to make smooth, whenever he can, the legislative paths of his party; but it does not seem likely that all importan measures originate with him, or that he is the author of every distinct policy. And in fact he is not. He is a great party chief, but the hedging circumstances of his official position as presiding officer prevent his performing the part of active leadership. He appoints the leaders of the House, but he is not himself its leader.

The leaders of the House are the chairmen of the principal Standing Committees. Indeed, to be exactly accurate, the House has as many leaders as there are subjects of legislation, for there are as many Standing Committees as there are leading classes of legislation, and in the consideration of every topic of business the House is guided by a special leader in the person of the chairman of the Standing Committee, charged with the superintendence of measures of the particular class to which that topic belongs. It is this multiplicity of leaders, this many-headed leadership, which makes the organization of the House too complex to afford uninformed people and unskilled observers any easy clue to its methods of rule. For the chairmen of the Standing Committees do not constitute a cooperative body like a ministry. They do not consult and concur in the adoption of homogeneous and mutually helpful measures; there is no thought of acting in concert. Each Committee goes its own way at its own pace. It is impossible to discover any unity or method in the disconnected and therefore unsystematic, confused, and desultory action of the House, or any common purpose in the measures which its Committees from time to time recommend. . . .

Of course it goes without saying that the practical effect of this Committee organization of the House is to consign to each of the Standing Committees the entire direction of legislation upon those subjects which properly come to its consideration. As to those subjects it is entitled to the initiative, and all legislative action with regard to them is under its overruling guidance. It gives shape and course to the determinations of the House. In one respect, however, its initiative is limited. Even a Standing Committee cannot report a bill whose subject-matter has not been referred to it by the House, "by the rules or otherwise"; it cannot volunteer advice on questions upon which its advice has not been asked. But this is not a serious, not even an operative, limitation upon its functions of suggestion and leadership; for it is a very simple matter to get referred to it any subject it wishes to introduce to the attention of the House. Its chairman, or one of its leading members, frames a bill covering the point upon which the Committee wishes to suggest legislation; brings it in, in his capacity as a private member, on Monday, when the call of States is made; has it referred to his Committee; and thus secures an opportunity for the making of the desired report.

It is by this imperious authority of the Standing Committees that the new member is stayed and thwarted whenever he seeks to take an active part in the business of the House. Turn which way he may, some privilege of the Committees stands in his path. The rules are so framed as to put all business under their management; and one of the discoveries which the new member is sure to make, albeit after many trying experiences and sobering adventures and as his first session draws towards its close, is, that under their sway freedom of debate finds no place of allowance, and that his long-delayed speech must remain unspoken. For even a long congressional session is too short to afford time for a full consideration of all the reports of the forty-seven Committees, and debate upon them must be rigidly cut short, if not altogether excluded, if any considerable part of the necessary business is to be gotten through with before adjournment. . . .

One very noteworthy result of this system is to shift the theatre of debate upon legislation from the floor of Congress to the privacy of the committee-rooms. Provincial gentlemen who read the Associated Press dispatches in their morning papers as they sit over their coffee at breakfast are doubtless often very sorely puzzled by certain of the items which sometimes appear in the brief telegraphic notes from Washington. What can they make of this for instance: "The House Committee on Commerce to-day heard arguments from the congressional delegation from" such and such States "in advocacy of appropriations for river and harbor improvements which the members desire incorporated in the River and Harbor Appropriations Bill"? They probably do not understand that it would have been useless for members not of the Committee on Commerce to wait for any opportunity to make their suggestions on the floor of Congress, where the measure to which they wish to make additions would be under the authoritative control of the Committee, and where, consequently, they could gain a hearing only by the courteous sufferance of the committee-man in charge of the report. Whatever is to be done must be done by or through the Committee.

It would seem, therefore, that practically Congress, or at any rate the House of Representatives, delegates not only its legislative but also its deliberative functions to its Standing Committees. The little public debate that arises under the stringent and urgent rules of the House is formal rather than effective, and it is the discussions which take place in the Committees that give form to legislation. . . .

But there are other reasons still more organic than these why the debates of Congress cannot, under our present system, have that serious purpose of search into the merits of policies and that definite and determine party—or, if you will, partisan—aim without which they can never be effective for the instruction of public opinion, or the cleansing of political action. The chief of these reasons, because the parent of all the rest, is that there are in Congress no authoritative leaders who are the recognized spokesmen of their parties. Power is nowhere concentrated: it is rather deliberately and of set policy scattered amongst many small chiefs. It is divided up, as it were, into forty-seven seigniories, in each of which a Standing Committee is the court-baron and its chairman lord-proprietor. These petty barons, some of them not a little powerful, but none of them within reach of the full powers of rule, may at will exercise an almost despotic sway within their own shires, and may sometimes threaten to convulse even the realm itself; but both their mutual jealousies and their brief and restricted opportunities forbid their combining, and each is very far from the office of common leader.

I know that to some this scheme of distributed power and disintegrated rule seems a very excellent device whereby we are enabled to escape a dangerous "one-man power" and an untoward concentration of functions; and it is very easy to see and appreciate the considerations which make this view of committee government so popular. It is based upon a very proper and salutary fear of *irresponsible* power; and those who most resolutely maintain it always fight from the position that all leadership in legislation is hard to restrain in proportion to its size and to the strength of its prerogatives, and that to divide it is to make it manageable. They aver, besides, that the less a man has to do—that is to say, the more he is confined to single departments and to definite details—the more intelligent and thorough will his work be. They like the Committees, therefore, just because they are many and weak, being quite willing to abide their being despotic within their narrow spheres.

It seems evident, however, when the question is looked at from another stand-point, that, as a matter of fact and experience, the more power is divided the more irresponsible it becomes. A mighty baron who can call half the country to arms is watched with greater jealousy, and, therefore, restrained with more vigilant care than is ever vouchsafed the feeble master of a single and solitary castle. The one cannot stir abroad upon an innocent pleasure jaunt without attracting the suspicious attention of the whole country-side; the other may vex and harry his entire neighborhood without fear of let or hindrance. It is ever the little foxes that spoil the grapes. At any rate, to turn back from illustration to

the facts of the argument, it is plain enough that the petty character of the leadership of each Committee contributes towards
making its despotism sure by making its duties uninteresting. . . .

In a word, the national parties do not act in Congress under the
restraint of a sense of immediate responsibility. Responsibility is
spread thin; and no vote or debate can gather it. It rests not so
much upon parties as upon individuals; and it rests upon individuals in no such way as would make it either just or efficacious to
visit upon them the iniquity of any legislative act. Looking at government from a practical and businesslike, rather than from a
theoretical and abstractly-ethical point of view,—treating the business of government as a business,—it seems to be unquestionably
and in a high degree desirable that all legislation should distinctly
represent the action of parties as parties. I know that it has been
proposed by enthusiastic, but not too practical, reformers to do
away with parties by some legerdemain of governmental recon-
struction, accompanied and supplemented by some rehabilitation,
devoutly to be wished, of the virtues least commonly controlling
in fallen human nature; but it seems to me that it would be
more difficult and less desirable than these amiable persons suppose to conduct a government of the many by means of any other
device than party organization, and that the great need is, not to
get rid of parties, but to find and use some expedient by which
they can be managed and made amenable from day to day to
public opinion. Plainly this cannot be effected by punishing here
and there a member of Congress who has voted for a flagrantly
dishonest appropriation bill, or an obnoxious measure relating
to the tariff. Unless the punishment can be extended to the party
—if any such be recognizable—with which these members have
voted, no advantage has been won for self-government, and no
triumph has been gained by public opinion. It should be desired
that parties should act in distinct organizations, in accordance
with avowed principles, under easily recognized leaders, in order
that the voters might be able to declare by their ballots, not only
their condemnation of any past policy, by withdrawing all support from the party responsible for it; but also and particularly
their will as to the future administration of the government, by
bringing into power a party pledged to the adoption of an ac-
ceptable policy.

It is, therefore, a fact of the most serious consequence that by our system of congressional rule no such means of controlling legislation is afforded. Outside of Congress the organization of the national parties is exceedingly well-defined and tangible; no one could wish it, and few could imagine it, more so; but within Congress it is obscure and intangible. Our parties marshal their adherents with the strictest possible discipline for the purpose of carrying elections, but their discipline is very slack and indefinite in dealing with legislation. At least there is within Congress no *visible*, and therefore no *controllable* party organization. The only bond of cohesion is the caucus, which occasionally whips a party together for cooperative action against the time for casting its vote upon some critical question. There is always a majority and a minority, indeed, but the legislation of a session does not represent the policy of either; it is simply an aggregate of the bills recommended by Committees composed of members from both sides of the House, and it is known to be usually, not the work of the majority men upon the Committees, but compromise conclusions bearing some shade or tinge of each of the variously-colored opinions and wishes of the committeemen of both parties.

It is plainly the representation of both parties on the Committees that makes party responsibility indistinct and organized party action almost impossible. If the Committees were composed entirely of members of the majority, and were thus constituted representatives of the party in power, the whole course of congressional proceedings would unquestionably take on a very different aspect. There would then certainly be a compact opposition to face the organized majority. Committee reports would be taken to represent the views of the party in power, and, instead of the scattered, unconcerted opposition, without plan or leaders, which now sometimes subjects the propositions of the Committees to vexatious hindrances and delays, there would spring up debate under skillful masters of opposition, who could drill their partisans for effective warfare and give shape and meaning to the purposes of the minority. . . .

The British system is perfected party government. No effort is made in the Commons, such as is made in the House of Representatives in the composition of the Committees, to give the minority a share in law-making. Our minorities are strongly represented on the Standing Committees; the minority in the Commons is not represented at all in the cabinet. It is this feature of closely organized party government, whereby the responsibility for legislation is saddled upon the majority, which, as I have already pointed out, gives to the debates and action of parliament an interest altogether denied to the proceedings of Congress. All legislation is made a contest for party supremacy, and if legislation goes wrong, or the majority becomes discontented with the course of policy, there is nothing for it but that the ministers should resign and give place to the leaders of the Opposition, unless a new election should procure for them a recruited following. Under such a system mere silent voting is out of the question; debate is a primary necessity. It brings the representatives of the people and the ministers of the Crown face to face. The principal measures of each session originate with the ministers, and embody the policy of the administration. Unlike the reports of our Standing Committees, which are intended to be simply the digested substance of the more sensible bills introduced by private members, the bills introduced into the House of Commons by the cabinet embody the definite schemes of the government; and the fact that the Ministry is made up of the leaders of the majority and represents always the principles of its party, makes the minority only the more anxious to have a chance to criticise its proposals. Cabinet government is a device for bringing the executive and legislative branches into harmony and cooperation without uniting or confusing their functions. . . .

As at present constituted, the federal government lacks strength because its powers are divided, lacks promptness because its authorities are multiplied, lacks wieldiness because its processes are roundabout, lacks efficiency because its responsibility is indistinct and its action without competent direction. It is a government in which every officer may talk about every other officer's duty without having to render strict account for not doing his own, and in which the masters are held in check and offered contradiction by the servants. . . .

The charm of our constitutional ideal has now been long enough wound up to enable sober men who do not believe in political witchcraft to judge what it has accomplished, and is likely still to accomplish, without further winding. The Constitution is not honored by blind worship. The more open-eyed we become, as a nation, to its defects, and the prompter we grow in applying with the unhesitating courage of conviction all thoroughly-tested or well-considered expedients necessary to make self-government among us a straightforward thing of simple method, single, unstinted power, and clear responsibility, the nearer will we approach to the sound sense and practical genius of the great and honorable statesmen of 1787. And the first step towards emancipation from the timidity and false pride which have led us to seek to thrive despite the defects of our national system rather than seem to deny its perfection is a fearless criticism of that system. When we shall have examined all its parts without sentiment, and gauged all its functions by the standards of practical common sense, we shall have established anew our right to the claim of political sagacity; and it will remain only to act intelligently upon what our opened eyes have seen in order to prove again the justice of our claim to political genius.

25. Rutherford B. Hayes—Executive Order on Political Assessments (1887)

The inadequacies of the political system that men like Bryce and Wilson described were a constant source of alarm to many thoughtful Americans in the 1870's and 1880's. That much could be done about these inadequacies, however, seemed problematical; it was easy to complain about such things as uninspired presidential leadership and the inefficiency of Congress, but difficult to suggest practicable means of improving the situation. Civil service reform was an exception to this generalization. The hoary spoils system, never a very good way of recruiting and maintaining an efficient bureaucracy, was becoming each year more burdensome and ineffective as both the number of government jobs and the technical requirements of the posts increased. The scandals of the Grant era brought demands for reform to a head, and the chief campaign promise of Rutherford B. Hayes during the election campaign of 1876 had been to institute significant changes. One of the evils most bitterly complained about was the practice of "assessing" government officeholders in order to obtain funds for running campaigns. Hayes's Executive Order of May 1877, marking the beginning of his drive to improve the system, was aimed at eliminating this practice.

SOURCE: J. D. Richardson, ed., *Messages and Papers of the Presidents* (Washington, D.C., 1898), VII, 450–1.

EXECUTIVE MANSION,
Washington, May 26, 1877

HON. JOHN SHERMAN,
  Secretary of the Treasury

MY DEAR SIR: I have read the partial report of the commission appointed to examine the New York custom-house. I concur with the commission in their recommendations. It is my wish that the collection of the revenues should be free from partisan control, and organized on a strictly business basis, with the same guaranties for efficiency and fidelity in the selection of the chief and subordinate officers that would be required by a prudent merchant. Party leaders should have no more influence in appointments than other equally respectable citizens. No assessments for political purposes on officers or subordinates should be allowed. No useless officer or employee should be retained. No officer should be required or permitted to take part in the management of political organizations, caucuses, conventions, or election campaigns. Their right to vote and to express their views on public questions, either orally or through the press, is not denied, provided it does not interfere with the discharge of their official duties.

Respectfully,   R. B. HAYES

EXECUTIVE MANSION,
Washington, June 22, 1877

SIR: [1] I desire to call your attention to the following paragraph in a letter addressed by me to the Secretary of the Treasury on the conduct to be observed by officers of the General Government in relation to the elections:

> No officer should be required or permitted to take part in the management of political organizations, caucuses, conventions, or election campaigns. Their right to vote and to express their views on public questions, either orally or through the press, is not denied, provided it does not interfere with the discharge of their official duties. No assessment for political purposes on officers or subordinates should be allowed.

This rule is applicable to every department of the civil service. It should be understood by every officer of the General Govern-

---

[1] Addressed to Federal Officers generally.

ment that he is expected to conform his conduct to its requirements.

Very respectfully,　　　　　　　　　R. B. HAYES

26. Roscoe Conkling—
Defense of the Spoils System (1877)

Attempts to modify or destroy the patronage system roused powerful
emotions in the breasts of the professional politicians. They reasoned
that parties were an integral part of the American government and
that parties could not exist unless loyal workers could be rewarded
with government jobs for their efforts in organizing campaigns and
publicizing issues. If the bureaucracy was divorced from partisan politics, the whole political system would collapse, and along with it the
sources of the personal power of the politicians. Or so the spoilsmen
argued.

Some of the most vitriolic political oratory of all time was produced
by these men in their attacks on civil service reformers. The following
is one of the most notorious examples of the genre—an assault
launched by Senator Roscoe Conkling at the New York State Republican Convention of 1877 at Rochester against George W. Curtis, a
leader of the reform movement.

. . . We are Republicans. We represent a great party. That party
has a battle to fight just now in every county, district and town,
and our duty is to Republicans and to their candidates in every
locality and school district in the State. Administrations do not
make parties. Parties make Administrations. Parties go before
Administrations, and live after them. The people make parties.
The people made the Republican party, and the people have
upheld it in a career of usefulness and achievement such as no
other party in history can boast. . . .

This is a State Convention. Its business is to nominate candidates for State officers, and to declare the principles on which
these candidates shall stand and act if they are chosen. Its business
is not to hinder, but to help, by the wisdom and harmony of its
action, every candidate, not only in the State at large, but upon all
tickets which are to run in all counties, towns and localities
throughout the State. . . . I will not assume that any man has been
entrusted to introduce matters foreign to our duties and calcu-

SOURCE: A. R. Conkling, *The Life and Letters of Roscoe Conkling*, (New
York, 1889), pp. 538–41, 546–7.

lated to foment discord among those of the same household of faith. I repel the idea that the national Administration suggests or sanctions any such proceeding. He who volunteers for such a purpose may be found wanting in the discretion of friendship, if not in its sincerity also. . . .

. . . To speak plainly, there are special reasons, just now, inviting the Convention to adhere calmly and firmly to its own sense of propriety and wisdom. The Republicans of this State have been summoned for weeks, with somewhat of menace and truculent dictation, to declare this and declare that, and broad hints have been given of retribution if they dare even to remain silent. . . . Americans, it seems, are now to be chastised for holding their peace. NOT YET. Exotic despotism, revised and improved, will not grow in American soil. It will perish. It would be trodden out, if it did not die out. Who are these oracular censors so busy of late in brandishing the rod over me and every other Republican in this State? Some man has said, "I am of age in the Republican party." So am I. For the last twenty-two years I have labored for it and stood by its flag; and never in twenty-two years have I been false to its principles, its cause, or its candidates. Who are these men who, in newspapers and elsewhere, are cracking their whips over Republicans and playing school-master to the Republican party and its conscience and convictions? They are of various sorts and conditions. Some of them are the non-milliners, the dilettanti and carpet knights of politics men whose efforts have been expended in denouncing and ridiculing and accusing honest men[1] who, in storm and in sun, in war and peace, have clung to the Republican flag and defended it against those who have tried to trail and trample it in the dust. Some of them are men who, when they could work themselves into conventions, have attempted to belittle and befoul Republican administrations and to parade their own thin veneering of superior purity. Some of them are men who, by insisting that it is corrupt and bad for men in office to take part in politics, are striving now to prove that the Republican party has been unclean and vicious all its life, and that the last campaign was venal and wrong and fraudulent, not in some of the States, but in all the States, North and South. For it is no

---

[1] ". . . to accusing and denouncing men more honest than themselves," in the New York Tribune's account, September 28, 1877.

secret that in all States office-holders, in committees, in organizations and everywhere, did all that men could fairly do to uphold the candidates of our party, and that they were encouraged and urged to do so. Some of these worthies masquerade as reformers. Their vocation and ministry is to lament the sins of other people. Their stock in trade is rancid, canting self-righteousness. They are wolves in sheep's clothing. Their real object is office and plunder. When Dr. Johnson defined patriotism as the last refuge of a scoundrel, he was unconscious of the then undeveloped capabilities and uses of the word "Reform." . . .

. . . Some of those now laying down new and strange tenets for Republicans, sat but yesterday in Democratic Conventions, some have sought nominations at the hands of Democrats in recent years, and some, with the zeal of neophytes and bitterness of apostates, have done more than self-respecting Democrats would do to vilify and slander their Government and their countrymen. Grant, and all who stood by that upright, fearless magistrate, have been objects of the bitter, truthless aspersions of these men. And now, opposed or laggard in the battles of the past, they leap forward to the feast. They forget that parties are not built up by deportment, or by ladies' magazines, or gush. It used to be said of certain Democrats in Massachusetts that they wanted, by their obnoxious officiousness, to keep the party in that State as small as they could in order to make the stockholders as few and the dividends as large as possible. I hope these new-fledged dictators are not aiming at the same thing in New York. The grasshoppers in the corner of a fence, even without a newspaper to be heard in, sometimes make more noise than the flocks and herds that graze upon a thousand hills. . . .

. . . Let us agree to put contentions aside and complete our task. Let us declare the purposes and methods which should guide the government of our great State. On this platform let us place upright, capable men, and then let us appeal to the people to decide whether such men shall conduct their affairs on such principles, or whether they would rather trust spurious reformers under the lead and dominion of our political opponents. . . .

27. Chester A. Arthur—The Movement for a Federal Civil Service Law (1882, 1883)

Senator Conkling's uncompromising opposition to civil service reform and his overweening urge to dominate Republican politics led him into a showdown battle with President James A. Garfield after the election of 1880. Garfield won this battle, but an indirect result (for which Conkling was certainly not responsible) was the assassination of the President by Charles J. Guiteau, an admirer of the colorful New York spoilsman. This tragic event greatly strengthened the hands of the reformers. The new President, Chester A. Arthur, was a member of the Conkling faction and no friend of reform, but the circumstances of his accession moderated his enthusiasm for the spoils system. In his annual message to Congress in 1881, he came out, albeit somewhat unenthusiastically, for a civil service law. Congress failed to act, however, and public demands for such a law increased. The effects of this mounting pressure are clearly revealed in Arthur's much more forthright endorsement of reform in his annual message of 1882. At last, in January 1883, the Pendleton Civil Service Act was passed. The relevant portions of Arthur's civil service message and of the Pendleton law follow.

A: President Arthur's Messages to Congress, 1881, 1882

[1881] In my letter accepting the nomination for the Vice-Presidency I stated that in my judgment—

No man should be the incumbent of an office the duties of which he is for any cause unfit to perform; who is lacking in the ability, fidelity, or integrity which a proper administration of such office demands. This sentiment would doubtless meet with general acquiescence, but opinion has been widely divided upon the wisdom and practicability of the various reformatory schemes which have been suggested and of certain proposed regulations governing appointments to public office.

The efficiency of such regulations has been distrusted mainly because they have seemed to exalt mere educational and abstract, tests above general business capacity and even special fitness for the particular work in hand. It seems to me that the rules which should be applied to the management of the public service may properly conform in the main to such as regulate the conduct of successful private business:

SOURCE: A: J. D. Richardson, ed., *Messages and Papers of the Presidents* (Washington, D.C., 1898), VIII, 60–3, 145–7.

SOURCE: B: *United States Statutes at Large,* 47th Congress, 2d Session, pp. 403–4, 406.

Original appointments should be based upon ascertained fitness.

The tenure of office should be stable.

Positions of responsibility should, so far as practicable, be filled by the promotion of worthy and efficient officers.

The investigation of all complaints and the punishment of all official misconduct should be prompt and thorough.

The views expressed in the foregoing letter are those which will govern my administration of the executive office. They are doubtless shared by all intelligent and patriotic citizens, however divergent in their opinions as to the best methods of putting them into practical operation.

For example, the assertion that "original appointments should be based upon ascertained fitness" is not open to dispute.

But the question how in practice such fitness can be most effectually ascertained is one which has for years excited interest and discussion. The measure which, with slight variations in its details, has lately been urged upon the attention of Congress and the Executive has as its principal feature the scheme of competitive examination. Save for certain exceptions, which need not here be specified, this plan would allow admission to the service only in its lowest grade, and would accordingly demand that all vacancies in higher positions should be filled by promotion alone. . . .

There are very many characteristics which go to make a model civil servant. Prominent among them are probity, industry, good sense, good habits, good temper, patience, order, courtesy, tact, self-reliance, manly deference to superior officers, and manly consideration for inferiors. The absence of these traits is not supplied by wide knowledge of books, or by promptitude in answering questions, or by any other quality likely to be brought to light by competitive examination.

To make success in such a contest, an indispensable condition of public employment would very likely result in the practical exclusion of the older applicants, even though they might possess qualifications far superior to their younger and more brilliant competitors.

These suggestions must not be regarded as evincing any spirit of opposition to the competitive plan, which has been to some extent successfully employed already, and which may hereafter vindicate the claim of its most earnest supporters; but it ought to be seriously considered whether the application of the same educational standard to persons of mature years and to young men fresh from school and college would not be likely to exalt mere intellectual proficiency above other qualities of equal or greater importance.

Another feature of the proposed system is the selection by promotion of all officers of the Government above the lowest grade, except such as would fairly be regarded as exponents of the policy of the Executive and the principles of the dominant party.

To afford encouragement to faithful public servants by exciting in their minds the hope of promotion if they are found to merit it is much to be desired.

But would it be wise to adopt a rule so rigid as to permit no other mode of supplying the intermediate walks of the service?

There are many persons who fill subordinate positions with great credit, but lack those qualities which are requisite for higher posts of duty; and, besides, the modes of thought and action of one whose service in a governmental bureau has been long continued are often so cramped by routine procedure as almost to disqualify him from instituting changes required by the public interests. An infusion of new blood from time to time into the middle ranks of the service might be very beneficial in its results.

The subject under discussion is one of grave importance. The evils which are complained of cannot be eradicated at once; the work must be gradual. . . .

The submission of a portion of the nominations to a central board of examiners selected solely for testing the qualifications of applicants may perhaps, without resort to the competitive test, put an end to the mischiefs which attend the present system of appointment, and it may be feasible to vest in such a board a wide discretion to ascertain the characteristics and attainments of candidates in those particulars which I have already referred to as being no less important than mere intellectual attainment.

If Congress should deem it advisable at the present session to establish competitive tests for admission to the service, no doubts such as have been suggested shall deter me from giving the measure my earnest support. . . .

I am unwilling, in justice to the present civil servants of the Government, to dismiss this subject without declaring my dissent from the severe and almost indiscriminate censure with which they have been recently assailed. That they are as a class indolent, inefficient, and corrupt is a statement which has been often made and widely credited; but when the extent, variety, delicacy, and importance of their duties are considered the great majority of the employees of the Government are, in my judgment, deserving of high commendation. . . .

The communication which I made to Congress at its first session, in December last, contained a somewhat full statement of my sentiments in relation to the principles and rules which ought to govern appointments to public service. . . .

Since these suggestions were submitted for your consideration there has been no legislation upon the subject to which they relate, but there has meanwhile been an increase in the public interest in that subject, and the people of the country, apparently without distinction of party, have in various ways and upon frequent occasions given expression to their earnest wish for prompt and definite action. In my judgment such action should no longer be postponed.

I may add that my own sense of its pressing importance has been quickened by observation of a practical phase of the matter, to which attention has more than once been called by my predecessors.

The civil list now comprises about 100,000 persons, far the larger part of whom must, under the terms of the Constitution, be selected by the President either directly or through his own appointees.

In the early years of the administration of the Government the personal direction of appointments to the civil service may not have been an irksome task for the Executive, but now that the burden has increased fully a hundredfold it has become greater than he ought to bear, and it necessarily diverts his time and attention from the proper discharge of other duties no less delicate and responsible, and which in the very nature of things cannot be delegated to other hands.

In the judgment of not a few who have given study and reflection to this matter, the nation has outgrown the provisions which the Constitution has established for filling the minor offices in the public service.

But whatever may be thought of the wisdom or expediency of changing the fundamental law in this regard, it is certain that much relief may be afforded, not only to the President and to the heads of the Departments, but to Senators and Representatives in Congress, by discreet legislation. They would be protected in a great measure by the bill now pending before the Senate, or by any other which should embody its important features, from the pressure of personal importunity and from the labor of examining conflicting claims and pretensions of candidates.

I trust that before the close of the present session some decisive action may be taken for the correction of the evils which inhere in the present methods of appointment, and I assure you of my hearty cooperation in any measures which are likely to conduce to that end.

As to the most appropriate term and tenure of the official life of the subordinate employees of the Government, it seems to be generally agreed that, whatever their extent or character, the one should be definite and the other stable, and that neither should be regulated by zeal in the service of party or fidelity to the fortunes of an individual.

It matters little to the people at large what competent person is at the head of this department or of that bureau if they feel assured that the removal of one and the accession of another will not involve the retirement of honest and faithful subordinates whose duties are purely administrative and have no legitimate connection with the triumph of any political principles or the success of any political party or faction. It is to .this latter class of officers that the Senate bill, to which I have already referred, exclusively applies.

While neither that bill nor any other prominent scheme for improving the civil service concerns the higher grade of officials, who are appointed by the President and confirmed by the Senate, I feel bound to correct a prevalent misapprehension as to the frequency with which the present Executive has displaced the incumbent of an office and appointed another in his stead.

It has been repeatedly alleged that he has in this particular signually departed from the course which has been pursued under recent Administrations of the Government. The facts are as follows:

The whole number of the Executive appointments during the four years immediately preceding Mr. Garfield's accession to the Presidency was 2,696. Of this number 244, or 9 per cent, involved the removal of previous incumbents.

The ratio of removals to the whole number of appointments was much the same during each of those four years. . . .

I declare my approval of such legislation as may be found necessary for supplementing the existing provisions of law in relation to political assessments.

In July last I authorized a public announcement that employees of the Government should regard themselves as at liberty to exercise their pleasure in making or refusing to make political contributions, and that their action in that regard would in no manner affect their official status.

In this announcement I acted upon the view, which I had always maintained and still maintain, that a public officer should be as absolutely free as any other citizen to give or to withhold a contribution for the aid of the political party of his choice. It has, however, been urged, and doubtless not without foundation in fact, that by solicitation of official superiors and by other modes such contributions have at times been obtained from persons whose only motive for giving has been the fear of what might befall them if they refused. It goes without saying that such contributions are not voluntary, and in my judgment their collection should be prohibited by law. A bill which will effectually suppress them will receive my cordial approval. . . .

B: The Pendleton Civil Service Act, 1883

Be it enacted by the Senate and House of Representatives of the United States of America in Congress assembled, That the President is authorized to appoint, by and with the advice and consent of the Senate, three persons, not more than two of whom shall be adherents of the same party, as Civil Service Commissioners, and said three commissioners shall constitute the United States Civil Service Commission. . . .

SEC. 2. That it shall be the duty of said commissioners:

FIRST. To aid the President, as he may request, in preparing suitable rules for carrying this act into effect, and when said rules shall have been promulgated it shall be the duty of all officers of the United States in the departments and offices to which any such rules may relate to aid, in all proper ways, in carrying said rules, and any modifications thereof, into effect.

SECOND. And, among other things, said rules shall provide and declare, as nearly as the conditions of good administration will warrant, as follows:

First, for open, competitive examinations for testing the fitness of applicants for the public service now classified or to be classified hereunder. Such examinations shall be practical in their character, and so far as may be shall relate to those matters which will fairly test the relative capacity and fitness of the persons examined to discharge the duties of the service into which they seek to be appointed.

Second, that all the offices, places, and employments so arranged or to be arranged in classes shall be filled by selections according to grade from among those graded highest as the results of such competitive examinations.

Third, appointments to the public service aforesaid in the departments at Washington shall be apportioned among the several States and Territories and the District of Columbia upon the basis of population as ascertained at the last preceding census. . . .

Fourth, that there shall be a period of probation before any absolute appointment or employment aforesaid.

Fifth, that no person in the public service is for that reason under any obligations to contribute to any political fund, or to render any political service, and that he will not be removed or otherwise prejudiced for refusing to do so.

Sixth, that no person in said service has any right to use his official authority or influence to coerce the political action of any person or body. . . .

SEC. 8. That no person habitually using intoxicating beverages to excess shall be appointed to, or retained in, any office, appointment, or employment to which the provisions of this act are applicable. . . .

SEC. 11. That no Senator, or Representative, or Territorial Delegate of the Congress, or Senator, Representative, or Delegate elect, or any officer or employee of either of said houses, and no executive, judicial, military, or naval officer of the United States, and no clerk or employee of any department, branch or bureau of the executive, judicial, or military or naval service of the United States, shall, directly, or indirectly, solicit or receive, or be in any manner concerned in soliciting or receiving, any assessment, subscription, or contribution for any political purpose whatever, from any officer, clerk, or employee of the United States, or any department, branch, or bureau thereof, or from any person receiving any salary or compensation from moneys derived from the Treasury of the United States. . . .

28. George W. Curtis—Achievements of the Civil Service Reformers (1891)

Although the subject of civil service reform remained controversial, the new system worked reasonably well and the number of government jobs placed in the "classified service" was steadily expanded. By the early 1890's, the reformers could look back over the recent past with considerable satisfaction. Speaking at a meeting of the National Civil-Service Reform League at Buffalo, New York, in 1891, George W. Curtis, longtime president of the League, may well have reflected upon Conkling's unbridled denunciation of him and his fellow reformers in nearby Rochester, fifteen years, almost to the day, earlier. In any case his speech, after presenting a somewhat overdrawn portrait of the horrors of the old spoils system, was a proud summary of the work of the reformers and of the United States Civil Service Commission they had helped to bring into being.

The formation of the League was not, as sometimes it has been pleasantly represented, a whim of amiable gentlemen who had a fancy for new fashions in politics, for spinning moonbeams and dipping water in a sieve. The spirit of reform is the instinct of order and progress and as old as government. It is the creative instinct moving upon the face of the waters. When the Republican platform of 1884, reaffirmed in 1888, spoke of the dangers to free institutions which lurk in the power of official patronage, it did not announce a new discovery; it merely stated a historical fact. In the famous declaration of 1688 which, after consultation with his English advisers, William the Third issued upon embarking for England, he mentioned as the sixth among the thirteen particulars in which the laws of England had been set at naught by the dethroned dynasty, interference with elections by turning out of all employment such as refused to vote as they were

SOURCE: G. W. Curtis, "Ten Years of Reform," National Civil-Service Reform League, *Proceedings* (New York, 1891), pp. 5–11, 14, 23–4.

required. . . . Webster draws a similar picture of its ravages in this country. It was sixty years ago that he said, in arraigning the Jackson administration, "As far as I know there is no civilized country on earth in which, on a change of rulers, there is such an inquisition for spoils as we have witnessed in this free republic." The evil that both described was the baldest form of political corruption. It was making booty of the public service, and Marcy, who defended the outrage, justly described a service so seized as spoils. In one country the public patronage was a bribery fund to prop the crown, in the other, to help a party. In both it was organized corruption.

It is not surprising that the passionate ardor of party spirit during a civil war which identified support of a party with the existence of the government should have strengthened the tradition that extreme partisanship is the rightful condition of public employment, nor that the immense increase of such employment at the very time when this conviction was strongest should have developed at once and flagrantly the evils of an exclusively partisan civil service. The exaltation of patriotic feeling during the war is an inspiring recollection. But the reaction that always follows such exaltation was not less signal, and corruption in our politics was never felt to be so general, so vast and penetrating, as during the last quarter of a century. The formation of the Civil Service Reform League, therefore, did not announce the discovery of a new abuse, but the conviction that an old one was at once so deeply extended and so threatening as to demand constant exposure and resolute reform. The story of the progress of ten years is the evidence of the scope of that conviction and of the awakening of public opinion. . . .

The National Civil Service Reform League was organized at Newport, R.I., on the 11th of August, 1881. It was the result of a conference among members of civil service reform associations that had spontaneously arisen in various parts of the country for the purpose of awakening public interest in the question, like the clubs of the Sons of Liberty among our fathers, and the antislavery societies among their children. The first act of the League was a resolution of hearty approval of the bill then pending in Congress, known as the Pendleton bill. Within less than two years afterward the Civil Service law was passed in Congress. . . .

The passage of the law was the first great victory of the ten years of the reform movement. The second is the demonstration of the complete practicability of reform attested by the heads of the largest offices of administration in the country. In the Treasury and Navy departments, the New York Custom House and Post Office, and other important custom houses and post offices, without the least regard to the wishes or the wrath of that remarkable class of our fellow citizens, known as political bosses, it is conceded by officers, wholly beyond suspicion of party independence, that, in these chief branches of the public service, reform is perfectly practicable and the reformed system a great public benefit. And, although as yet these offices are by no means thoroughly reorganized upon reform principles, yet a quarter of the whole number of places in the public service to which the reformed methods apply are now included within those methods.

I say reformed methods and not principles, because the principle of reform is applicable to the entire public service. When under their oaths to discharge the duties of their offices to their best ability and with the divine aid, the President nominates and the Senate confirms a member of the Cabinet or a minister to England, the collector of a port or a postmaster, both the President and the Senate are morally bound to select the fittest agents for those high public trusts without regard to personal or party interests and with reference solely to the public welfare. For the public service is the service of the people. Its offices are not the perquisites of the chief magistrate to whom the people commit the appointment of persons to fill them. Nor are they the property of the constitutional majority of the people which selects that magistrate. The majority which selects him is simply the agency by which the whole people act, and in executing the trust of appointment to office, he is discharging a duty, not to a majority not to a party, but to the whole people; and in making the appointment he is morally bound to consider only qualification for the service and not agreement with the opinion of the majority upon subjects that do not affect the duties of the office. Undoubtedly, our political system intends the action of the President to give effect to the will of the majority in legislation. He officially confirms the policy of the country as expressed at the polls and declared by Congress, a policy which varies with varying opinion. But whatever the changing policy, the actual transaction of the public business under that policy is unchangeable. It demands only capacity, honesty, diligence, subordination. . . .

Another happy advantage of the reform in this retrospect has been the character and efficiency of the National Civil Service Commission. The prosperity of the reformed system depended almost wholly in the beginning upon the sincerity, the special knowledge and the tenacity of those to whom was entrusted the duty of putting it into operation. To farm out the infant to an enemy would have been to smother it. It was easy for President Arthur, after he had approved the bill, to paralyze reform by the appointment of Commissioners who had no faith in the law and no heart in its proper enforcement. But he honestly placed at the head of the commission one of the most conspicuous, intelligent, and earnest friends of reform, who had made a complete study upon the spot of the English system, and whose report is the most important contribution ever made to the literature of the subject; who had taken a leading part in the preparation of the reform law, and whose large familiarity with the question especially qualified him to organize the practical operation of the law, Mr. Dorman B. Eaton. Cordially sustained by President Arthur in the novel and difficult work, Mr. Eaton and his colleagues laid the secure foundations upon which their successors have wrought in the same spirit. . . .

. . . As President, Mr. Cleveland enlarged the range of the classified service, revised and strengthened the rules of the Commission and sustained it in the strict enforcement of the law. President Harrison's selection of Civil Service Commissioners, also, was in strict conformity to the spirit of the platform upon which he was elected, and to his own professions and pledges as a candidate, and also has extended somewhat the classified service.

The enforcement of the law through the Commission by the three Presidents who have served since its passage, has been honest and honorable. It is certain that neither of them has struck at reform by entrusting the execution of the law to its enemies. They have not adopted, indeed, all the progressive recommendations of the Commission, but political pressure for the practical betrayal of its work, or for the dismissal of any actively aggressive Commissioner, has been manfully resisted by them. This is well done, for I can imagine a Commissioner of so high a faith, so alert a mind, so aggressive a temperament, a public officer so impatient of humbug, lies and hypocrisy, and with so shrewd an eye to see and so sharp a sting to avenge even senatorial violations and sneaking cabinet evasions of the law, that he must be as welcome to lofty official delinquents as a swarm of hornets to a crowd of Sunday-School boys on a high fence stealing fruit. . . .

Still another victory is the fact that the system of party assessments on the civil service and the kindred evil of the interference of office-holders in elections are now so effectually stigmatized by public opinion that although not abandoned, they have become disgraceful. The effort to justify the levying of blackmail by party committees of Congress or of local districts, and to defend the moral coercion of public employees by irresponsible officers of the government, has dissappeared in the contemptuous scorn of public common sense. . . .

Upon a survey even so general as this of the progress of civil service reform within the ten years of the existence of this League, it is idle to deny the prodigious advance which it has made, both in public opinion and in practical application. . . . The League has represented not party strategy to carry an election, but public conviction to reform an acknowledged evil of administration. If it had done nothing more its service would be great in having forced the spoils system to its defence. The political pirates are at last driven to show the black flag and defiantly to declare that at every election the whole public service in every detail, with all its emoluments and opportunities, shall be made the prize of a vast struggle of greed and intrigue, of bribery and dishonesty of every kind, all inflamed to fury by party spirit. We demand that all public business, which is not political, shall be kept free from politics and shall be transacted upon the simple principles which are approved by universal private experience. The masters of Tammany Hall, with the dealers in mules, soap, and blocks of floaters, who hold that in politics fraud is not fraudulent, nor dishonesty dishonest, declare that everywhere, except in Sancho Panza's Barataria, No Man's Land, and the Isle of Fools, the public service is spoils and belongs to the victors. But Washington warned us in advance against these voices. Webster said that whoever controlled a man's means of living controlled his will. Clay said that Marcy's doctrine would end in despotism. Lincoln, hounded by the remorseless demand for spoils, said that the evil would destroy the Government. Those who would use the patronage of public employment as the vast bribery fund of a party are on one side. Washington and Lincoln, patriotism and good sense, the wisdom of age, the instinct of youth, are on the other. Let all good men choose their part. We have chosen ours.

Part VIII

Social Reformers

29. Henry George—The Baleful Effects of the Private Ownership of Land (1879)

The marvelous economic growth of the post-Civil War years did not, of course, eliminate the material problems of every American. Many persons remained desperately poor, and the condition of these unfortunates appeared steadily more intolerable as other people improved their lot and a relative handful of successful men achieved unprecedented riches. The age, therefore, was not lacking in indignant critics or in suggestions for basic changes in the structure of society.

Of the critics, none roused more controversy or attracted more devoted followers than Henry George. As a young man George held a variety of jobs—seaman, clerk, reporter, and printer. Living in California in the late 1860's, he was alarmed by the extent to which a few men were gaining control of the natural resources of the state and using their power to enrich themselves at the expense, George felt, of those who labored in the actual development of these resources. Later observations of life in the crowded eastern cities, where property values rose astronomically as population density increased, reinforced him in his belief that private ownership of land should be abolished. Landlords, he reasoned, extracted in the form of rent an enormous unearned increment, wealth that properly belonged to society. In 1879 he published *Progress and Poverty,* an emotionally charged, brilliantly argued exposition of the problem as he saw it. The solution that he proposed was what became known as the single tax, the confiscation of all rent. In the following selection, George explains how "the enslavement of laborers [is] the ultimate result of private property in land."

If chattel slavery be unjust, then is private property in land unjust.

For, let the circumstances be what they may—the ownership of

SOURCE: Henry George, *Progress and Poverty* (New York, 1887), pp. 312–13, 315, 317, 320–1.

land will always give the ownership of men, to a degree measured by the necessity (real or artificial) for the use of land. This is but a statement in different form of the law of rent.

And when that necessity is absolue—when starvation is the alternative to the use of land, then does the ownership of men involved in the ownership of land become absolute.

Place one hundred men on an island from which there is no escape, and whether you make one of these men the absolute owner of the other ninety-nine, or the absolute owner of the soil of the island, will make no difference either to him or to them.

In the one case, as the other, the one will be the absolute master of the ninety-nine—his power extending even to life and death, for simply to refuse them permission to live upon the island would be to force them into the sea.

Upon a larger scale, and through more complex relations, the same cause must operate in the same way and to the same end the ultimate result, the enslavement of laborers, becoming apparent just as the pressure increases which compels them to live on and from land which is treated as the exclusive property of others. Take a country in which the soil is divided among a number of proprietors, instead of being in the hands of one, and in which, as in modern production, the capitalist has been specialized from the laborer, and manufactures and exchange, in all their many branches, have been separated from agriculture. Though less direct and obvious, the relations between the owners of the soil and the laborers will, with increase of population and the improvement of the arts, tend to the same absolute mastery on the one hand and the same abject helplessness on the other, as in the case of the island we have supposed. Rent will advance, while wages will fall. Of the aggregate produce, the land owner will get a constantly increasing, the laborer a constantly diminishing share. Just as removal to cheaper land becomes difficult or impossible laborers, no matter what they produce, will be reduced to a bare living and the free competition among them, where land is monopolized, will force them to a condition which, though they may be mocked with the titles and insignia of freedom, will be virtually that of slavery.

There is nothing strange in the fact that, in spite of the enormous increase in productive power which this century has witnessed, and which is still going on, the wages of labor in the lower and wider strata of industry should everywhere tend to the wages of slavery—just enough to keep the laborer in working condition. For the ownership of the land on which and from which a man must live, is virtually the ownership of the man himself, and in acknowledging the right of some individuals to the exclusive use and enjoyment of the earth, we condemn other individuals to slavery as fully and as completely as though we had formally made them chattels. . . .

The necessary relation between labor and land, the absolute power which the ownership of land gives over men who cannot live but by using it, explains what is otherwise inexplicable—the growth and persistence of institutions, manners, and ideas so utterly repugnant to the natural sense of liberty and equality.

When the idea of individual ownership, which so justly and naturally attaches to things of human production, is extended to land, all the rest is a mere matter of development. The strongest and most cunning easily acquire a superior share in this species of property, which is to be had, not by production, but by appropriation, and in becoming lords of the land they become necessarily lords of their fellow-men. The ownership of land is the basis of aristocracy. It was not nobility that gave land, but the possession of land that gave nobility. All the enormous privileges of the nobility of medieval Europe flowed from their position as the owners of the soil. The simple principle of the ownership of the soil produced, on the one side, the lord, on the other, the vassal—the one having all rights, the other none. The right of the lord to the soil acknowledged and maintained, those who lived upon it could only do so upon his terms. The manners and conditions of the times made those terms include services and servitudes, as well as rents in produce or money, but the essential thing that compelled them was the ownership of land. This power exists wherever the ownership of land exists, and can be brought out wherever the competition for the use of land is great enough to enable the landlord to make his own terms. . . .

Now, as I think I have conclusively proved, it is the same cause which has in every age degraded and enslaved the laboring masses, that is working in the civilized world today. Personal liberty—that is to say, the liberty to move about—is everywhere conceded, while of political and legal inequality there are in the United

States no vestiges, and in the most backward civilized countries but few. But the great cause of inequality remains, and is manifesting itself in the unequal distribution of wealth. The essence of slavery is that it takes from the laborer all he produces save enough to support an animal existence, and to this minimum the wages of free labor, under existing conditions, unmistakably tend. Whatever be the increase of productive power, rent steadily tends to swallow up the gain, and more than the gain.

Thus the condition of the masses in every civilized country is, or is tending to become, that of virtual slavery under the forms of freedom. And it is probable that of all kinds of slavery this is the most cruel and relentless. For the laborer is robbed of the produce of his labor and compelled to toil for a mere subsistence; but his taskmasters, instead of human beings, assume the form of imperious necessities. . . .

It is not without reason that the wise crow in the Ramayana, the crow Bushands, "who has lived in every part of the universe and knows all events from the beginnings of time," declares that, though contempt of worldly advantages is necessary to supreme felicity, yet the keenest pain possible is inflicted by extreme poverty. The poverty to which in advancing civilization great masses of men are condemned, is not the freedom from distraction and temptation which sages have sought and philosophers have praised; it is a degrading and embruting slavery, that cramps the higher nature, dulls the finer feelings, and drives men by its pain to acts which the brutes would refuse. It is into this helpless, hopeless poverty, that crushes manhood and destroys womanhood, that robs even childhood of its innocence and joy, that the working classes are being driven by a force which acts upon them like a resistless and unpitying machine. The Boston collar manufacturer who pays his girls two cents an hour may commiserate their condition, but he, as they, is governed by the law of competition, and cannot pay more and carry on his business, for exchange is not governed by sentiment. And so, through all intermediate gradations, up to those who receive the earnings of labor without return, in the rent of land, it is the inexorable laws of supply and demand, a power with which the individual can no more quarrel or dispute than with the winds and the tides, that seem to press down the lower classes into the slavery of want.

But in reality, the cause is that which always has and always must result in slavery—the monopolization by some of what nature has designed for all.

Our boasted freedom necessarily involves slavery, so long as we recognize private property in land. Until that is abolished, Declarations of Independence and Acts of Emancipation are in vain. So long as one man can claim the exclusive ownership of the land from which other men must live, slavery will exist, and as material progress goes on, must grow and deepen! . . .

. . . Private ownership of land is the nether mill-stone. Material progress is the upper mill-stone. Between them, with an increasing pressure, the working classes are being ground.

30. Laurence Gronlund—
Marxism, American Style (1884)

Despite the wide popular interest in proposals for drastic social and economic reform, very few Americans in the 1880's were familiar with the ideas of Karl Marx, and still fewer took kindly to these ideas. To the general public, there was little difference between communism (usually called socialism) and anarchism, which was used as a kind of bogey man by defenders of the status quo and viewed more as an attack on moral values than as a form of social organization.

In an effort to explain Marxian socialism to Americans, a Danish-born writer, Laurence Gronlund, published *The Cooperative Commonwealth* in 1884. Although he played down Marx's emphasis on class conflict and the inevitability of revolution, Gronlund, besides denouncing rampant economic individualism and the exploitation of workers by the capitalists, made a strong argument for increasing role of government in American life. He did so by appealing to the democratic instincts of the nation: a government *of* the people (a commonwealth) need not be feared *by* the people. He also, as the following selection shows, tried to reconcile the traditional American admiration of the self-reliant individual with socialist ideas. The cooperative commonwealth, he concluded, "will help everybody to help himself."

We have concluded the Socialist critique of the present order of things. In a nutshell it is this: The Fleecings increase in our country and in all industrial countries at a very great rate. In order

SOURCE: Laurence Gronlund, *The Cooperative Commonwealth* (Boston, 1884) [Stow Persons, ed., Cambridge, 1966, pp. 66–7, 71–4, 76–7, 82–4.]

that Capital (the sum of these Fleecings) may be simply *maintained*, (mark that!) it must be constantly employed in production and a market must be found for the products which it enables Labor to create. Foreign markets will soon dry up; our autocrats, therefore, will be confined to their respective home-markets. But the masses at home are more and more becoming wage-workers from the operation of "Individualism"; wage-workers receive in wages only about half of what they produce; the masses, consequently, are becoming more and more unable to buy back the Values they create. Thus for lack of consumption, Capital will be more and more threatened with depreciation. The more Capital, the more "overproduction." The Wage-System and Private "Enterprise" *will*, indeed, involve capitalists and laborers in one common ruin.

This is the foundation for what may be called: "constructive" Socialism. We are not under the delusion, that Nations can be *persuaded* by the grandeur, excellence and equity of our system. The Future is ours, because the present system will soon be *unbearable;* because, as we said, we might fold our arms and calmly wait to see the Established Order fall to pieces by its own weight. Our conception of Value, therefore, truly comprises the *whole* of Socialism.

When the culmination has been reached, the reins will drop from the impotent hands of our autocrats and will be taken up by an impersonal Power, coeval with human nature: The STATE. . . .

The "Government"—the punishing and restraining authority—may possibly be dispensed with at some future time. But the STATE—*never*. To dispense with the State would be to dissolve Society.

It follows that the relation of the State, the body politic, to us, its citizens, is *actually* that of a tree to its cells, and *not* that of a heap of sand to its grains, to which it is entirely indifferent how many other grains of sand are scattered and trodden under foot.

This is a conception of far-reaching consequence.

In the *first* place, it, together with the modern doctrine of *Evolution*, as applied to all organisms, deals a mortal blow to the theory of "man's natural rights," the theory of man's "inalienable right" to life, liberty, property, "happiness" &c., the theory of which mankind during the last century has heard and read so much; the theory that has been so assiduously preached to our dispossessed classes, and which has benefited them *so* little!

Natural rights! The highest "natural right" we can imagine is for the stronger to kill and eat the weaker, and for the weaker to be killed and eaten. One of the "natural rights," left "man" now, is to act the brute towards wife and children, and that "right" the State has already curtailed and will by-and-by give it the finishing stroke. Another "natural right," very highly prized by our autocrats, is the privilege they now possess of "saving" for themselves what other people produce. In brief, "natural rights" are the rights of the muscular, the cunning, the unscrupulous. . . .

It is Society, organized Society, the State that gives us all the rights we have. To the State we owe our freedom. To it we owe our living and property, for outside of organized Society man's needs far surpasses his means. The humble beggar owes much to the State, but the haughty millionaire far more, for outside of it they both would be worse off than the beggar now is. To it we owe all that we are and all that we have. To it we owe our civilization. It is by its help that we have reached such a condition as man individually never would have been able to attain. Progress is the struggle with Nature for mastery, is war with the misery and inabilities of our "natural" condition. The State is the organic union of us all to wage that war, to subdue Nature, to redress natural defects and inequalities. The State therefore, so far from being a burden to the "good," a "necessary evil," is man's greatest good.

This conception of the State as an organism thus consigns the "rights of man" to obscurity and puts *Duty* in the foreground.

In the *second* place, we now can ascertain the true sphere of the State. That is, we now can commence to build something solid.

We say *Sphere* on purpose; we do not ask what are the "rights," "duties" or "functions" of the State, for if it truly is an organism it is just as improper to speak of *its* rights, duties or functions towards its citizens as it is to speak of a man's rights, duties and functions in relation to his heart, his legs, or his head. The State has rights, duties and functions in relation to other organisms, but towards its own members it has only a sphere of activities.

The sphere of the State simply consists in caring for its own welfare, just as a man's sphere, as far as himself is concerned, consists in caring for his own well-being. If that be properly done, then his brain, his lungs and his stomach will have nothing to complain of.

So with the State. Its whole sphere is the making all special activities work together for one general end: its own welfare, or the *Public Good.* Observe that the Public Good, the General Welfare, implies far more than "the greatest good to the greatest number" on which our "practical" politicians of today base their trifling measures. Their motto broadly sanctions the sacrifice of minorities to majorities, while the "General Welfare" means the greatest good of every individual citizen.

To that end the State may do anything whatsoever which is shown to be expedient. . . .

The State is thus fully entitled to take charge of *all* instruments of Labor and Production, and to say that all social activities shall be carried on in a perfectly different manner.

Undoubtedly the whole fleecing class will interpose their socalled "vested rights." That is to say because the State for a long time tacitly allowed a certain class to divide the common stock of social advantages among themselves and appropriate it to their own individual benefit therefore the State is estopped, they say, from ever recovering it. And not alone will they claim undisturbed possession of what they have, but also the right to use it in the future as they have in the past; that is, they will claim a "vested right" to fleece the masses to all eternity.

But such a protest will be just as vain as was that of the Pope against the loss of his temporal sovereignty. The theory of "vested rights" never applies when a revolution has taken place; when the whole structure of Society is changed. The tail of a tadpole that is developing into a frog may protest as much as it pleases; Nature heeds it not. And when the frog is an accomplished fact, there is no tail to protest. . . .

But let it, in the *third* place, be emphatically understood, that when we insist that the State ought to extend its sphere over all social activities, we do not mean the *present* State at all.

Our Republic is a State. Parliamentary Great Britain is a State. Imperial Germany, autocratic Russia and bureaucratic China are all social organisms. But not one of them is a *full grown* State, a fully developed organism. In all of them, our own country included, CLASSES *exercise the authority* and direct all social activity. . . .

Class-rule is always detrimental to the welfare of the whole social organism, because classes, when in power, cannot help considering themselves pre-eminently the State. They, furthermore, cannot help being biased in favor of their special interests and therefore are necessarily hostile to the rest of the Nation, and as we daily see in our free traders and protectionists, hostile to each other. Matthew Arnold speaks truly when he says that State-action by a hostile class ought to be deprecated.

Our Republic, therefore, just as all other modern States, may properly be compared to some imaginable animal organism, where the blood, proceeding from the collective digestion, is principally diverted to the stomach or the brain, while the arms and legs are stinted as much as possible.

The *Class*-State will develop into a *Commonwealth*—bless the Puritans for that splendid English word! It will develop into a State that will know of no "classes" either in theory or practice; in other words into a State *where the whole population is incorporated into Society*. In the place of the present partially evolved organism in which the arms and legs, and to a great extent the brain, are stinted in blood as much as possible, we shall have an organism "whose every organ shall receive blood in proportion to the work it does" in the language of Spencer.

That is to say: *the Commonwealth will be a State of* EQUALITY.

Again, our Commonwealth will put *Interdependence* in the place of the phrases of our Declaration of Independence, which claims for every citizen the "right" to life, liberty and the pursuit of "happiness." This declaration was evidently adopted by "Individualists," as the French Revolution was a revolution of "Individualism," for of what use is it to possess the "right" to do something, when you have not the power, the means, the opportunity to do it? Is this "right to the pursuit of happiness" not a mocking irony to the masses who *cannot* pursue "happiness"? We saw how the millionaire and beggar would be equally miserable outside of the State, and behold, how much this Rights-of-Man doctrine has done for the former and how very little for the latter!

The future Commonwealth will *help* every individual to attain the highest development he or she has capacity for. It will lay a cover for every one at Nature's table. "State" and "State-*help*" will be as inseparable as a piano and music. . . .

State-help is not to do away with a man's own efforts. I do not do away with a man's own efforts, when I hand him a ladder. I do not set aside his own exertions in cultivating a field, because I give him a plow. Our State does not render useless the powers of a boy, when it furnishes him schools, teachers and libraries. Our Commonwealth will relieve none of self-help, but make self-help possible to all. *It will help everybody to help himself. . . .*

31. Lester Frank Ward—
The Evolution of Civilization (1886)

Opponents of government regulation of economic and social affairs made extensive use of arguments drawn by analogy from Charles Darwin's theory of evolution. These American social Darwinists, most notably William Graham Sumner and John Fiske, insisted that social institutions evolved slowly and inexorably, like living species. Human efforts to tamper with them were, if not entirely useless, harmful, because they interfered with the competition which, through natural selection, led to the development of higher and more efficient forms.

Aside from the dubious character of the analogy—Darwin himself never claimed that societies were affected by the laws of evolution—the conservative argument was subject to attack on biological grounds. No one demonstrated this more effectively than the sociologist Lester Frank Ward. A phenomenally learned man, Ward wrote a long, obtuse, and largely unread analysis of social Darwinism, *Dynamic Sociology* (1883). In an effort to bring his ideas to a wider audience, however, he also wrote a series of popular magazine articles, of which the following, published in 1886, is an outstanding example.

The relative claims of the inherited and the acquired have long been argued. How men of mark come to make their mark is always an open question. How much to attribute to genius, how much to circumstances—who shall say? Whether "blood will tell;" whether what is within will come out; or whether, under certain conditions, it may not always stay in; whether the born poet has not also to be made or make himself; whether there really is any such thing as a "self-made man," and if there is, whether he is superior to other men—these are some of the problems which the thoughtful student of life always finds before him demanding solution.

For our present purpose, these problems may all be reduced to that of the relative claims of genius on the one hand, and opportunity on the other. No one will deny the potency of genius as a

SOURCE: L. F. Ward, "Broadening the Way to Success," *The Forum*, II (1886), 340–2, 344–50.

factor in success; neither will any candid person deny that even genius may encounter insuperable barriers; and all must admit that, as a matter of fact, success in all cases is the product of two forces—the force from within and the force from without—in the entire absence of either of which, however great may be the other, its achievement is impossible. The question, therefore, always really is, not whether the result was accomplished by the one or by the other, but, rather, which one of the two contributed most to its accomplishment.

Hence, in discussing the causes of success or failure in human effort, there may be found no difference in the degree of efficacy of these two forces, or, if there be a difference, it can never be measured by any accepted standard. But, whatever the equality in the factors themselves, it is evident at a glance that they have attracted a very unequal degree of attention. We find, in fact, that far greater praise is bestowed upon the internal than upon the external elements of success.

The reason for this is not far to seek. These personal elements reside in and seem to characterize the individual. They mark him off from the rest of the world, and single him out as the special object of admiration. It is the exhibitions of genius, the special displays of physical or intellectual power, the judicious use of talents combined with industry and perseverance, that rivet the gaze, and, when the result is attained, all honor is accorded to these qualities. Little or no notice is taken of the peculiar circumstances which favored its accomplishment, and without which it would have been impossible. These are not accounted as factors in the result; they are rarely recognized as existing, or, if recognized, they are assumed to offer themselves to the unsuccessful as well as to the successful. The idea prevails that genius is omnipotent, an idea which has been crystallized into the homely proverb, "Where there's a will there's a way;" and we often hear of men who "create the circumstances" which are requisite to their success.

But, aside from crude popular opinion, which should not, perhaps, be expected to perceive the impersonal agencies at work in society, we find that the current of scientific opinion runs exactly parallel to it, and we here see the individual still held up to view as the central figure in the panorama of events. Scientific men talk of heredity, of the cumulative transmission of qualities, of the conservation of latent attributes and their reappearance through atavism, while Galton has combined the scientific and the popular conceptio̊ns in his expression, "hereditary genius." The literature of the world centers round a few great geniuses, and the history of our epoch will be very much such a record of the achievements of the kings of thought and action in modern times, as the history of past ages has been of those of the kings of political states.

Into this department of history I do not now propose to enter, and, in leaving it to those who have chosen it, I do not know that I need apologize for choosing the less fascinating, less tangible side of this two-sided problem, and venturing to appear for those impersonal influences outside of the agent, which by their presence or absence permit, or do not prevent, the accomplishment of cherished results. I thus shirk the dilemma by choosing the horn on which others never hang their hopes. I leave the claims of genius to the panegyrists of genius, and pass from the individual to the evnironment.

I have not, however, selected this thankless task merely because it is new and difficult. I have chosen it chiefly because it is important. In biology the importance of the environment is fully recognized. In the arts of agriculture and stock raising, which consist in the creation of an artificial environment advantageous to man, the recognition of this principle has yielded his chief sustenance. But it applies to sociology as rigidly as to biology, and the exact homologue of this culture of plants and animals, when extended to man, is education in its broadest sense. . . .

The improvement of the race of men is the highest object that can enlist our energies. There are two ways in which this can be successfully attempted artificially. One of these consists in the practical recognition of the laws of heredity, the other in the practical recognition of the influence of the environment. The former must be something more than the mere admiration of high qualities when they appear. This adds nothing to the present occasional and spasmodic appearance of these qualities. It must consist in their rational and systematic culture, not different from that which has been so successfully applied to animals and plants, where the laws of heredity are no more uniform than among human beings. While I am not now defending this side of the great question of race improvement, I nevertheless regard this as the only course, from the point of view of heredity, that holds out the least promise of practical results.

What, then, can be said of the other plan of race improvement, that through post-natal development? At the outset let it be frankly conceded that the capacity for the display of high qualities must exist, else these qualities cannot be displayed; the germs of excellence must have been previously implanted by heredity, if they are ever to be developed by education. But the possession of the elements of worth—the capacity for excellence—is a very different thing from the manifestation of worth—the attainment of excellence. To those who believe that high attributes only exist in those who actually display them, it must indeed seem impossible to improve the race by education. But this is not the case. The germs of some form of talent exist in a latent state in nearly every undeveloped intellect, and may be brought out by opportunity. The possessor is himself usually unconscious of them. Opportunity, therefore, must not merely be offered and accepted; it must be actively thrust upon him. The greater part of the energy of the race is thus dormant, and simply needs to be aroused. The few scattered scintillations of genius that now display themselves, instead of being the objects of vacant astonishment, are to be interpreted as the evidences of enormous hidden forces to be set free.

There is no need to search for talent. It exists already, and everywhere. The thing that is rare is opportunity, not ability. . . .

When we study history, and see who the true promoters of civilization have been, we perceive how these statements are sustained by examples. The men who have increased the world's stock of knowledge, and placed the race in possession of the secrets of nature and the keys to its control and utilization, are the true benefactors of mankind. A study of the personal history of such men shows that without exception they have been in possession of rare opportunities. They have either been entirely free from the distractions of want and the necessity of toil, or they have found themselves situated in the midst of those scenes and objects which are to constitute their special field of labor, and which furnish the incentive to the effort, however great, which they must put forth in order to achieve success. Examples would be superfluous, as they cannot fail to present themselves to the reader's mind; and as to the alleged exceptions, I doubt whether a single one of them will bear the light of candid biographical scrutiny.

Many persons of an optimistic turn of mind look benignantly

over the history of man, and, seeing the great number of individuals who have distinguished themselves by the display of towering
qualities, break out in admiration of the grandeur of the race. But
the true philosopher, who correctly discerns the significance of
these examples, sees in them only signs of the possibilities of the
race. The grandeur that he sees is only a possible grandeur. For
every actual great name in history he sees a hundred potential
great names. The present corps of workers in every department of
science and culture, and in every land, are viewed kaleidoscopi-
cally, and multiplied indefinitely.

Science is only just beginning to reveal the true extent of the
latent energies of organic life. . . . It is now known that the plants
of every region possess the potency of a far higher life than they
enjoy, and that they are prevented from attaining that higher state
by the adverse influences that surround them in their normal hab-
itat. The singling out of certain species by man, and their development through his care into far higher and more perfect forms
to supply his needs, both physical and aesthetic, further demonstrate this law. Man gives these plants a new and artificial environment favorable to their higher development, and they develop
accordingly. In a word, he gives them opportunity to progress, and
they progress by inherent powers with which all plants are
endowed. Once, when herborizing in a rather wild, neglected
spot, I collected a little depauperate grass that for a time greatly
puzzled me, but which upon analysis proved to be none other
than genuine wheat. It had been accidentally sown in this abandoned nook, where it had been obliged to struggle for existence
along with the remaining vegetation. There it had grown up, and
sought to rise into that majesty and beauty that is seen in a field of
waving grain. But at every step it had felt the resistance of an
environment no longer regulated by intelligence. It missed the
fostering care of man, who destroys competition, removes enemies,
and creates conditions favorable to the highest development. This
is called cultivation, and the difference between my little starvel-
ing grass and the wheat of the well-tilled field is a difference of
cultivation only, and not at all of capacity. I could adduce any
number of similar examples from the vegetable kingdom; and the
zoologist, the stock-breeder, and the fancier could furnish equally
pointed illustrations from the animal world. But the laws of life
are the same in all departments, and even man is no exception to

them. Man has developed thus far as the wild animal has developed, as the wild grasses have developed. He has come up slowly, as these have, under a natural environment, under the influence of adverse agencies and of competition. And if as an individual he has at last learned to exercise control over the lower kingdoms of nature, as a social being he has never yet consciously attempted his own liberation from the retarding influence of his natural environment. He has never yet taken measures for the removal of competition and other obstacles to social progress.

There is a school of philosophers, never more strongly intrenched than at the present time, who not only deny the possibility of such action on the part of society, and insist that to attempt it would entail great evil, but who go further, and maintain that competition and adversity are the most effective aids to social progress. They point to the development that has taken place among animals and plants under the laws of natural selection, and deprecate in the strongest terms any attempt on the part of man to interfere with the operation of these laws in society. They forget entirely that civilization itself has been the result of successful interference with these very laws. The cereals, the fruit-trees, and the finest breeds of animals are not the results of natural but of artificial and intelligent selection, and they might as well maintain that these would have produced themselves, as that man can ever attain his highest development without conscious, intelligent, and systematic culture.

The central truth which I have sought to enforce is that, like plants and animals, men possess latent capacities which for their development simply require opportunity. Heredity will surely do its part, and therefore need not be specially attended to, but without opportunity, however great the native powers, nothing can result. I look upon existing humanity as I look upon a pristine vegetation. The whole struggling mass is held by the relentless laws of competition in a condition far below its possibilities. Just as what might be grain is mere grass, just as the potential greening is a diminutive crab-apple, so the potential giants of the intellectual world may now be the hewers of wood and drawers of water. On the theory of equality, which I would defend, the number of individuals of exceptional usefulness will be proportional to the number possessing the opportunity to develop their powers; and this regardless of any of the class distinctions that now exist. This number, in the present condition of society, is not a fixed percentage of the total population; it is a fixed percentage only of those who possess opportunity. This class is very small in proportion to the whole, but is capable of being indefinitely extended. But if, with the relative handful who at present possess opportunities, we have such results as we now see, what may we not expect when this favored class is made co-extensive with the entire population?

To the intelligent reader it need scarcely be explained that there is a legitimate and fairly practical way of enlarging this favored class. It consists in arbitrarily placing them under a changed environment favorable to the development of all their faculties. To this process the term education is usually applied, but it must be understood in that comprehensive sense which embraces this complex and fundamental conception. It is so rarely used in this sense, that, to prevent the necessity of explanation and the danger of misconstruction, I have purposely avoided its use. And yet, so great is the progress now being made in the direction of truer and broader ideas of education, that I doubt not many will readily recognize its appropriateness in the present discussion.

In conclusion, I may add that, while I am far from being over-sanguine as to the early realization of such far-reaching reforms, I do not regard such a glimpse into the future as in the least utopian. In a country like ours, where all power resides in the opinions of the people, we have only to suppose them to possess a clear conception of their interests and of the measures necessary to secure them, in order to see much measures adopted and enforced. And while I agree with the *noli-tangere* philosophers and the hereditarians, that legislation cannot be successfully applied to the alteration of the great laws of nature, such, for example, as those of heredity. I regard the work of creating opportunities, by which gifted individuals can utilize their powers, as simply in the nature of policy regulation, capable of being conducted by any body politic.

32. Richard T. Ely—
The "New" Economics (1886)

If conservatives relied upon Darwinian evolution to justify a hands-off attitude on the part of government, they relied still more heavily upon classical economics. Although the great classical economists from Adam Smith to David Ricardo and John Stuart Mill had never claimed that *all* government interference in economic affairs was wrong, they had made a powerful argument for individual freedom of decision in economic matters. Laissez faire was the central principle of this argument: if every individual was left free to pursue his own interests, the interests of society as a whole would inevitably be advanced.

This point of view, however, was rejected by a group of younger American economists, most of them trained in German universities where the "historical school" of economic analysis predominated. Without specifically repudiating the teachings of the great economists of the past, these men reasoned that economic principles had constantly to be adjusted to changing conditions. Laissez faire made good sense for a relatively simple society in which tyrannical monarchs hampered economic activity with a host of petty restrictions, as had been the case in the eighteenth century. It made much less sense under late-nineteenth-century conditions, where the economy was complex and democratic governments dedicated to advancing the general welfare existed. In 1885 a group of these "new" economists met to form the American Economic Association. The report of their deliberations prepared by secretary Richard T. Ely, and the constitution of the Association, reveal their ideas clearly.

The need of an association designed to promote independent economic inquiry and to disseminate economic knowledge was keenly felt long before any determined effort was made to establish the desired organization. Suggestions looking to the formation of a society of economists were heard from time to time, but no active steps in this direction appear to have been taken before the spring of 1885, when it was agreed that the time was ripe for action, and it was determined to test the feelings in this matter of those who would be likely to prove helpful in associated scientific work in economics. The class of men required for this purpose was, it was believed, a large and constantly growing one. Men were wanted who were investigators, men, consequently,

SOURCE: R. T. Ely, "Report of the Organization of the American Economic Association," American Economic Association, *Publications*, I (1886), 5–7, 13–17, 20–2, 24–30, 35–6.

who did not believe that the entire range of economic knowledge had been compassed. It follows from this that it was not proposed to form a society of advocates of any political opinion or set of political opinions, as for example, free-trade or protection. It was not meant to deny that a free-trade club or a protectionist club might have its legitimate sphere, but it was held that this sphere lay outside the realm of science. Likewise it was not aimed to form a society to champion any class interests, either of rich or of poor, either of employer or of employé. What was desired was a society which, free from all trammels, should seek truth from all sources, should be ready to give a respectful hearing to every new idea, and should shun no revelation of facts, but, on the contrary, should make the collection, classification and interpretation of facts its chief task. The ideal of this new society, as it presented itself to the minds of its projectors, was to seek light, to bear light, to diffuse light—ever the highest aim of all true science.

A statement of the objects of the proposed association and a platform were drawn up, which, while intended to be merely provisional, would be calculated to attract those who believed in economic research, who thought that there was a great work to be done in economics, and who for other reasons might be able to work together profitably. This platform, it must be distinctly asserted, was never meant as a hard and fast creed which should be imposed on all members, and least of all was it intended to restrict the freest investigation. The statement of objects and the proposed platform read as follows:

OBJECTS OF THIS ASSOCIATION

I.   The encouragement of economic research.
II. The publication of economic monographs.
III. The encouragement of perfect freedom in all economic discussion.
IV. The establishment of a bureau of information designed to aid all members with friendly counsels in their economic studies.

PLATFORM

1. We regard the state as an educational and ethical agency whose positive aid is an indispensable condition of human progress. While we recognize the necessity of individual initiative in

industrial life, we hold that the doctrine of *laissez-faire* is unsafe in politics and unsound in morals; and that it suggests an inadequate explanation of the relations between the state and the citizens.

2. We do not accept the final statements which characterized the political economy of a past generation; for we believe that political economy is still in the first stages of its scientific development, and we look not so much to speculation as to an impartial study of actual conditions of economic life for the satisfactory accomplishment of that development. We seek the aid of statistics in the present, and of history in the past.

3. We hold that the conflict of labor and capital has brought to the front a vast number of social problems whose solution is impossible without the united efforts of Church, state and science.

4. In the study of the policy of government, especially with respect to restrictions on trade and to protection of domestic manufactures, we take no partisan attitude. We are convinced that one of the chief reasons why greater harmony has not been attained, is because economists have been too ready to assert themselves as advocates. We believe in a progressive development of economic conditions which must be met by corresponding changes of policy.

A prospectus containing this statement and platform was sent to a majority of those interested in political economy in our colleges and met with a hearty response in nearly every quarter. While there were not wanting criticisms of some of the phrases, there was general approval of the aims of the projected American Economic Association. . . .

It was finally decided to meet at Saratoga at the time of the annual meeting of the American Historical Association, which had been announced for September 8–11. This seemed desirable, as nearly all who wished to form the Economic Association belonged at the same time to the Historical Association. . . .

DR. [EDMUND J.] JAMES called the meeting to order and nominated Professor Henry C. Adams as temporary Chairman. Professor J[ohn] B[ates] Clark then nominated Dr. R[ichard] T. Ely as temporary Secretary. These gentlemen were thereupon elected.

DR. ELY was then called upon to make a statement in regard to the purposes of the proposed association.

One aim of our association should be the education of public opinion in regard to economic questions and economic literature.

In no other science is there so much quackery and it must be our province to expose it and bring it into merited contempt. A review at each of our meetings of the economic works of the past year, if published in our proceedings, might help in the formation of enlightened judgment.

Coming to the platform, a position is first of all taken in regard to the state, because it is thought necessary precisely at this time to emphasize its proper province. No one invited to join this association, certainly no one who has been active in calling this meeting, contemplates a form of pure socialism. "We recognize the necessity of individual initiative." We would do nothing to weaken individual activity, but we hold that there are certain spheres of activity which do not belong to the individual, certain functions which the great co-operative society, called the state— must perform to keep the avenues open for those who would gain a livelihood by their own exertions. The avenues to wealth and preferment are continually blocked by the greed of combinations of men and by monopolists, and individual effort and initiative are thus discouraged. . . .

We hold that the doctrine of *laissez-faire* is unsafe in politics and unsound in morals, and that it suggests an inadequate explanation of the relations between the state and the citizens. In other words we believe in the existence of a system of social ethics; we do not believe that any man lives for himself alone, nor yet do we believe social classes are devoid of mutual obligations corresponding to their infinitely varied inter-relations. All have duties as well as rights, and, as Emerson said several years ago, it is time we heard more about duties and less about rights. We who have resolved to form an American Economic Association hope to do something towards the development of a system of social ethics.

It is asked: what is meant by *laissez-faire?* It is difficult to define *laissez-faire* categorically, because it is so absurd that its defenders can never be induced to say precisely what they mean. Yet it stands for a well-known, though rather vague set of ideas, to which appeal is made every day in the year by the bench, the bar, the newspapers and our legislative bodies. It means that government, the state, the people in their collective capacity, ought not to interfere in industrial life; that, on the contrary, free contract should regulate all the economic relations of life and public authority should simply enforce this, punish crime and preserve peace. It means that the laws of economic life are natural laws like those of physics and chemistry, and that this life must be left to the free play of natural forces. One adherent uses these words: "This industrial world is governed by natural laws. . . These laws are superior to man. Respect this providential order—let alone the work of God."

The platform then emphasizes the mission of the State and the mission of the individual in that State. *To distinguish between the proper functions of the two must be one of the purposes of our association. . . .*

At the conclusion of the paper presented by Dr. Ely, the provisional platform and statement of objects were presented and discussed in detail, nearly all present taking part in the animated debate.

Professor Henry C. Adams expressed himself as most heartily in favor of the purposes of the proposed association, and, so far as he was personally concerned, would be quite willing to undertake a defense of the statement of principles as presented. He thought, however, that it might be wise to modify them in one or two particulars; for they were too explicit to be held merely as general statements, while at the same time they did not say enough to guard against possible misapprehension. In two particulars was there danger of misunderstanding. In the first place, a formal denial of the claims of *laissez-faire* might be construed to mean the acceptance of what is popularly known as the German view of social relations. This, he thought, would be unfortunate, for it would not properly represent the opinions of some who were interested in the present movement. It may be admitted that the English political philosophy (or what goes by that name), which regards the state as a necessary evil, is untenable. The state is not an appendage to private action. But on the other hand, German political philosophy, which presents the state as the final analysis of human relations, is equally erroneous. The truth is, that society is the organic entity about which all reasoning should center, and both state action and the industrial activity of individuals are but functions of the organism, society. The great problem of the present day is properly to correlate public and private activity so as to preserve harmony and proportion between the various parts of organic society; and he believed that the path by which this purpose might be attained had been indicated by neither English nor German economists. In the second place, the speaker ventured the opinion that the Association would gain material strength by formally expressing its high appreciation of the work of former economists. This movement should be considered as a further development of the work which they so well began. The radical changes in society have forced new problems to the front for study and solution, but the claim to be historical students would be forfeited, should even a suggestion of isolation make its appearance. Much is heard to-day among the philosophers of a return to Kant; current political economy needs nothing at present so much as a return to the spirit of Adam Smith.

Professor [Alexander] Johnston, agreeing, in the main, with the propositions offered by the secretary, wished that their expression could be considerably modified. He apprehended that the words might seem to imply an absolute rejection of the work of the great thinkers upon economics. On the contrary, their work must stand, since it has not been successfully assailed. The definitions which they have thought out so laboriously and put into apt words as a basis for the work of future generations, we ought not even to seem to treat with disrespect. This is not a rebellion against Adam Smith, Malthus, Ricardo and Mill; only a struggle for freedom of development of their work. . . .

President Andrew D. White expressed himself as ready to stand on the platform as presented. He was glad to see this movement and paid a high tribute to those present who were assisting in the establishment of the new society. He considered the return of "these young men from Germany" as of sufficient importance to constitute an epoch in American history. He was also glad to see it explicitly stated that the association did not design to become either a free-trade club or a protectionist club, as the fact needed to be emphasized, that political economy was something broader than controversies about the tariff. A prominent journal had ventured to express disapproval when, as President of Cornell University, he invited two gentlemen to present the two sides of this issue, it being implied that political economy was identical with one view of the subject. President White spoke of the total inadequacy of the so-called *laissez-faire* theory of political economy, saying that in Europe it had entirely broken down.

President C[harles] K. Adams followed with an expression of his understanding of the purposes of the association. He said that in signing the call he had understood that the design of the new organization was to promote the study of economic science from what may be called the historical point of view. He had the impression that the time had come to organize into an association all those who are ready to admit that it is impossible to formulate what there is of political economy into an economic code of universal application. He believed that economic science must be studied in the light of history, inasmuch as experience has shown that many of its doctrines must be regarded, not as truths of universal application, but simply as truths to be adapted to the changing conditions of human development. In the way of illustration, he called attention to the fact that the so-called doctrines of *laissez-faire* are now generally regarded by economists as of much less wide-spread application than was supposed by the economists of fifty or even twenty-five years ago. Thus the course of history has compelled economists to modify some of their beliefs, and, consequently, how far their beliefs are subject to still further modification is a legitimate subject of inquiry. Such inquiry he supposed to be one of the most prominent objects of the new organization.

Professor E. J. James expressed himself as very much pleased with the hearty response to the proposal to organize an Economic Association which was indicated by the presence at this meeting of so many representative workers in the field of economics. It was a matter of surprise that there should be so much unanimity of sentiment among men who had never before had the opportunity of coming together to exchange opinions on questions which were the subject of so much dispute. It argued well for the future success of the association. He thought the proposed platform might well be modified in certain particulars, as the language might convey false impressions as to the views of the men who were present. It should contain a hearty acknowledgment of the work done by the so-called orthodox school, and insist on the fact that the association proposed to work on the basis of whatever truth had been discovered and formulated by previous workers in this field, no matter to what school they belong. It should, however, also contain a vigorous expression of the intention of the association to go forward in the investigation of economic truth as far as possible, without any of those prepossessions and limitations which are inevitably connected with the habit of regarding any past thinkers as having spoken the last word, even on the topics which they discovered. . . .

Dr. [E. R. A.] Seligman feared that the statement of principles as originally drafted might create in some minds a misconception of the true object of the association. He believed, and thought that the majority of the members agreed with him in believing, that the reaction against the principle of free competition had perhaps been somewhat exaggerated by certain recent economists. Competition is not in itself bad. It is a neutral force which has already produced immense benefits, but which may, under certain conditions, bring in its train sharply defined evils. Modern economics has, however, not yet attained that certainty in results which would authorize us to invoke increased governmental action as a check to various abuses of free competition. He thought that care should be taken to preserve an impartial scientific attitude, and that the great aim of the association, as of all political economy, should be to investigate the actual facts of each particular question thoroughly, and without any prepossessions on the side of complete liberty, or of necessary restriction. . . .

It was finally decided to refer the platform to a committee of five, consisting of the chairman, the secretary, and three other gentlemen to be appointed by the chair. Messrs. [Washington,] Gladden, Johnston and Clark were subsequently appointed. . . .

The Second Session

SARATOGA, SEPTEMBER 9TH, 1885

At four o'clock, Professor Henry C. Adams, acting as chairman, called the meeting to order. The first business before the meeting was the report of the committee on the objects of the association and the statement of principles. The members of the committee concluded, as a result of the debate on the preceding day, that a simplification of the declaration of purposes was desired; also a positive rather than a negative statement in every practicable instance; finally, a modification of some of the views expressed in the "Platform." It was also felt that it was desirable to make it plain that it was not the intention of the founders of the association to formulate a creed which should restrict freedom of inquiry or independence of thought. The committee endeavored to attain this object by a note to that effect, to be appended to the statement of principles. The report, as submitted, was debated passage by passage, was slightly amended, and then accepted and became our present declaration of "Objects" and "Statement of Principles." . . .

Constitution

ARTICLE I

NAME

This Society shall be known as the AMERICAN ECONOMIC ASSOCIATION.

ARTICLE II

OBJECTS

1. The encouragement of economic research.
2. The publication of economic monographs.
3. The encouragement of perfect freedom in all economic discussion.
4. The establishment of a Bureau of Information designed to aid members in their economic studies.

ARTICLE III

STATEMENT OF PRINCIPLES

1. We regard the state as an agency whose positive assistance is one of the indispensable conditions of human progress.
2. We believe that political economy as a science is still in an early state of its development. While we appreciate the work of former economists, we look not so much to speculation as to the historical and statistical study of actual conditions of economic life for the satisfactory accomplishment of that development.
3. We hold that the conflict of labor and capital has brought into prominence a vast number of social problems, whose solution requires the united efforts, each in its own sphere, of the church, of the state, and of science.
4. In the study of the industrial and commercial policy of governments we take no partisan attitude. We believe in a progres-

sive development of economic conditions, which must be met by a corresponding development of legislative policy.

Note.—This statement was proposed and accepted as a general indication of the views and purposes of those who founded the American Economic Association, but is not to be regarded as binding upon individual members. . . .

33. Henry Carter Adams—
The Limits of *Laissez Faire* (1887)

The most thoughtful of the new American economists was probably Henry Carter Adams. After graduating from Grinnell College in Iowa in 1874, he entered the new Johns Hopkins University, where he was awarded the first Ph.D. granted by that institution. He then spent two years studying in Germany, at the universities of Berlin and Heidelberg. Beginning in 1879, he taught economics at Cornell and the University of Michigan.

As befitted his training, Adams espoused the theories of the German historical school. He was one of the founders of the American Economic Association. His monograph "Relation of the State to Industrial Action," part of which is reproduced below, was a landmark in American economics. Instead of denouncing laissez faire or presenting a general argument for state regulation of the economy, Adams analyzed the particular economic conditions of his own times and sought to explain what types of businesses were best left entirely in the hands of their owners and managers, and what ones required regulation by government.

. . . The fundamental error of English political philosophy lies in regarding the state as a necessary evil; the fundamental error of German political philosophy lies in its conception of the state as an organism complete within itself. Neither the one nor the other of these views is correct. *Society* is the organic entity about which all our reasoning should center. Both state action and the industrial activity of individuals are functions of the complete social organism. The state is not made out of the chips and blocks left over after framing industrial society, nor does industrial society serve its full purpose in furnishing a means of existence for the

SOURCE: H. C. Adams, "Relation of the State to Industrial Action," American Economic Association, *Publications,* I (1887), 494–6, 498–502, 511–12, 515–21, 523–6, 528.

poor unfortunates who are thrust out of the civil or the military service. Society, as a living and growing organism, is the ultimate thing disclosed by an analysis of human relations; and because this is true it is not right to speak of a presumption in favor of individual initiative or of state control, as though these stood like contestants opposed to each other. It is not proper to consider individual activity as supplementary to state powers, or to look upon the functions of the state as supplementary to personal activity. It is futile to expect sound principles for the guidance of intricate legislation so long as we over-estimate either public or private duties; the true principle must recognize society as a unity, subject only to the laws of its own development.

Much of the confusion that now surrounds the question of the appropriate duties of government, so far as the people in this country are concerned, is due to the failure to distinguish between *laissez-faire* as a dogma and free competition as a principle. The former, as we have seen, is a rule or maxim intended for the guidance of public administration; the latter is a convenient expression for bringing to mind certain conditions of industrial society. Thus when one speaks of the benefits of free competition, one means the benefits conferred by industrial freedom. And when one argues for free competition, one is called upon to show that the best possible results may be expected for society, as a whole, and for each member of it, when labor is free and independent, when the right to acquire and enjoy property is guaranteed, when contracts are defended, and when every man is obliged to stand on his own legs, enjoying to the full the fruits of his own labor and suffering to the full the barren harvest of idleness. It seems that there should be no reasonable doubt respecting the benefits that must flow from such an organization of society, and I for one have no quarrel with those who urge its realization as a worthy object of endeavor. But I do take serious issue (and this is the important point to be observed), with those who hold that the rule of *laissez-faire* indicates the way by means of which such a state of affairs may be established and maintained. . . .

. . . Competition is neither malevolent nor beneficient, but will work malevolence or beneficence according to the conditions under which it is permitted to act. If this very reasonable view of the case be admitted, it follows that we may escape the practical conclusions of both socialists and individualists. . . . It should be the purpose of all laws, touching matters of business, to maintain the beneficent results of competitive action while guarding society from the evil consequences of unrestrained competition. . . .

But what are the beneficial workings of competition? Modern industrial society is built upon four legal facts: Private property in land, private property in labor, private property in capital, and the right of contract for all alike. The development of these rights, which required centuries for its accomplishment, portrays the growth of individualism and the decay of communalism; and no one who fully appreciates the opportunities thus offered by an industrial society based on slavery, or on undeveloped or general proprietary rights, can seriously advocate a return to the conditions of the past. The peculiar claims urged in favor of a society organized on the competitive basis are familiar to all. Perhaps the most important of these is that men are in this manner guaranteed full enjoyment in the fruits of their labor, and on this account will be jealous in its application. Competitive society also provides for ease of movement from one grade of labor to another, or from one business to another, and thus ensures elasticity in thought and expansion of purpose as the result of the manner in which motives are applied to individual conduct. . . .

Again, wherever the conditions for competitive action are maintained, society has a guarantee that goods will be produced at the lowest possible cost; for the hope of personal gain leads to the best disposal of labor, to invention, and to the adoption of the best machinery. Assuming the same premise, society has also a guarantee that the goods produced will be placed upon the market at fair prices. . . .

But what are the evils of unrestrained competition; or, more accurately stated, what are the pernicious results of the attempted realization of competitive action under the direction of the doctrine of *laissez-faire?* I cannot hope to present a complete answer to this question, but must rest content with certain suggestions that may lead to a clear understanding of such rules for governmental action as will be proposed. The important evils of unrestrained competition are of three sorts.

First. The free play of individual interests tends to force the moral sentiment pervading any trade down to the level of that which characterizes the worst man who can maintain himself in it. So far as morals are concerned, it is the character of the worst men and not of the best men that gives color to business society.

Second. The application of the rule of non-interference renders it impossible for men to realize the benefits that arise, in certain lines of business, from organization in the form of a monopoly. The theory of *laissez-faire* sees clearly the beneficent principle in free competition, but fails wholly to recognize a beneficent principle in monopoly.

Third. The policy of restricting public powers within the narrowest possible limits tend to render government weak and inefficient, and a weak government placed in the midst of a society controlled by the commercial spirit will quickly become a corrupt government; this in its turn reacts upon commercial society by encouraging private corporations to adopt bold measures for gaining control of government machinery. Thus the doctrine of *laissez-faire* overreaches itself; for the application of the rule which it lays down will surely destroy that harmony between public and private duties essential to the best results in either domain of action. . . .

Let us now turn to consider the second point introduced by the enumeration of the evils that flow from unrestricted competition. The application of the rule of non-interference, it was said, rendered it impossible for society to realize for its members the benefits that arise, in certain lines of business, from organizations in the form on monopoly. It may seem at first strange to speak of a beneficent principle in connection with monopolies, for we are accustomed to associate them with all that is odious, grasping, and tyrannous. . . . But what is an industrial monopoly? An industrial monopoly may be defined as a business superior to the regulating control of competition. The peculiar privileges of the past, so far as they were of an industrial character, usually rested on royal grants or charters; but those of which complaint is now heard, spring from the conditions of modern business activity, or from the peculiar nature of certain lines of business. The distrust with which monopolies are universally regarded arises from the fact that the public is deprived of its ordinary guarantee of fair treatment, so far as it must have dealings with them. But the important thing for us to notice is, that men do not so much complain of the existence of monopolies, for they recognize the existence as inevitable, but that the peculiar privileges and unusual powers which they bestow are perverted from their high purpose to serve private ends. . . .

. . . I am arguing neither for nor against state socialism. The position here assumed is, that the doctrine of *laissez-faire* does not permit society to realize in any adequate degree the benefits of organization in the form of monopoly. This is true, for several reasons, but especially because there are many industries which, from their nature, are monopolies, and cannot, therefore, be safely consigned to the guidance of the rule of private financiering. . . .

The practical conclusion to which this analysis leads is that society should be guaranteed against the oppression of exclusive privileges administered for personal profit, while at the same time it should be secured such advantages as flow from concentrated organization. I do not at present undertake to say whether this should be done through carefully guarded franchises, through official commissions, through competition of the state with private industries, or through direct governmental management; but in some manner this purpose should be accomplished. Such monopolies as exist should rest on law and be established in the interests of the public; a well-organized society will include no extra-legal monopolies of any sort. . . .

All industries, as it appears to me, fall into three classes, according to the relation that exists between the increment of product which results from a given increment of capital or labor. These may be termed industries of constant returns, industries of diminishing returns, and industries of increasing returns. The first two classes of industries are adequately controlled by competitive action; the third class, on the other hand, requires the superior control of state power. Let us consider these a little more in detail:

Industries of the first class—Industries of the first class are such as demand a proportional increase in capital and labor to secure a given increase in product. That is to say, if $2x$ capital and labor result in $2y$ product, the application of $3x$ capital and labor would gain $3y$ product. The increment of return is equal to the increment of capital. All those businesses in which success depends largely on attention to detail, and where the personal element of the laborer is brought prominently into view, fall under this class. For example, the retail business of merchants is subject to the rule here stated. It is not necessary for public officials to inquire if sugar is sold as low as fair dealings demand, for this business is one that admits easily of multiplication and consequently invites competition. . . . Prices are determined by the ordinary or average cost of production, but if by superior business talent the cost of producing goods in a few establishments is less than the average, or if superior organization permits more work to be done in one establishment than in another, there is in this manner created an unusual margin between cost and price which gives rise to unusual profits. Or to state this distinction in another way: a fortune built out of a monopoly is made up from the excess of the market price over the necessary cost of production, while a fortune created by business talent springs from depressing the cost of rendering a service below the average necessary price. . . .

Industries of the second class.—The same conclusion applies to the second class of industries, where a given increment of product calls for a proportionally greater increment of capital and labor. Assuming the same relation to exist in an established business as before, if $2x$ capital is required for $2y$ product, an additional x of capital will not produce an additional y of product, but something less. That is to say, $3x$ capital may produce but $3\ 2^3/_4y$ product. Industries of this sort are said to be subject to the law of diminishing returns, and it calls for no abstruse argument to recognize that society is quite safe in submitting such lines of industry to the control of competition. The rate of produce in the new industry is greater than that in the one that is farther developed, and for this reason we may rely upon individual interest to maintain a large number of separate producers. The agricultural industry is usually cited as an illustration to which the principle of diminishing returns may be said to apply, and, if we leave out of view the element of accruing rent, the conclusion which we have suggested may be applied in its most extreme form to the business of farming. There is no call for government farming. . . .

Industries of the third class. The peculiarity of those industries belonging to the third class, which we now come to consider, lies in the fact that they conform to the law of increasing, rather than to the law of constant or decreasing returns. The increment of product from an expanding enterprise is greater than the increment of capital and labor required to secure its expansion. Adopting the algebraic formula as before, if $2x$ capital give $2y$ product, an economic application of $3x$ capital will give more than $3y$ product. . . . Where the law of increasing returns works with any degree of intensity, the principle of free competition is powerless to exercise a healthy regulating influence. This is true, because it is easier for an established business to extend its facilities for satisfactorily meeting a new demand than for a new industry to spring into competitive existence. If this analysis of industries be accepted as correct, there can be no question as to the line which marks the duties of the state. The control of the state over industries should be co-extensive with the application of the law of increasing returns in industries. . . .

The railroad business may be cited as a good illustration of this third class of industries. When a railroad is first built through a thinly settled country, it is the problem of the engineer to put the enterprise into running order at the least possible outlay of money. The survey avoids cuts and bridges even at the expense of distance; the rails are light and the rolling stock not the best. The cost of plant is necessarily great in proportion to the business that may be immediately expected. But the development of the country soon taxes the facilities of the road to its utmost, and a new road must be built, or the capacity of the old one extended through the application of fresh capital. It is not difficult to decide which of these methods will be adopted. The capacity of the old road may be extended at a cost comparatively less than would be required by the building of a new road; and, so decided are the advantages of an established business over one struggling into existence, that it is fair to regard the old road as practically free, for a long time at least, from the competitive interference of new capital. . . .

There are many other lines of business which conform to the principle of increasing returns, and for that reason come under the rule of centralized control. Such businesses are by nature monopolies. We certainly deceive ourselves in believing that competition can secure for the public fair treatment in such cases, or that laws compelling competition can ever be enforced. If it is for the interest of men to combine no law can make them compete. For all industries, therefore, which conform to the principle of increasing returns, the only question at issue is, whether society shall support an irresponsible, extra-legal monopoly, or a monopoly established by law and managed in the interest of the public. In this latter way may the benefits of organization in the form of monopoly be secured to the people, and in no other. . . .

34. Woodrow Wilson—
The Role of Government (1889)

The pervasive influence of German scholarship, and incidentally of the main center of German scholarship in the United States in the 1880's, Johns Hopkins University, is well illustrated by the career of Woodrow Wilson. Wilson was temperamentally a conservative, predisposed to a narrow view of the scope of government and suspicious of democracy; but his contacts at Johns Hopkins with the new social thinking, so antithetical to laissez faire, had a profound impact upon him. While teaching at Bryn Mawr and Wesleyan in the late eighties he wrote *The State,* a broad survey of political systems which was to become for many years a leading textbook in political science. In the final section of that work, Wilson discussed the general functions and purposes of government, as distinct from the particular governmental institutions developed by the various nations of the world. His treatment, relevant parts of which follow, shows how thoroughly he was committed to the historical approach and the degree to which he had accepted the idea that in modern industrial states the areas of governmental activity had to be greatly enlarged.

It will contribute to clearness of thought to observe the functions of government in two groups, I. *The Constituent* Functions, II. *The Ministrant.* Under the *Constituent* I would place that usual category of governmental function, the protection of life, liberty, and property, together with all other functions that are necessary to the civic organization of society,—functions which are *not optional* with governments, even in the eyes of strictest *laissez faire,*—which are indeed the very bonds of society. Under the *Ministrant* I would range those other functions (such as education, posts and telegraphs, and the care, say, of forests) which are undertaken, not by way of *governing,* but by way of advancing the general interests of society, functions which *are* optional, being necessary only according to standards of convenience or expediency, and not according to standards of existence; functions

SOURCE: Woodrow Wilson, *The State* (Boston, 1889), pp. 638–40, 651–2, 656–61.

which assist without constituting social organization. . . .

It is hardly possible to give a complete list of those functions which I have called Ministrant, so various are they under different systems of government; the following partial list will suffice, however, for the purposes of the present discussion:

(1)   The regulation of trade and industry. Under this head I would include the coinage of money and the establishment of standard weights and measures, laws against forestalling, engrossing, the licensing of trades, etc., as well as the great matters of tariffs, navigation laws, and the like.

(2)   The regulation of labor.

(3)   The maintenance of thoroughfares,—including state management of railways and that great group of undertakings which we embrace within the comprehensive terms 'Internal Improvements' or 'The Development of the Country.'

(4)   The maintenance of postal and telegraph systems, which is very similiar in principle to (3) .

(5)   The manufacture and distribution of gas, the maintenance of water-works, etc.

(6)   Sanitation, including the regulation of trades for sanitary purposes.

(7)   Education.

(8)   Care of the poor and incapable.

(9)   Care and cultivation of forests and like matters, such as the stocking of rivers with fish.

(10) Sumptuary laws, such as 'prohibition' laws, for example.

These are all functions which, in one shape or another, all governments alike have undertaken. Changed conceptions of the nature and duty of the state have arisen, issuing from changed historical conditions, deeply altered historical circumstance, and part of the change which has thus affected the idea of the state has been a change in the method and extent of the exercise of governmental functions; but changed conceptions have left the functions of government *in kind* the same. Diversities of conception are very much more marked than diversities of practice. . . .

. . . In this field of the Ministrant functions one would expect the state to be less active now than formerly: it is natural enough that in the field of the Constituent functions the state should serve society now as always. But there is in fact no such difference: *government does now whatever experience permits or the times demand;* and though it does not do exactly the same things it still does substantially the same kind of things that the ancient state did. . . .

What part shall government play in the affairs of society?—that is the question which has been the gauge of controversial battle. Stated in another way, it is the very question which I postponed when discussing the functions of government, *'What,'* namely, *'ought the functions of government to be?'* On the one hand there are extremists who cry constantly to government, 'Hands off,' *'laissez faire,' 'laissez passer'!* who look upon every act of government which is not merely an act of policy with jealousy, who regard government as necessary, but as a necessary evil, and who would have government hold back from everything which could by any possibility be accomplished by individual initiative and endeavor. On the other hand, there are those who with equal extremeness of view in the opposite direction, would have society lean fondly upon government for guidance and assistance in every affair of life, who, captivated by some glimpse of public power and beneficence caught in the pages of ancient or mediaeval historian or by some dream of cooperative endeavor cunningly imagined by the great fathers of Socialism, believe that the state can be made a wise foster-mother to every member of the family politic. Between these two extremes, again, there are all grades, all shades and colors, all degrees of enmity or of partiality to state action.

Enmity to exaggerated state action, even a keen desire to keep that action down to its lowest possible terms, is easily furnished with impressive jusification. It must unreservedly be admitted that history abounds with warnings of no uncertain sound against indulging the state with a too great liberty of interference with the life and work of its citizens. Much as there is that is attractive in the political life of the city states of Greece and Rome, in which the public power was suffered to be omnipotent, their splendid public spirit, their incomparable organic wholeness, their fine play of rival talents, serving both the common thought and the common action, their variety, their conception of public virtue, there is also much to blame,—their too wanton invasion of that privacy of the individual life in which alone family virtue can dwell secure, their callous tyranny over minorities in matters which might have been left to individual choice, their sacrifice of personal independence for the sake of public solidarity, their hasty average judgments, their too confident trust in the public voice. They, it is true, could not have had the individual liberty which we cherish without breaking violently with their own history, with the necessary order of their development; but neither can we, on the other hand, imitate them without an equally violent departure from our own normal development and a reversion to the now too primitive methods of their pocket republics. . . .

It by no means follows, however, that because the state may unwisely interfere in the life of the individual, it must be pronounced in itself and by nature a necessary evil. It is no more an evil than is society itself. It is the organic body of society: without it society would be hardly more than a mere abstraction. If the name had not been restricted to a single, narrow, extreme, and radically mistaken class of thinkers, we ought all to regard ourselves and to act as *socialists,* believers in the wholesomeness and beneficence of the body politic. If the history of society proves anything, it proves the absolute naturalness of government, its rootage in the nature of man, its origin in kinship, and its identification with all that makes man superior to the brute creation. Individually man is but poorly equipped to dominate other animals: his lordship comes by combination, his strength is concerted strength, his sovereignty is the sovereignty of union. Outside of society man's mind can avail him little as an instrument of supremacy, and government is the visible form of society: if society itself be not an evil, neither surely is government an evil, for government is the indispenable organ of society.

Every means, therefore, by which society may be perfected through the instrumentality of government, every means by which individual rights can be fitly adjusted and harmonized with public duties, by which individual self-development may be made at once to serve and to supplement social development, ought certainly to be diligently sought, and, when found, sedulously fostered by every friend of society. Such is the socialism to which every true lover of his kind ought to adhere with the full grip of every noble affection that is in him.

It is possible indeed, to understand, and even in a measure to

sympathize with, the enthusiasm of those special classes of agitators whom we have dubbed with the too great name of 'Socialists.'
The schemes of social reform and regeneration which they support with so much ardor, however mistaken they may be,—and
surely most of them are mistaken enough to provoke the laughter
of children,—have the right end in view: they seek to bring the
individual with his special interst, personal to himself, into complete harmony with society with its general interests, common to
all. Their method is always some sort of co-operation, meant to
perfect mutual helpfulness. They speak, too, a revolt from selfish,
misguided individualism; and certainly modern individualism has
much about it that is hateful, too hateful to last. The modern
industrial organization has so distorted competition as to put it
into the power of some to tyrannize over many, as to enable the
rich and the strong to combine against the poor and the weak. It
has given a woeful material meaning to that spiritual law that "to
him that hath shall be given, and from him that hath not shall be
taken away even the little that he seemeth to have." It has magnified that self-interest which is grasping selfishness and has thrust
out love and compassion not only, but free competition in part, as
well. Surely it would be better, exclaims the Socialist, altogether
to stamp out competition by making all men equally subject to
the public order, to an imperative law of social co-operation! But
the Socialist mistakes: it is not competition that kills, but unfair
competition, the pretence and form of it where the substance and
reality of it cannot exist.

But there is a middle ground. The schemes which Socialists
have proposed society assuredly cannot accept, and no scheme
which involves the complete control of the individual by government can be devised which differs from theirs very much for the
better. A truer doctrine must be found, which gives wide freedom
to the individual for his self-development and yet guards that freedom against the competition that kills, and reduces the antago-
nism between self-development and social development to a minimum. And such a doctrine can be formulated, surely, without too
great vagueness.

Government, as I have said, is the organ of society, its only
potent and universal instrument: its objects must be the objects of
society. What, then, are the objects of society? What *is* society? It
is an organic association of individuals for mutual aid. Mutual aid

to what? To self-development. The hope of society lies in an infinite individual variety, in the freest possible play of individual forces: only in that can it find that wealth of resource which constitutes civilization, with all its appliances for satisfying human wants and mitigating human sufferings, all its incitements to thought and spurs to action. It should be the end of government *to accomplish the objects of organized society:* there must be constant adjustments of governmental assistance to the needs of a changing social and industrial organization. Not license of interference on the part of government, only strength and adaptation or regulation. The regulation that I mean is not interference: it is the equalization of conditions, so far as possible, in all branches of endeavor; and the equalization of conditions is the very opposite of interference.

Every rule of development is a rule of adaptation, a rule for meeting 'the circumstances of the case'; but the circumstances of the case, it must be remembered, are not, so far as government is concerned, the circumstances of any individual case, but the circumstances of society's case, the general conditions of social organization. The case for society stands thus: the individual must be assured the best means, the best and fullest opportunities, for complete self-development: in no other way can society itself gain variety and strength. But one of the most indispensable conditions of opportunity for self-development government alone, society's controlling organ, can supply. All combination which necessarily creates monopoly, which necessarily puts and keeps indispensable means of industrial or social development in the hands of a few, and those few, not the few selected by society itself but the few selected by arbitrary fortune, must be under either the direct or the indirect control of society. To society alone can the power of dominating combination belong: and society cannot suffer any of its members to enjoy such a power for their own private gain independently of its own strict regulation or oversight. . . .